W9-ALU-156

3 Practice Tests for the

SAT®

The Princeton Review®

3 Practice Tests for the

SAT®

The Staff of The Princeton Review

PrincetonReview.com

PENGUIN RANDOM HOUSE

Random House, Inc. New York

The Princeton Review, Inc.
24 Prime Parkway, Suite 201
Natick, MA 01760
E-mail: editorialsupport@review.com

Copyright © 2013 by TPR Education IP Holdings, LLC.
All rights reserved.

Published in the United States by Random House LLC,
New York, and simultaneously in Canada by
Random House of Canada Limited, Toronto.
A Penguin Random House Company.

Some content in this book previously appeared in
11 Practice Tests for the SAT and PSAT, 2014
Edition, published by Random House as a trade
paperback in 2013.

SAT is a registered trademark of the College Board,
which does not sponsor or endorse this product.

ISBN 978-0-307-94602-7

The Princeton Review is not affiliated with Princeton
University.

Editor: Selena Coppock
Production Editor: James Tyler
Production Artist: Deborah A. Silvestrini

Printed in the United States of America on partially
recycled paper.

10 9 8 7 6 5 4 3 2

Editorial
Rob Franek, Senior VP, Publisher
Casey Cornelius, VP Content Development
Mary Beth Garrick, Director of Production
Selena Coppock, Managing Editor
Calvin Cato, Editor
Meave Shelton, Editor
Alyssa Wolff, Editorial Assistant

Random House Publishing Team
Tom Russell, Publisher
Alison Stoltzfus, Publishing Manager
Dawn Ryan, Associate Managing Editor
Ellen Reed, Production Manager
Erika Pepe, Associate Production Manager
Kristin Lindner, Production Supervisor
Andrea Lau, Designer

Acknowledgments

An SAT course is much more than clever techniques and powerful computer score reports. The reason our results are great is that our teachers care so much about their students. Many teachers have gone out of their way to improve the course, often going so far as to write their own materials, some of which we have incorporated into our course manual as well as into this book. The list of these teachers could fill this page.

Special thanks to our National Content Director for the SAT, Jonathan Chiu.

Contents

Foreword

Welcome to *3 Practice Tests for the SAT.* The SAT is not a test of aptitude, how good of a person you are, or how successful you will be in life. The SAT simply tests how well you take the SAT. And performing well on the SAT is a skill, one that can be learned like any other. The Princeton Review was founded more than 20 years ago on this very simple idea, and—as our students' test scores show—our approach is the one that works.

Sure, you want to do well on the SAT, but you don't need to let the test intimidate you. As you prepare, remember these two important things about the SAT:

- **It doesn't measure the stuff that matters.** It measures neither intelligence nor the depth and breadth of what you're learning in high school. It doesn't predict college grades as well as your high school grades do, and many schools are still hesitant to use the score from your 25-minute essay in their application decisions at all. Colleges know there is more to you as a student—and as a person—than what you do at a single 4-hour test administration on a random Saturday morning.
- **It underpredicts the college performance of women, minorities, and disadvantaged students.** Historically, women have done better than men in college but worse on the SAT. For a test that is used to help predict performance in college, that's a pretty poor record.

Your preparation for the SAT starts here. We at The Princeton Review spend millions of dollars every year improving our methods and materials. Our teachers take each and every SAT to make sure nothing slips by us, and our books contain the most accurate, up-to-date information available. We're always ready for the SAT, and we'll get you ready too.

However, there is no magic pill: Just buying this book isn't going to improve your scores. Solid score improvement takes commitment and effort from you. If you read this book carefully and work through the problems and practice tests included in the book, not only will you be thoroughly versed in the format of the SAT and the concepts it tests, you will also have a sound overall strategy and a powerful arsenal of test-taking skills that you can apply to whatever you encounter on test day.

This test is challenging, but you're on the right track. We'll be with you all the way.

Good luck!

The Staff of The Princeton Review

Chapter 1
Orientation

GENERAL INFORMATION ABOUT THE SAT

You may have bought this book because you know nothing about the SAT, or perhaps you took the test once and want to raise your score. Either way, it's important to know about the test and the people who write it. Let's take a second to discuss some SAT facts; some of them may surprise you.

What Does the SAT Test?

Just because the SAT features math, reading, and writing questions doesn't mean that it reflects what you learned in school. You can ace calculus or write like Faulkner and still struggle with the SAT. The test writers claim that the test measures "reasoning ability," but all the SAT really measures is how well you take the SAT. It does *not* reveal how smart or how good a person you are.

Wait, *Who* Writes This Test?

You may be surprised to learn that the people who write SAT test questions are NOT necessarily teachers or college professors. The people who write the SAT are professional test writers, not superhuman geniuses, so you can beat them at their own game.

WHO PUTS THE TEST OUT?

Even though colleges and universities make wide use of the SAT, they're not the ones who write the test. That's the job of Educational Testing Service (ETS), a nonprofit company that writes tests for college and graduate school admissions. ETS also writes tests for groups as diverse as butchers and professional golfers (who knew?).

ETS is often criticized for the SAT. Many educators have argued that the test does not measure the skills you really need for college. In fact, several years ago the University of California, one of the nation's largest university systems, decided that the SAT didn't provide enough information for admissions. ETS scrambled to change the test and introduced the current version of the SAT. It's almost an hour longer than the old SAT and—unlike the old version—tests grammar and includes an essay.

WHAT'S ON IT?

The SAT runs 3 hours and 45 minutes and is divided into 10 sections. These include

- one 25-minute Essay section, requiring you to present your viewpoint on a topic
- two 25-minute Math sections, containing multiple-choice questions and response questions (we call these "grid-ins")
- two 25-minute Critical Reading sections, made up of sentence completions and reading comprehension questions
- one 25-minute Writing section, containing error identification questions, improving sentences questions, and improving paragraphs questions
- one 20-minute Math section, including only multiple-choice questions
- one 20-minute Critical Reading section, again featuring sentence completions and reading comprehension questions
- one 10-minute Writing section containing only improving sentences questions
- one 25-minute Experimental section, which may be Writing, Math, or Critical Reading. There's no way to tell which section is the Experimental, so treat every section as if it will be scored

The Essay section on the SAT always comes first, while the 10-minute Writing section always comes last. The other six 25-minute sections can be in any order, as can the two 20-minute sections.

More great titles from The Princeton Review
The Best 377 Colleges
Best Value Colleges

SCORING

Each subject area on the SAT—Math, Writing, and Critical Reading—is scored on a scale of 200 to 800. The three scores are then totaled, for a combined score between 600 and 2,400. The average SAT score is about 500 per section, or 1,500 total.

You'll receive your score report about two to four weeks after you take the test. It will include your scaled score as well as your percentile rank, which tells you how you performed relative to other people who took the same test. If your score is in the 60th percentile, it means that you scored better than 60 percent of test takers.

One way of thinking of your SAT score is to imagine yourself in a line with 100 other students, all waiting to be seen by an admissions officer. However, the officer can't see every student—some students won't make it through the door. If your SAT score is in the 50th percentile, you'd have 50 other kids in front of you. Maybe you'll be seen, maybe not. Wouldn't it be nice to jump the line? If you can boost your SAT score, even by a couple of points, you move up the line and increase your odds of getting through the door. We can help you do that…

HOW TO USE THIS BOOK

Scoring Your Own SAT Practice Test

The College Board figures out your score by using the following formula:

> # of questions you get correct − (# of questions you get incorrect ÷ 4) = Raw Score

They take your Raw Score, along with the Raw Score of every other test taker in the country, and figure out a curve. Finally, they assign each Raw Score to a number on a scale of 200 to 800. This is your Scaled Score.

How Do I Figure Out My Score?

Let's look at the subjects one at a time. Fill in the numbers on your SAT scoring worksheet on page 111/203/295.

Writing

Step One   Count up the number of your correct answers for the multiple-choice Writing Skills section. This is the number that goes in the first box.

Step Two   Count up the number of your incorrect answers for the multiple-choice Writing Skills section. Divide this number by four and place the resulting number in the second box.

Step Three	Subtract the second number from the first. This is your Grammar Raw Score. This is the number that goes in the third box.
Step Four	Look up the number from the third column in the Writing Multiple-Choice Subscore Conversion Table on page 112/204/296. This is your Grammar Scaled Subscore.
Step Five	The essay is scored on a scale from 2 to 12. It is based on the score that two graders give you, each on a scale from 1 to 6. The number that you should put in the fourth box depends on how it was scored. If your essay is self-graded on a 1 to 6 scale, then double that number so that it is from 2 to 12. Take your 2 to 12 grade and double it so that it is from 4 to 24. This is the number that goes in the fourth box.
Step Six	Add the fourth box to the third. This is your Writing Raw Score. This number goes in the fifth box.
Step Seven	Look up the number from the fifth box in the SAT Score Conversion Table. This is your Writing Scaled Score.

Critical Reading

Step One	Count up the number of your correct answers for the three Critical Reading sections of the test. This is the number that goes in the first box.
Step Two	Count up the number of your incorrect answers for the three Critical Reading sections of the test. Divide this number by four. The resulting number goes in the second box.

Step Three	Subtract the second number from the first. This is your Critical Reading Raw Score. This is the number that goes in the third box.
Step Four	Look up the number from the third column in the SAT Score Conversion Table on page 112/204/ 296. This is your Critical Reading Scaled Score.

Math

Step One	Count up the number of your correct grid-in answers. This is the number that goes in the first box.
Step Two	Count up the number of your correct answers for the multiple-choice questions in the three Math sections of the test. This is the number that goes in the second box.
Step Three	Count up the number of your incorrect answers for the multiple-choice questions in the three Math sections of the test. **Do NOT include any grid-in questions you may have answered incorrectly.** Divide this number by four and place the resulting number in the third box.
Step Four	Subtract the third number from the second, and then add the first number. This is your Math Raw Score. This is the number that goes in the fourth box.
Step Five	Look up the number from the fourth column in the SAT Score Conversion Table on page 112/204/ 296. This is your Math Scaled Score.

Score Choice™

The College Board restarted a program called Score Choice. Normally, colleges get to see every single time you take the SAT. With Score Choice, however, you can tell the College Board which test date or dates (as many or as few as you want) to send to colleges. At first glance, this seems great. "Hey, colleges don't have to see that one bad score from the first time I took the SAT without preparing? Great!" But there are some major problems with it, which you may want to consider before using Score Choice.

First and foremost is that some colleges require that you send them all scores from all times you took the SAT. Score Choice is still new (it first took effect in March 2009), and some colleges aren't very happy about it. They want to know about every single time you take the SAT, and they don't want the College Board telling them which of your SAT scores they're allowed to see. For these colleges, you must submit all scores, and Score Choice is not an option.

Second, many colleges actually just look at your highest scores either for one sitting of a test or, in many cases, per subject across several sittings. If the college just looks at your highest sitting, Score Choice doesn't make any difference, and it's probably not worth bothering with it. The college admissions officer will just look at your highest-scored test date and ignore the other scores. But for the colleges that cherry pick your scores by subject, Score Choice can actually hurt you. For instance, let's say you take the SAT in March and get a 510 in Math, a 400 in Reading, and a 450 in Writing. You retake the SAT in May and get a 410 in Math (ouch), a 500 in Reading (much better), and a 470 in Writing (OK). Many schools look at your best scores per subject and would consider your SAT score to be 510 Math, 500 Reading, and 470 Writing. But if you submitted only one score, the colleges wouldn't have the high points to choose from.

Whether or not you decide to use Score Choice, plan on taking the SAT two or three times. Many colleges frown on taking the SAT four or more times.

A searchable list of colleges and their requested SAT score submission requirements, as well as more information on Score Choice, can be found at the College Board website at www.collegeboard.com.

THE ACT VS. THE SAT

In your SAT preparation, you have probably heard about another popular exam, the ACT. Most colleges accept both SAT and ACT scores as part of a student's application and you might be interested in taking both tests. Whereas the ACT says it measures "achievement," the SAT says it measures "ability" and the differences between the two can be quite confusing.

What Exactly Are the Differences?

The SAT tends to be less time-pressured than the ACT. However, many of the questions on the SAT are trickier than those on the ACT. The SAT Verbal sections have a stronger emphasis on vocabulary than do the ACT English and Reading tests. The SAT Math section tests primarily algebra and plane geometry and includes no trigonometry at all.

Both tests include an Essay section, although ACT has made this new essay optional because some colleges require it while others do not. ACT doesn't want to force students to take (and pay for) a test they don't need. The implication then is that

More great titles by The Princeton Review

1,296 ACT Practice Questions,

ACT or SAT? Choosing the Right Exam For You

many students can ignore the new Writing Test altogether depending on what the schools to which they are applying require.

To find out if the schools in which you are interested require the ACT essay, visit the ACT writing test page at www.actstudent.org/writing or contact the schools directly.

While it's your call as to whether you'd prefer to take the SAT, the ACT, or both. But you should know that some students end up scoring substantially higher on the SAT than they do on the ACT and vice versa. It may be to your advantage to take a practice test for each one and see which is more likely to get you a better score.

Chapter 2
Strategy

The first step to cracking the SAT is to know how best to approach the test. The SAT is not like the tests you've taken in school, so you need to learn to look at it in a different way. This chapter will show test-taking strategies that immediately improve your score.

PROCESS OF ELIMINATION (POE)

There won't be many questions on the SAT in which incorrect choices will be as easy to eliminate as they were on the Azerbaijan question. But if you read this book carefully, you'll learn how to eliminate at least one choice on almost any SAT multiple-choice question, if not two, three, or even four choices.

What good is it to eliminate just one or two choices on a five-choice SAT question?

Plenty. In fact, for most students, it's an important key to earning higher scores. Here's another example:

> **2.** The capital of Qatar is
>
>   (A) Paris
>   (B) Dukhan
>   (C) Tokyo
>   (D) Doha
>   (E) London

On this question you'll almost certainly be able to eliminate three of the five choices by using POE. That means you're still not sure of the answer. You know that the capital of Qatar has to be either Doha or Dukhan, but you don't know which.

Should you skip the question and go on? Or should you guess?

Close Your Eyes and Point

You've probably heard a lot of different advice about guessing on multiple-choice questions on the SAT. Some teachers and guidance counselors tell their students never to guess and to mark an answer only if they're absolutely certain that it's correct. Others tell their students not to guess unless they are able to eliminate two or three of the choices.

Both of these pieces of advice are incorrect.

Even ETS is misleading about guessing. Although it tells you that you *can* guess, it doesn't tell you that you *should*. In fact, if you can eliminate even *one* incorrect choice on an SAT multiple-choice question, guessing from among the remaining choices will usually improve your score. And if you can eliminate two or three choices, you'll be even more likely to improve your score by guessing.

The Big Bad Guessing Penalty

Your raw score on the SAT is the number of questions you got right, minus a fraction of the number you got wrong (except on the grid-ins, which are scored a little differently). Every time you answer an SAT question correctly, you get 1 raw point. Every time you leave an SAT question blank, you get 0 raw points. Every time you answer an SAT question incorrectly, ETS subtracts $\frac{1}{4}$ of a raw point if the question has five answer choices, or nothing if it is a grid-in.

ETS refers to the subtracted fraction as the "guessing penalty." The penalty is supposed to discourage students from guessing on multiple-choice questions (and getting the right answer out of luck). However, let's take a closer look at how the penalty works.

Raw scores can be a little confusing, so let's think in terms of money instead. For every question you answer correctly on the SAT, ETS will give you a dollar. For every multiple-choice question you leave blank, ETS will give you nothing. For every multiple-choice question you get wrong, you will have to give 25 cents back to ETS. That's exactly the way raw scores work.

What happens to your score if you select the correct answer on one question and incorrect choices on four questions? Remember what we said about money: ETS gives you a dollar for the one answer you got right; you give ETS a quarter for each of the four questions you missed. Four quarters equal a dollar, so you end up exactly where you started, with nothing—which is the same thing that would have happened if you had left all five questions blank. Now, what happens if you guess on four questions, but—for each of those questions—you can eliminate one incorrect answer choice? Random odds say you will get one question right—get a dollar—and miss the other three questions—give back 75 cents. You've just gained a quarter! So, guessing can work in your favor.

TO GUESS OR NOT TO GUESS: THAT IS THE QUESTION

If you are confident that you know the answer to a question or that you know how to solve it, just go ahead and select an answer. If you are uncertain about either the answer to a question or how to solve it, see if you can eliminate any wrong answers. We're going to give you lots of tools to eliminate wrong answers, so you'll probably be able to eliminate answers *even* on the hardest questions.

But, should you guess on every question? Well, that depends. In the next chapter, we're going to show you how to set a pacing goal for each section. The pacing goal will tell you how many questions you need to answer for each section. Your goal is to answer that number of questions. If you can get to your pacing goal without guessing, that's great. But most students will need to guess on at least a few questions to reach their pacing goals. When you get to a question you're not sure of, ask yourself, "Can I reach my pacing goal without this question?"

Finally, guess only if you can eliminate *at least one* answer choice. If you can't eliminate one, leave that question blank.

Credit for Partial Information

Earning points for a guess probably seems a little bit like cheating or stealing: You get something you want, but you didn't do anything to earn it.

This is not a useful way to think about the SAT. It's also not true. Look at the following example:

3. The Sun is
    (A) a main-sequence star
    (B) a meteor
    (C) an asteroid
    (D) a white dwarf star
    (E) a planet

If you've paid any attention at all in school for the past 10 years or so, you probably know that the Sun is a star. You can easily tell, therefore, that the answer to this question must be either A or D. You can tell this not only because it seems clear from the context that "white dwarf" and "main-sequence" are kinds of stars—as they are—but also because you know for a fact that

Want more practice? Check out
Cracking the SAT

Essential SAT Vocabulary Flashcards

the Sun is not a planet, a meteor, or an asteroid. Still, you aren't sure which of the two possible choices is correct.

Heads, You Win a Dollar; Tails, You Lose a Quarter

By using POE you've narrowed down your choice to two possibilities. If you guess randomly you'll have a fifty-fifty chance of being correct, like flipping a coin—heads you win a dollar, tails you lose a quarter. Those are extremely good odds on the SAT. So go ahead and guess!

(The answer, by the way, is A. And don't worry, there won't be any questions about astronomy on the SAT.)

Chapter 3
Practice Test 1

THIS PAGE INTENTIONALLY LEFT BLANK

SECTION 1

○ I prefer NOT to grant the College Board the right to use, reproduce, or publish my essay for any purpose beyond the assessment of my writing skills, even though my name will not be used in any way in conjunction with my essay. I understand that I am free to mark this circle with no effect on my score.

IMPORTANT: **USE A NO. 2 PENCIL. DO NOT WRITE OUTSIDE THE BORDER!**
Words written outside the essay box or written in ink **WILL NOT APPEAR** in the copy sent to be scored and your score will be affected.

Begin your essay on this page. If you need more space, continue on the next page.

Continue on the next page, if necessary.

Continuation of ESSAY Section 1 from previous page. Write below only if you need more space.

IMPORTANT: DO NOT START on this page—if you do, your essay may appear blank and your score may be affected.

COMPLETE MARK ● EXAMPLES OF INCOMPLETE MARKS Ⓐ Ⓑ Ⓒ Ⓓ Ⓐ Ⓑ Ⓒ Ⓓ

You must use a No. 2 pencil and marks must be complete. Do not use a mechanical pencil. It is very important that you fill in the entire circle darkly and completely. If you change your responses, erase as completely as possible. Incomplete marks or erasures may affect your score.

SECTION 2

1 Ⓐ Ⓑ Ⓒ Ⓓ Ⓔ
2 Ⓐ Ⓑ Ⓒ Ⓓ Ⓔ
3 Ⓐ Ⓑ Ⓒ Ⓓ Ⓔ
4 Ⓐ Ⓑ Ⓒ Ⓓ Ⓔ
5 Ⓐ Ⓑ Ⓒ Ⓓ Ⓔ
6 Ⓐ Ⓑ Ⓒ Ⓓ Ⓔ
7 Ⓐ Ⓑ Ⓒ Ⓓ Ⓔ
8 Ⓐ Ⓑ Ⓒ Ⓓ Ⓔ
9 Ⓐ Ⓑ Ⓒ Ⓓ Ⓔ
10 Ⓐ Ⓑ Ⓒ Ⓓ Ⓔ

11 Ⓐ Ⓑ Ⓒ Ⓓ Ⓔ
12 Ⓐ Ⓑ Ⓒ Ⓓ Ⓔ
13 Ⓐ Ⓑ Ⓒ Ⓓ Ⓔ
14 Ⓐ Ⓑ Ⓒ Ⓓ Ⓔ
15 Ⓐ Ⓑ Ⓒ Ⓓ Ⓔ
16 Ⓐ Ⓑ Ⓒ Ⓓ Ⓔ
17 Ⓐ Ⓑ Ⓒ Ⓓ Ⓔ
18 Ⓐ Ⓑ Ⓒ Ⓓ Ⓔ
19 Ⓐ Ⓑ Ⓒ Ⓓ Ⓔ
20 Ⓐ Ⓑ Ⓒ Ⓓ Ⓔ

21 Ⓐ Ⓑ Ⓒ Ⓓ Ⓔ
22 Ⓐ Ⓑ Ⓒ Ⓓ Ⓔ
23 Ⓐ Ⓑ Ⓒ Ⓓ Ⓔ
24 Ⓐ Ⓑ Ⓒ Ⓓ Ⓔ
25 Ⓐ Ⓑ Ⓒ Ⓓ Ⓔ
26 Ⓐ Ⓑ Ⓒ Ⓓ Ⓔ
27 Ⓐ Ⓑ Ⓒ Ⓓ Ⓔ
28 Ⓐ Ⓑ Ⓒ Ⓓ Ⓔ
29 Ⓐ Ⓑ Ⓒ Ⓓ Ⓔ
30 Ⓐ Ⓑ Ⓒ Ⓓ Ⓔ

31 Ⓐ Ⓑ Ⓒ Ⓓ Ⓔ
32 Ⓐ Ⓑ Ⓒ Ⓓ Ⓔ
33 Ⓐ Ⓑ Ⓒ Ⓓ Ⓔ
34 Ⓐ Ⓑ Ⓒ Ⓓ Ⓔ
35 Ⓐ Ⓑ Ⓒ Ⓓ Ⓔ
36 Ⓐ Ⓑ Ⓒ Ⓓ Ⓔ
37 Ⓐ Ⓑ Ⓒ Ⓓ Ⓔ
38 Ⓐ Ⓑ Ⓒ Ⓓ Ⓔ
39 Ⓐ Ⓑ Ⓒ Ⓓ Ⓔ
40 Ⓐ Ⓑ Ⓒ Ⓓ Ⓔ

SECTION 3

1 Ⓐ Ⓑ Ⓒ Ⓓ Ⓔ
2 Ⓐ Ⓑ Ⓒ Ⓓ Ⓔ
3 Ⓐ Ⓑ Ⓒ Ⓓ Ⓔ
4 Ⓐ Ⓑ Ⓒ Ⓓ Ⓔ
5 Ⓐ Ⓑ Ⓒ Ⓓ Ⓔ
6 Ⓐ Ⓑ Ⓒ Ⓓ Ⓔ
7 Ⓐ Ⓑ Ⓒ Ⓓ Ⓔ
8 Ⓐ Ⓑ Ⓒ Ⓓ Ⓔ
9 Ⓐ Ⓑ Ⓒ Ⓓ Ⓔ
10 Ⓐ Ⓑ Ⓒ Ⓓ Ⓔ

11 Ⓐ Ⓑ Ⓒ Ⓓ Ⓔ
12 Ⓐ Ⓑ Ⓒ Ⓓ Ⓔ
13 Ⓐ Ⓑ Ⓒ Ⓓ Ⓔ
14 Ⓐ Ⓑ Ⓒ Ⓓ Ⓔ
15 Ⓐ Ⓑ Ⓒ Ⓓ Ⓔ
16 Ⓐ Ⓑ Ⓒ Ⓓ Ⓔ
17 Ⓐ Ⓑ Ⓒ Ⓓ Ⓔ
18 Ⓐ Ⓑ Ⓒ Ⓓ Ⓔ
19 Ⓐ Ⓑ Ⓒ Ⓓ Ⓔ
20 Ⓐ Ⓑ Ⓒ Ⓓ Ⓔ

21 Ⓐ Ⓑ Ⓒ Ⓓ Ⓔ
22 Ⓐ Ⓑ Ⓒ Ⓓ Ⓔ
23 Ⓐ Ⓑ Ⓒ Ⓓ Ⓔ
24 Ⓐ Ⓑ Ⓒ Ⓓ Ⓔ
25 Ⓐ Ⓑ Ⓒ Ⓓ Ⓔ
26 Ⓐ Ⓑ Ⓒ Ⓓ Ⓔ
27 Ⓐ Ⓑ Ⓒ Ⓓ Ⓔ
28 Ⓐ Ⓑ Ⓒ Ⓓ Ⓔ
29 Ⓐ Ⓑ Ⓒ Ⓓ Ⓔ
30 Ⓐ Ⓑ Ⓒ Ⓓ Ⓔ

31 Ⓐ Ⓑ Ⓒ Ⓓ Ⓔ
32 Ⓐ Ⓑ Ⓒ Ⓓ Ⓔ
33 Ⓐ Ⓑ Ⓒ Ⓓ Ⓔ
34 Ⓐ Ⓑ Ⓒ Ⓓ Ⓔ
35 Ⓐ Ⓑ Ⓒ Ⓓ Ⓔ
36 Ⓐ Ⓑ Ⓒ Ⓓ Ⓔ
37 Ⓐ Ⓑ Ⓒ Ⓓ Ⓔ
38 Ⓐ Ⓑ Ⓒ Ⓓ Ⓔ
39 Ⓐ Ⓑ Ⓒ Ⓓ Ⓔ
40 Ⓐ Ⓑ Ⓒ Ⓓ Ⓔ

CAUTION

Grid answers in the section below for SECTION 2 or SECTION 3 only if directed to do so in your test book.

Student-Produced Responses

ONLY ANSWERS THAT ARE GRIDDED WILL BE SCORED. YOU WILL NOT RECEIVE CREDIT FOR ANYTHING WRITTEN IN THE BOXES.

Quality Assurance Mark ●

9 10 11 12 13

14 15 16 17 18

(Each grid contains columns with circles for / . 0 1 2 3 4 5 6 7 8 9)

COMPLETE MARK ● EXAMPLES OF INCOMPLETE MARKS ⒶⒷⒸⒹ / ⊘⊗⊛

You must use a No. 2 pencil and marks must be complete. Do not use a mechanical pencil. It is very important that you fill in the entire circle darkly and completely. If you change your responses, erase as completely as possible. Incomplete marks or erasures may affect your score.

SECTION 4

1 Ⓐ Ⓑ Ⓒ Ⓓ Ⓔ
2 Ⓐ Ⓑ Ⓒ Ⓓ Ⓔ
3 Ⓐ Ⓑ Ⓒ Ⓓ Ⓔ
4 Ⓐ Ⓑ Ⓒ Ⓓ Ⓔ
5 Ⓐ Ⓑ Ⓒ Ⓓ Ⓔ
6 Ⓐ Ⓑ Ⓒ Ⓓ Ⓔ
7 Ⓐ Ⓑ Ⓒ Ⓓ Ⓔ
8 Ⓐ Ⓑ Ⓒ Ⓓ Ⓔ
9 Ⓐ Ⓑ Ⓒ Ⓓ Ⓔ
10 Ⓐ Ⓑ Ⓒ Ⓓ Ⓔ

11 Ⓐ Ⓑ Ⓒ Ⓓ Ⓔ
12 Ⓐ Ⓑ Ⓒ Ⓓ Ⓔ
13 Ⓐ Ⓑ Ⓒ Ⓓ Ⓔ
14 Ⓐ Ⓑ Ⓒ Ⓓ Ⓔ
15 Ⓐ Ⓑ Ⓒ Ⓓ Ⓔ
16 Ⓐ Ⓑ Ⓒ Ⓓ Ⓔ
17 Ⓐ Ⓑ Ⓒ Ⓓ Ⓔ
18 Ⓐ Ⓑ Ⓒ Ⓓ Ⓔ
19 Ⓐ Ⓑ Ⓒ Ⓓ Ⓔ
20 Ⓐ Ⓑ Ⓒ Ⓓ Ⓔ

21 Ⓐ Ⓑ Ⓒ Ⓓ Ⓔ
22 Ⓐ Ⓑ Ⓒ Ⓓ Ⓔ
23 Ⓐ Ⓑ Ⓒ Ⓓ Ⓔ
24 Ⓐ Ⓑ Ⓒ Ⓓ Ⓔ
25 Ⓐ Ⓑ Ⓒ Ⓓ Ⓔ
26 Ⓐ Ⓑ Ⓒ Ⓓ Ⓔ
27 Ⓐ Ⓑ Ⓒ Ⓓ Ⓔ
28 Ⓐ Ⓑ Ⓒ Ⓓ Ⓔ
29 Ⓐ Ⓑ Ⓒ Ⓓ Ⓔ
30 Ⓐ Ⓑ Ⓒ Ⓓ Ⓔ

31 Ⓐ Ⓑ Ⓒ Ⓓ Ⓔ
32 Ⓐ Ⓑ Ⓒ Ⓓ Ⓔ
33 Ⓐ Ⓑ Ⓒ Ⓓ Ⓔ
34 Ⓐ Ⓑ Ⓒ Ⓓ Ⓔ
35 Ⓐ Ⓑ Ⓒ Ⓓ Ⓔ
36 Ⓐ Ⓑ Ⓒ Ⓓ Ⓔ
37 Ⓐ Ⓑ Ⓒ Ⓓ Ⓔ
38 Ⓐ Ⓑ Ⓒ Ⓓ Ⓔ
39 Ⓐ Ⓑ Ⓒ Ⓓ Ⓔ
40 Ⓐ Ⓑ Ⓒ Ⓓ Ⓔ

SECTION 5

1 Ⓐ Ⓑ Ⓒ Ⓓ Ⓔ
2 Ⓐ Ⓑ Ⓒ Ⓓ Ⓔ
3 Ⓐ Ⓑ Ⓒ Ⓓ Ⓔ
4 Ⓐ Ⓑ Ⓒ Ⓓ Ⓔ
5 Ⓐ Ⓑ Ⓒ Ⓓ Ⓔ
6 Ⓐ Ⓑ Ⓒ Ⓓ Ⓔ
7 Ⓐ Ⓑ Ⓒ Ⓓ Ⓔ
8 Ⓐ Ⓑ Ⓒ Ⓓ Ⓔ
9 Ⓐ Ⓑ Ⓒ Ⓓ Ⓔ
10 Ⓐ Ⓑ Ⓒ Ⓓ Ⓔ

11 Ⓐ Ⓑ Ⓒ Ⓓ Ⓔ
12 Ⓐ Ⓑ Ⓒ Ⓓ Ⓔ
13 Ⓐ Ⓑ Ⓒ Ⓓ Ⓔ
14 Ⓐ Ⓑ Ⓒ Ⓓ Ⓔ
15 Ⓐ Ⓑ Ⓒ Ⓓ Ⓔ
16 Ⓐ Ⓑ Ⓒ Ⓓ Ⓔ
17 Ⓐ Ⓑ Ⓒ Ⓓ Ⓔ
18 Ⓐ Ⓑ Ⓒ Ⓓ Ⓔ
19 Ⓐ Ⓑ Ⓒ Ⓓ Ⓔ
20 Ⓐ Ⓑ Ⓒ Ⓓ Ⓔ

21 Ⓐ Ⓑ Ⓒ Ⓓ Ⓔ
22 Ⓐ Ⓑ Ⓒ Ⓓ Ⓔ
23 Ⓐ Ⓑ Ⓒ Ⓓ Ⓔ
24 Ⓐ Ⓑ Ⓒ Ⓓ Ⓔ
25 Ⓐ Ⓑ Ⓒ Ⓓ Ⓔ
26 Ⓐ Ⓑ Ⓒ Ⓓ Ⓔ
27 Ⓐ Ⓑ Ⓒ Ⓓ Ⓔ
28 Ⓐ Ⓑ Ⓒ Ⓓ Ⓔ
29 Ⓐ Ⓑ Ⓒ Ⓓ Ⓔ
30 Ⓐ Ⓑ Ⓒ Ⓓ Ⓔ

31 Ⓐ Ⓑ Ⓒ Ⓓ Ⓔ
32 Ⓐ Ⓑ Ⓒ Ⓓ Ⓔ
33 Ⓐ Ⓑ Ⓒ Ⓓ Ⓔ
34 Ⓐ Ⓑ Ⓒ Ⓓ Ⓔ
35 Ⓐ Ⓑ Ⓒ Ⓓ Ⓔ
36 Ⓐ Ⓑ Ⓒ Ⓓ Ⓔ
37 Ⓐ Ⓑ Ⓒ Ⓓ Ⓔ
38 Ⓐ Ⓑ Ⓒ Ⓓ Ⓔ
39 Ⓐ Ⓑ Ⓒ Ⓓ Ⓔ
40 Ⓐ Ⓑ Ⓒ Ⓓ Ⓔ

CAUTION Grid answers in the section below for SECTION 4 or SECTION 5 only if directed to do so in your test book.

Student-Produced Responses ONLY ANSWERS THAT ARE GRIDDED WILL BE SCORED. YOU WILL NOT RECEIVE CREDIT FOR ANYTHING WRITTEN IN THE BOXES.

Quality Assurance Mark ●

9, 10, 11, 12, 13

14, 15, 16, 17, 18

COMPLETE MARK ●
EXAMPLES OF INCOMPLETE MARKS Ⓐ Ⓑ Ⓒ Ⓓ / Ⓐ Ⓑ Ⓒ Ⓓ

You must use a No. 2 pencil and marks must be complete. Do not use a mechanical pencil. It is very important that you fill in the entire circle darkly and completely. If you change your responses, erase as completely as possible. Incomplete marks or erasures may affect your score.

SECTION 6

1 Ⓐ Ⓑ Ⓒ Ⓓ Ⓔ	11 Ⓐ Ⓑ Ⓒ Ⓓ Ⓔ	21 Ⓐ Ⓑ Ⓒ Ⓓ Ⓔ	31 Ⓐ Ⓑ Ⓒ Ⓓ Ⓔ
2 Ⓐ Ⓑ Ⓒ Ⓓ Ⓔ	12 Ⓐ Ⓑ Ⓒ Ⓓ Ⓔ	22 Ⓐ Ⓑ Ⓒ Ⓓ Ⓔ	32 Ⓐ Ⓑ Ⓒ Ⓓ Ⓔ
3 Ⓐ Ⓑ Ⓒ Ⓓ Ⓔ	13 Ⓐ Ⓑ Ⓒ Ⓓ Ⓔ	23 Ⓐ Ⓑ Ⓒ Ⓓ Ⓔ	33 Ⓐ Ⓑ Ⓒ Ⓓ Ⓔ
4 Ⓐ Ⓑ Ⓒ Ⓓ Ⓔ	14 Ⓐ Ⓑ Ⓒ Ⓓ Ⓔ	24 Ⓐ Ⓑ Ⓒ Ⓓ Ⓔ	34 Ⓐ Ⓑ Ⓒ Ⓓ Ⓔ
5 Ⓐ Ⓑ Ⓒ Ⓓ Ⓔ	15 Ⓐ Ⓑ Ⓒ Ⓓ Ⓔ	25 Ⓐ Ⓑ Ⓒ Ⓓ Ⓔ	35 Ⓐ Ⓑ Ⓒ Ⓓ Ⓔ
6 Ⓐ Ⓑ Ⓒ Ⓓ Ⓔ	16 Ⓐ Ⓑ Ⓒ Ⓓ Ⓔ	26 Ⓐ Ⓑ Ⓒ Ⓓ Ⓔ	36 Ⓐ Ⓑ Ⓒ Ⓓ Ⓔ
7 Ⓐ Ⓑ Ⓒ Ⓓ Ⓔ	17 Ⓐ Ⓑ Ⓒ Ⓓ Ⓔ	27 Ⓐ Ⓑ Ⓒ Ⓓ Ⓔ	37 Ⓐ Ⓑ Ⓒ Ⓓ Ⓔ
8 Ⓐ Ⓑ Ⓒ Ⓓ Ⓔ	18 Ⓐ Ⓑ Ⓒ Ⓓ Ⓔ	28 Ⓐ Ⓑ Ⓒ Ⓓ Ⓔ	38 Ⓐ Ⓑ Ⓒ Ⓓ Ⓔ
9 Ⓐ Ⓑ Ⓒ Ⓓ Ⓔ	19 Ⓐ Ⓑ Ⓒ Ⓓ Ⓔ	29 Ⓐ Ⓑ Ⓒ Ⓓ Ⓔ	39 Ⓐ Ⓑ Ⓒ Ⓓ Ⓔ
10 Ⓐ Ⓑ Ⓒ Ⓓ Ⓔ	20 Ⓐ Ⓑ Ⓒ Ⓓ Ⓔ	30 Ⓐ Ⓑ Ⓒ Ⓓ Ⓔ	40 Ⓐ Ⓑ Ⓒ Ⓓ Ⓔ

SECTION 7

1 Ⓐ Ⓑ Ⓒ Ⓓ Ⓔ	11 Ⓐ Ⓑ Ⓒ Ⓓ Ⓔ	21 Ⓐ Ⓑ Ⓒ Ⓓ Ⓔ	31 Ⓐ Ⓑ Ⓒ Ⓓ Ⓔ
2 Ⓐ Ⓑ Ⓒ Ⓓ Ⓔ	12 Ⓐ Ⓑ Ⓒ Ⓓ Ⓔ	22 Ⓐ Ⓑ Ⓒ Ⓓ Ⓔ	32 Ⓐ Ⓑ Ⓒ Ⓓ Ⓔ
3 Ⓐ Ⓑ Ⓒ Ⓓ Ⓔ	13 Ⓐ Ⓑ Ⓒ Ⓓ Ⓔ	23 Ⓐ Ⓑ Ⓒ Ⓓ Ⓔ	33 Ⓐ Ⓑ Ⓒ Ⓓ Ⓔ
4 Ⓐ Ⓑ Ⓒ Ⓓ Ⓔ	14 Ⓐ Ⓑ Ⓒ Ⓓ Ⓔ	24 Ⓐ Ⓑ Ⓒ Ⓓ Ⓔ	34 Ⓐ Ⓑ Ⓒ Ⓓ Ⓔ
5 Ⓐ Ⓑ Ⓒ Ⓓ Ⓔ	15 Ⓐ Ⓑ Ⓒ Ⓓ Ⓔ	25 Ⓐ Ⓑ Ⓒ Ⓓ Ⓔ	35 Ⓐ Ⓑ Ⓒ Ⓓ Ⓔ
6 Ⓐ Ⓑ Ⓒ Ⓓ Ⓔ	16 Ⓐ Ⓑ Ⓒ Ⓓ Ⓔ	26 Ⓐ Ⓑ Ⓒ Ⓓ Ⓔ	36 Ⓐ Ⓑ Ⓒ Ⓓ Ⓔ
7 Ⓐ Ⓑ Ⓒ Ⓓ Ⓔ	17 Ⓐ Ⓑ Ⓒ Ⓓ Ⓔ	27 Ⓐ Ⓑ Ⓒ Ⓓ Ⓔ	37 Ⓐ Ⓑ Ⓒ Ⓓ Ⓔ
8 Ⓐ Ⓑ Ⓒ Ⓓ Ⓔ	18 Ⓐ Ⓑ Ⓒ Ⓓ Ⓔ	28 Ⓐ Ⓑ Ⓒ Ⓓ Ⓔ	38 Ⓐ Ⓑ Ⓒ Ⓓ Ⓔ
9 Ⓐ Ⓑ Ⓒ Ⓓ Ⓔ	19 Ⓐ Ⓑ Ⓒ Ⓓ Ⓔ	29 Ⓐ Ⓑ Ⓒ Ⓓ Ⓔ	39 Ⓐ Ⓑ Ⓒ Ⓓ Ⓔ
10 Ⓐ Ⓑ Ⓒ Ⓓ Ⓔ	20 Ⓐ Ⓑ Ⓒ Ⓓ Ⓔ	30 Ⓐ Ⓑ Ⓒ Ⓓ Ⓔ	40 Ⓐ Ⓑ Ⓒ Ⓓ Ⓔ

CAUTION Grid answers in the section below for SECTION 6 or SECTION 7 only if directed to do so in your test book.

Student-Produced Responses

ONLY ANSWERS THAT ARE GRIDDED WILL BE SCORED. YOU WILL NOT RECEIVE CREDIT FOR ANYTHING WRITTEN IN THE BOXES.

Quality Assurance Mark ●

The following gridded response fields are numbered 9, 10, 11, 12, 13, 14, 15, 16, 17, 18, each containing columns of bubbles marked ⊘ ⊘ ⊘ / . . . . / ⓪ ⓪ ⓪ ⓪ / ① ① ① ① / ② ② ② ② / ③ ③ ③ ③ / ④ ④ ④ ④ / ⑤ ⑤ ⑤ ⑤ / ⑥ ⑥ ⑥ ⑥ / ⑦ ⑦ ⑦ ⑦ / ⑧ ⑧ ⑧ ⑧ / ⑨ ⑨ ⑨ ⑨.

COMPLETE MARK ● EXAMPLES OF INCOMPLETE MARKS Ⓐ Ⓑ Ⓓ Ⓐ Ⓑ Ⓓ

You must use a No. 2 pencil and marks must be complete. Do not use a mechanical pencil. It is very important that you fill in the entire circle darkly and completely. If you change your responses, erase as completely as possible. Incomplete marks or erasures may affect your score.

SECTION 8

1 Ⓐ Ⓑ Ⓒ Ⓓ Ⓔ	11 Ⓐ Ⓑ Ⓒ Ⓓ Ⓔ	21 Ⓐ Ⓑ Ⓒ Ⓓ Ⓔ	31 Ⓐ Ⓑ Ⓒ Ⓓ Ⓔ
2 Ⓐ Ⓑ Ⓒ Ⓓ Ⓔ	12 Ⓐ Ⓑ Ⓒ Ⓓ Ⓔ	22 Ⓐ Ⓑ Ⓒ Ⓓ Ⓔ	32 Ⓐ Ⓑ Ⓒ Ⓓ Ⓔ
3 Ⓐ Ⓑ Ⓒ Ⓓ Ⓔ	13 Ⓐ Ⓑ Ⓒ Ⓓ Ⓔ	23 Ⓐ Ⓑ Ⓒ Ⓓ Ⓔ	33 Ⓐ Ⓑ Ⓒ Ⓓ Ⓔ
4 Ⓐ Ⓑ Ⓒ Ⓓ Ⓔ	14 Ⓐ Ⓑ Ⓒ Ⓓ Ⓔ	24 Ⓐ Ⓑ Ⓒ Ⓓ Ⓔ	34 Ⓐ Ⓑ Ⓒ Ⓓ Ⓔ
5 Ⓐ Ⓑ Ⓒ Ⓓ Ⓔ	15 Ⓐ Ⓑ Ⓒ Ⓓ Ⓔ	25 Ⓐ Ⓑ Ⓒ Ⓓ Ⓔ	35 Ⓐ Ⓑ Ⓒ Ⓓ Ⓔ
6 Ⓐ Ⓑ Ⓒ Ⓓ Ⓔ	16 Ⓐ Ⓑ Ⓒ Ⓓ Ⓔ	26 Ⓐ Ⓑ Ⓒ Ⓓ Ⓔ	36 Ⓐ Ⓑ Ⓒ Ⓓ Ⓔ
7 Ⓐ Ⓑ Ⓒ Ⓓ Ⓔ	17 Ⓐ Ⓑ Ⓒ Ⓓ Ⓔ	27 Ⓐ Ⓑ Ⓒ Ⓓ Ⓔ	37 Ⓐ Ⓑ Ⓒ Ⓓ Ⓔ
8 Ⓐ Ⓑ Ⓒ Ⓓ Ⓔ	18 Ⓐ Ⓑ Ⓒ Ⓓ Ⓔ	28 Ⓐ Ⓑ Ⓒ Ⓓ Ⓔ	38 Ⓐ Ⓑ Ⓒ Ⓓ Ⓔ
9 Ⓐ Ⓑ Ⓒ Ⓓ Ⓔ	19 Ⓐ Ⓑ Ⓒ Ⓓ Ⓔ	29 Ⓐ Ⓑ Ⓒ Ⓓ Ⓔ	39 Ⓐ Ⓑ Ⓒ Ⓓ Ⓔ
10 Ⓐ Ⓑ Ⓒ Ⓓ Ⓔ	20 Ⓐ Ⓑ Ⓒ Ⓓ Ⓔ	30 Ⓐ Ⓑ Ⓒ Ⓓ Ⓔ	40 Ⓐ Ⓑ Ⓒ Ⓓ Ⓔ

SECTION 9

1 Ⓐ Ⓑ Ⓒ Ⓓ Ⓔ	11 Ⓐ Ⓑ Ⓒ Ⓓ Ⓔ	21 Ⓐ Ⓑ Ⓒ Ⓓ Ⓔ	31 Ⓐ Ⓑ Ⓒ Ⓓ Ⓔ
2 Ⓐ Ⓑ Ⓒ Ⓓ Ⓔ	12 Ⓐ Ⓑ Ⓒ Ⓓ Ⓔ	22 Ⓐ Ⓑ Ⓒ Ⓓ Ⓔ	32 Ⓐ Ⓑ Ⓒ Ⓓ Ⓔ
3 Ⓐ Ⓑ Ⓒ Ⓓ Ⓔ	13 Ⓐ Ⓑ Ⓒ Ⓓ Ⓔ	23 Ⓐ Ⓑ Ⓒ Ⓓ Ⓔ	33 Ⓐ Ⓑ Ⓒ Ⓓ Ⓔ
4 Ⓐ Ⓑ Ⓒ Ⓓ Ⓔ	14 Ⓐ Ⓑ Ⓒ Ⓓ Ⓔ	24 Ⓐ Ⓑ Ⓒ Ⓓ Ⓔ	34 Ⓐ Ⓑ Ⓒ Ⓓ Ⓔ
5 Ⓐ Ⓑ Ⓒ Ⓓ Ⓔ	15 Ⓐ Ⓑ Ⓒ Ⓓ Ⓔ	25 Ⓐ Ⓑ Ⓒ Ⓓ Ⓔ	35 Ⓐ Ⓑ Ⓒ Ⓓ Ⓔ
6 Ⓐ Ⓑ Ⓒ Ⓓ Ⓔ	16 Ⓐ Ⓑ Ⓒ Ⓓ Ⓔ	26 Ⓐ Ⓑ Ⓒ Ⓓ Ⓔ	36 Ⓐ Ⓑ Ⓒ Ⓓ Ⓔ
7 Ⓐ Ⓑ Ⓒ Ⓓ Ⓔ	17 Ⓐ Ⓑ Ⓒ Ⓓ Ⓔ	27 Ⓐ Ⓑ Ⓒ Ⓓ Ⓔ	37 Ⓐ Ⓑ Ⓒ Ⓓ Ⓔ
8 Ⓐ Ⓑ Ⓒ Ⓓ Ⓔ	18 Ⓐ Ⓑ Ⓒ Ⓓ Ⓔ	28 Ⓐ Ⓑ Ⓒ Ⓓ Ⓔ	38 Ⓐ Ⓑ Ⓒ Ⓓ Ⓔ
9 Ⓐ Ⓑ Ⓒ Ⓓ Ⓔ	19 Ⓐ Ⓑ Ⓒ Ⓓ Ⓔ	29 Ⓐ Ⓑ Ⓒ Ⓓ Ⓔ	39 Ⓐ Ⓑ Ⓒ Ⓓ Ⓔ
10 Ⓐ Ⓑ Ⓒ Ⓓ Ⓔ	20 Ⓐ Ⓑ Ⓒ Ⓓ Ⓔ	30 Ⓐ Ⓑ Ⓒ Ⓓ Ⓔ	40 Ⓐ Ⓑ Ⓒ Ⓓ Ⓔ

SECTION 10

1 Ⓐ Ⓑ Ⓒ Ⓓ Ⓔ	11 Ⓐ Ⓑ Ⓒ Ⓓ Ⓔ	21 Ⓐ Ⓑ Ⓒ Ⓓ Ⓔ	31 Ⓐ Ⓑ Ⓒ Ⓓ Ⓔ
2 Ⓐ Ⓑ Ⓒ Ⓓ Ⓔ	12 Ⓐ Ⓑ Ⓒ Ⓓ Ⓔ	22 Ⓐ Ⓑ Ⓒ Ⓓ Ⓔ	32 Ⓐ Ⓑ Ⓒ Ⓓ Ⓔ
3 Ⓐ Ⓑ Ⓒ Ⓓ Ⓔ	13 Ⓐ Ⓑ Ⓒ Ⓓ Ⓔ	23 Ⓐ Ⓑ Ⓒ Ⓓ Ⓔ	33 Ⓐ Ⓑ Ⓒ Ⓓ Ⓔ
4 Ⓐ Ⓑ Ⓒ Ⓓ Ⓔ	14 Ⓐ Ⓑ Ⓒ Ⓓ Ⓔ	24 Ⓐ Ⓑ Ⓒ Ⓓ Ⓔ	34 Ⓐ Ⓑ Ⓒ Ⓓ Ⓔ
5 Ⓐ Ⓑ Ⓒ Ⓓ Ⓔ	15 Ⓐ Ⓑ Ⓒ Ⓓ Ⓔ	25 Ⓐ Ⓑ Ⓒ Ⓓ Ⓔ	35 Ⓐ Ⓑ Ⓒ Ⓓ Ⓔ
6 Ⓐ Ⓑ Ⓒ Ⓓ Ⓔ	16 Ⓐ Ⓑ Ⓒ Ⓓ Ⓔ	26 Ⓐ Ⓑ Ⓒ Ⓓ Ⓔ	36 Ⓐ Ⓑ Ⓒ Ⓓ Ⓔ
7 Ⓐ Ⓑ Ⓒ Ⓓ Ⓔ	17 Ⓐ Ⓑ Ⓒ Ⓓ Ⓔ	27 Ⓐ Ⓑ Ⓒ Ⓓ Ⓔ	37 Ⓐ Ⓑ Ⓒ Ⓓ Ⓔ
8 Ⓐ Ⓑ Ⓒ Ⓓ Ⓔ	18 Ⓐ Ⓑ Ⓒ Ⓓ Ⓔ	28 Ⓐ Ⓑ Ⓒ Ⓓ Ⓔ	38 Ⓐ Ⓑ Ⓒ Ⓓ Ⓔ
9 Ⓐ Ⓑ Ⓒ Ⓓ Ⓔ	19 Ⓐ Ⓑ Ⓒ Ⓓ Ⓔ	29 Ⓐ Ⓑ Ⓒ Ⓓ Ⓔ	39 Ⓐ Ⓑ Ⓒ Ⓓ Ⓔ
10 Ⓐ Ⓑ Ⓒ Ⓓ Ⓔ	20 Ⓐ Ⓑ Ⓒ Ⓓ Ⓔ	30 Ⓐ Ⓑ Ⓒ Ⓓ Ⓔ	40 Ⓐ Ⓑ Ⓒ Ⓓ Ⓔ

SECTION 1
ESSAY
Time — 25 minutes

Turn to Section 1 of your answer sheet to write your essay.

The essay gives you an opportunity to show how effectively you can develop and express ideas. You should, therefore, take care to develop your point of view, present your ideas logically and clearly, and use language precisely.

Your essay must be written on the lines provided on your answer sheet—you will receive no other paper on which to write. You will have enough space if you write on every line, avoid wide margins, and keep your handwriting to a reasonable size. Remember that people who are not familiar with your handwriting will read what you write. Try to write or print so that what you are writing is legible to those readers.

You have twenty-five minutes to write an essay on the topic assigned below. DO NOT WRITE ON ANOTHER TOPIC. AN OFF-TOPIC ESSAY WILL RECEIVE A SCORE OF ZERO.

Think carefully about the issue presented in the following excerpt and the assignment below.

> Society may limit our actions, but it cannot limit our thoughts. Even if society disapproves of our opinions, we are ultimately free to decide whatever we want. Those decisions may, of course, have consequences, but they are still ours to make.

Assignment: Do society's rules limit our decisions such that our choices are not freely made? Plan and write an essay in which you develop your point of view on this issue. Support your position with reasoning and examples taken from your reading, studies, experience, or observations.

DO NOT WRITE YOUR ESSAY IN YOUR TEST BOOK. You will receive credit only for what you write on your answer sheet.

BEGIN WRITING YOUR ESSAY IN SECTION 1 OF THE ANSWER SHEET.

STOP
If you finish before time is called, you may check your work on this section only.
Do not turn to any other section in the test.

SECTION 2
Time — 25 minutes
20 Questions

Turn to Section 2 of your answer sheet to answer the questions in this section.

Directions: For this section, solve each problem and decide which is the best of the choices given. Fill in the corresponding circle on the answer sheet. You may use any available space for scratchwork.

Notes

1. The use of a calculator is permitted.

2. All numbers used are real numbers.

3. Figures that accompany problems in this test are intended to provide information useful in solving the problems. They are drawn as accurately as possible EXCEPT when it is stated in a specific problem that the figure is not drawn to scale. All figures lie in a plane unless otherwise indicated.

4. Unless otherwise specified, the domain of any function f is assumed to be the set of all real numbers x for which $f(x)$ is a real number.

Reference Information

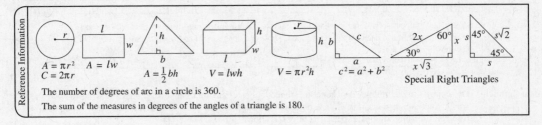

$A = \pi r^2$
$C = 2\pi r$
$A = lw$
$A = \frac{1}{2}bh$
$V = lwh$
$V = \pi r^2 h$
$c^2 = a^2 + b^2$

Special Right Triangles

The number of degrees of arc in a circle is 360.

The sum of the measures in degrees of the angles of a triangle is 180.

1. Leah is loading supplies from her garage into her truck. In the garage, she has 10 identical water containers that weigh a total of 250 pounds, 8 identical sacks of food that weigh a total of 400 pounds, and 120 identical blankets that weigh a total of 360 pounds. If Leah loads into her truck 5 containers of water, 3 sacks of food, and 40 blankets, what is the total weight, in pounds, of this cargo?

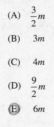

  (A)   250
  (B)   290
  (C)   395
  (D)   525
  (E) 1,010

2. The midpoint of segment $\overline{PQ}$ is F, and the length of $\overline{FQ}$ is $3m$. What is the length of $\overline{PQ}$ in terms of m ?

  (A) $\dfrac{3}{2}m$

  (B) $3m$

  (C) $4m$

  (D) $\dfrac{9}{2}m$

  (E) $6m$

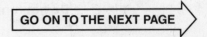

GO ON TO THE NEXT PAGE

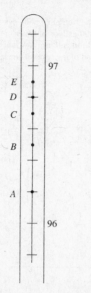

3. In the thermometer above, all the tick marks are equally spaced. Which lettered point is closest to 96.7 ?

(A) A
(B) B
(C) C
(D) D
(E) E

OFFICE SUPPLY COSTS

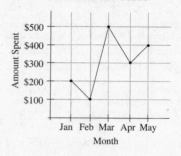

4. The line graph above shows the amount of money spent on office supplies by Jacksonville Tax Service during the first five months of the year. According to the graph, the amount it spent in May was how many times the amount it spent in January?

(A) 1
(B) 2
(C) 3
(D) 4
(E) 5

5. The cost for a bag of polished stones at a craft fair is $10 for a hand-stitched bag and 50 cents for each polished stone. Which of the following functions represents the total cost, in dollars, for p polished stones divided into two bags?

(A) $f(p) = 20 + 2p$

(B) $f(p) = 20 + \dfrac{1}{2}p$

(C) $f(p) = 10p + 2$

(D) $f(p) = 15p$

(E) $f(p) = 10p$

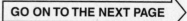
GO ON TO THE NEXT PAGE

$$-4, -3, -2, -1, 0, 1, 2, 3$$

6. If a number is randomly selected from the list above, what is the probability that it will be greater than –2 ?

(A) $\frac{1}{4}$

(B) $\frac{3}{8}$

(C) $\frac{1}{2}$

(D) $\frac{5}{8}$

(E) $\frac{3}{4}$

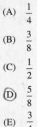

7. Three times a number is the same as that number subtracted from 12. What is the number?

$3x = 12 - x$

(A) –6

(B) –2

(C) 2

(D) 3

(E) 4

8. One-half of the water in a pond evaporates each week. There are 2,400 gallons of water in the pond at the end of the third week. In gallons, how much less water is in the pond at the end of the seventh week than at the end of the third week?

(A) 2,250

(B) 1,975

(C) 1,800

(D) 950

(E) 150

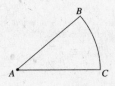

9. In the figure above, the length of arc $\overarc{BC}$ is $\frac{1}{9}$ the circumference of a circle with center A. If AB has length 6, what is the area of the sector of the circle shown above?

(A) $\frac{\pi}{9}$

(B) $\frac{\pi}{4}$

(C) 2π

(D) 4π

(E) 9π

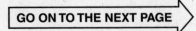

GO ON TO THE NEXT PAGE

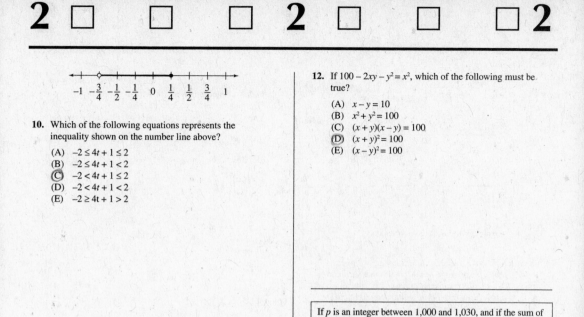

$$-1 \quad -\frac{3}{4} \quad -\frac{1}{2} \quad -\frac{1}{4} \quad 0 \quad \frac{1}{4} \quad \frac{1}{2} \quad \frac{3}{4} \quad 1$$

10. Which of the following equations represents the inequality shown on the number line above?

(A) $-2 \le 4t + 1 \le 2$
(B) $-2 \le 4t + 1 < 2$
(C) $-2 < 4t + 1 \le 2$
(D) $-2 < 4t + 1 < 2$
(E) $-2 \ge 4t + 1 > 2$

11. For any point on line ℓ, the product of the x-coordinate and the y-coordinate is less than or equal to zero. Which of the following could be the equation of line ℓ ?

(A) $y = -2$
(B) $x = -2$
(C) $y = -2x$
(D) $y = -2x - 2$
(E) $y = 2x - 2$

12. If $100 - 2xy - y^2 = x^2$, which of the following must be true?

(A) $x - y = 10$
(B) $x^2 + y^2 = 100$
(C) $(x + y)(x - y) = 100$
(D) $(x + y)^2 = 100$
(E) $(x - y)^2 = 100$

If p is an integer between 1,000 and 1,030, and if the sum of the digits of p is odd, then p must be odd.

13. Which of the following is one possible value of p that proves the above statement FALSE?

(A) 1,017
(B) 1,018
(C) 1,019
(D) 1,020
(E) 1,021

GO ON TO THE NEXT PAGE

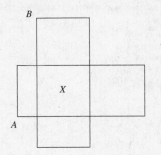

Note: Figure not drawn to scale.

14. In the figure above, rectangle *A* and rectangle *B* overlap to form square *X* and 4 smaller rectangles that surround square *X*. If *A* and *B* each have an area of 30, and all sides of the 4 surrounding rectangles are integers, which of the following is the area of square *X* ?

    (A) 49
    (B) 36
    (C) 25
    (D) 16
    (E)   9

15. Right triangle *A* has base *b*, height *h*, and area *x*. Rectangle *B* has length 2*b* and width 2*h*. What is the area of rectangle *B* in terms of *x* ?

    (A) 2*x*
    (B) 4*x*
    (C) 6*x*
    (D) 7*x*
    (E) 8*x*

16. If $a^{\frac{1}{2}} = b^2$ and *a* and *b* are both greater than 1, then what is the value of a^2 in terms of *b* ?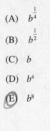

    (A) $b^{\frac{1}{4}}$

    (B) $b^{\frac{1}{2}}$

    (C) b

    (D) b^4

    (E) b^8

17. Shawn creates a meal by mixing the pastas, sauces, and toppings in his kitchen. Each meal he creates consists of one type of pasta, one sauce, and one type of topping. If Shawn can make exactly 30 different meals, which of the following could NOT be the number of sauces that Shawn has?

    (A) 1
    (B) 2
    (C) 3
    (D) 4
    (E) 5

GO ON TO THE NEXT PAGE ⇨

18. Each student in a cooking class of 50 students is assigned to create a dessert, an appetizer, or both. The total number of students creating an appetizer is seven more than the number of students creating a dessert. If the number of students who create two dishes is the same as the number of students who create exactly one dish, how many students created only a dessert?

(A) 9
(B) 16
(C) 25
(D) 34
(E) 41

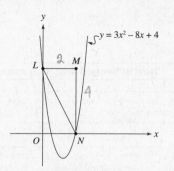

$y = 3x^2 - 8x + 4$

19. In the figure above, the graph of the function $3x^2 - 8x + 4$ is shown. The function intersects the y-axis at L and the x-axis at N. Line segments LM and MN are perpendicular, and LM is parallel to the x-axis. What is the area of triangle LMN ?

(A) $\dfrac{1}{2}$

(B) $\dfrac{3}{8}$

(C) 4

(D) 8

(E) 16

$\frac{2}{3}a = b$ $8 = \frac{3}{2}b$ $C = 18b^2 + 6$

20. If $2a = 3b$, $\dfrac{1}{3}c = 6b^2 + 2$, and $b > 0$, what is c in terms of a ?

(A) $8a^2 + 6$
(B) $8a^2 + 12$
(C) $12a^2 + 6$
(D) $18a^2 + 6$
(E) $18a^2 + 12$

$\left(\frac{a}{3}\right)^2$

$18 \cdot \frac{4}{9} = 8$

$C = 8a^2 + 6$

STOP
**If you finish before time is called, you may check your work on this section only.
Do not turn to any other section in the test.**

SECTION 4
Time — 25 minutes
24 Questions

Turn to Section 4 of your answer sheet to answer the questions in this section.

Directions: For each question in this section, select the best answer from among the choices given and fill in the corresponding circle on the answer sheet.

Each sentence below has one or two blanks, each blank indicating that something has been omitted. Beneath the sentence are five words or sets of words labeled A through E. Choose the word or set of words that, when inserted in the sentence, <u>best</u> fits the meaning of the sentence as a whole.

Example:

Desiring to ------- his taunting friends, Mitch gave them taffy in hopes it would keep their mouths shut.

(A) eliminate   (B) satisfy   (C) overcome
   (D) ridicule   (E) silence

Ⓐ Ⓑ Ⓒ Ⓓ ●

---

1. The witness's testimony was truly ------- , rambling and incoherent.

   (A) informative   (B) capricious   (C) disjointed
      (D) indignant   (E) essential

2. The recent addition of members who care less about fundraising than about throwing expensive parties has given rise to ------- that the club's funds will soon be -------.

   (A) recriminations . . enhanced
   (B) suspicions . . traditional
   (C) recommendations . . connected
   (D) concerns . . exhausted
   (E) allegations . . improved

3. The politician's speeches were -------: because he did not take a stand on any issue, voters felt ------- about his position on topics that mattered in the election.

   (A) misleading . . assured
   (B) vague . . uncertain
   (C) predictable . . determined
   (D) passionate . . absolute
   (E) legislative . . reasonable

4. The physicist did not support his theory with adequate -------; nonetheless, he was surprised that his claim was rejected as -------.

   (A) objectivity . . hearsay
   (B) significance . . sympathy
   (C) substantiation . . fallacy
   (D) equivocation . . guesswork
   (E) verification . . treachery

5. Although the candidates were respectful of each other during the debate, they ------- each other's character during their post-debate press conferences.

   (A) celebrated   (B) impugned   (C) elected
      (D) mollified   (E) filibustered

6. The library lends an abundance of science books -------- of technical jargon: the straightforward descriptions in such books help ------- new knowledge about scientific topics to beginners.

   (A) reminiscent . . divulge
   (B) devoid . . convey
   (C) redolent . . grant
   (D) deficient . . duplicate
   (E) indicative . . revive

7. The principal characterized his pupils as ------- because they were pampered and spoiled by their indulgent parents.

   (A) cosseted   (B) disingenuous   (C) corrosive
      (D) laconic   (E) mercurial

8. Greg was extremely ------- ; for he carefully accumulated money to ensure that he would have funds during his retirement.

   (A) reticent   (B) assiduous   (C) fallible
      (D) clairvoyant   (E) provident

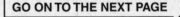
GO ON TO THE NEXT PAGE

Directions: Each passage below is followed by questions based on its content. Answer the questions on the basis of what is <u>stated</u> or <u>implied</u> in each passage and in any introductory material that may be provided.

Questions 9-10 are based on the following passage.

Since 1970, national parks have had to double the number of signs warning visitors of possible hazards. The new signs have a dual purpose in that they also protect the parks from
Line unnecessary litigation. In 1972, the National Parks Service
5 in Yellowstone was forced to pay more than $87,000 to the victim of a bear attack. This ruling prompted Yellowstone historian Lee Whittlesey to write, "Analogously I could ask, should New York's Central Park have signs every ten feet saying, 'Danger! Muggers!' just because a non-streetwise,
10 non–New Yorker might go walking there?"

9. The reference to "the victim" (lines 5-6) serves primarily to
(A) support a previous claim
(B) summarize a counterargument
(C) restate an inconsistency
(D) suggest a possible solution
(E) elaborate on a hypothesis

10. Lee Whittlesey's attitude toward the "ruling" in line 6 could best be described as
(A) disinterested
(B) apathetic
(C) appreciative
(D) enthusiastic
(E) sarcastic

Questions 11-12 are based on the following passage.

The notion that journalists should strive to remain objective has been challenged in recent years as new reporting styles have come into vogue. For instance, a novel
Line style of journalism, known as "gonzo journalism," emerged
5 in the 1970s. This form, which remains popular today, is characterized by a punchy style, rough and occasionally sarcastic language, and an apparent disregard for conventional journalistic writing customs. Unlike traditional journalists, gonzo journalists use the power of both emotions and
10 personal experience to convey their messages. Rather than adhering to the objectivity prized in standard journalistic writing, they believe in presenting an unedited perspective on a story in "true gonzo" form.

11. The passage suggests that the writing of "traditional journalists" (line 8) is typically
(A) controversial
(B) neutral
(C) superficial
(D) authoritative
(E) subjective

12. The passage primarily focuses on which aspect of gonzo journalism?
(A) Its comedic elements
(B) Its alterations of language
(C) Its editing
(D) Its subject matter
(E) Its unconventionality

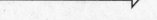
GO ON TO THE NEXT PAGE

Questions 13-24 are based on the following passages.

The following passages discuss the possibility of time travel. Passage 1 was written by a physicist, while passage 2 was written by a historian.

Passage 1

Ever since H.G. Wells published his classic novella, *The Time Machine*, in 1895, science fiction fans have been fascinated by the idea of contraptions that could effortlessly
Line transport passengers through time at the push of a button. The
5 truth, however, is that two-way travel from present to past would probably violate both the laws of causality and the laws of physics.

To be sure, certain celebrity scientists have postulated the existence of wormholes, warp drives, and other theoretical
10 constructs that might make time travel a reality. I have to confess that I find these notions rather unconvincing. While I agree with the view expressed by most physicists, which is that Einstein's Theory of Relativity ought to make some form of limited travel to the future possible, I consider it
15 highly implausible that an advanced civilization of the future would be able to send 'time-tourists' back into our own time. Eloquent support for my position comes from the eminent physicist Stephen Hawking, who has published a theory known as the "Chronological Protection Conjecture"
20 that conclusively debunks the concept of moving backwards through time.

Hawking raises two objections to the possibility of time travel. The first is that if time travelers were able to return to their own past, they might be able to alter the future.
25 Among time travel devotees, this conundrum is known as the Grandfather Paradox. Suppose a man was able to travel back in time and kill his own grandfather, thus preventing the man's father from being conceived. As a result, the man himself could never have been born. But since he was not
30 born, he could not have killed his grandfather. Thus, we are forced to conclude that the man both killed and could not have killed his grandfather! The implausibility of this scenario indicates a fundamental flaw in the concept of backwards time travel.
35 Another problem is that, as Hawking has observed, if time travel were possible, wouldn't we be swamped with visitors from the future? The logic of this argument is straightforward. On a grand scale, modern science is still in its infancy, yet the pace of technological advancement has been dramatic. In
40 less than a hundred years, we have gone from horse-drawn carriages to walking on the moon, and the rate of innovation shows no sign of slowing down. If it were possible to travel backwards in time, it seems almost inevitable that our distant descendants would eventually develop the necessary
45 technology, and return to visit their ancestors. The fact that hordes of time travelers are not walking around suggests that backwards time travel is unlikely to occur, no matter how technologically advanced our society becomes.

Passage 2

When the world's most respected physicist expresses
50 skepticism about an issue, his opinion carries a great deal of weight. Stephen Hawking's "Chronological Protection Conjecture," while allowing for the possibility of time travel to the future, presents a formidable logical argument against the possibility of traveling back through time, and has caused
55 many a professional scientist to dismiss the whole concept out of hand.

Not everyone, however, is convinced. Carl Sagan, for example, has called Hawking's argument "very dubious," and asserts that he can think of half a dozen reasons why "we
60 might not be awash in time travelers, and yet time travel is still possible." For one thing, there might be something about time travel that makes it impossible for us to see visitors from the future, even if they are in our midst. Or perhaps they simply don't want to be seen, and have developed the
65 necessary technology to prevent us from catching a glimpse of them. As for the oft-cited Grandfather Paradox, Sagan notes that while the idea of a self-consistent causality is appealing, "inconsistencies might very well be consistent with the universe." Though dismissive of Hawking's argument,
70 Sagan remains noncommittal about the possibility of time travel, preferring to "withhold judgment until there is better evidence."

Physicist Ronald Mallett, a professor at the University of Connecticut, is more optimistic. He believes that time
75 travel can be achieved within the next decade, and has actively pursued funding to build an experimental version of a time travel device. Mallett's time machine, known as the Spacetime Twisting by Light (STL) project, would use a ring laser and Einstein's Theory of Relativity to produce
80 a circulating cylinder of light. In theory, this device could produce "closed spacetime curves," allowing time travel into the past. Mallett's theories are controversial, but have gained adherents within the scientific community. One colleague expressed his support for Mallett's point of view by noting
85 that "while we shouldn't expect time machines to turn up in shops any time soon, we can be confident that one day, they will."

13. Which statement best describes a significant difference between the two passages?

(A) Passage 1 rejects the Chronological Protection Conjecture, while Passage 2 embraces it.
(B) Passage 1 analyzes a work of fiction, while Passage 2 presents scientific evidence.
(C) Passage 1 argues a position, while Passage 2 surveys current opinion about a topic.
(D) Passage 1 defends a point of view, while Passage 2 questions the objectivity of that point of view.
(E) Passage 1 details a phenomenon, while Passage 2 details an ideology that rejects that phenomenon.

GO ON TO THE NEXT PAGE ⟩

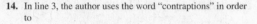
14. In line 3, the author uses the word "contraptions" in order to

(A) suggest that time travel may soon be within our grasp
(B) imply that science fiction novels have no merit
(C) praise the creativity of science fiction writers
(D) contrast fictional conceptions with a scientific point of view
(E) claim that literature exerts undue influence on scientific research

15. The "celebrity scientists" in line 8, Passage 1, most directly share the attitude of

(A) Stephen Hawking (Passage 1)
(B) H.G. Wells (Passage 1)
(C) "science fiction fans" (line 2, Passage 1)
(D) "a professional scientist" (line 55, Passage 2)
(E) Ronald Mallett (Passage 2)

16. The claim made in Passage 1 that the Chronological Protection Conjecture "conclusively debunks" (line 20) the notion of backwards time travel would most likely be characterized by the author of Passage 2 as

(A) an oversimplification of a complex issue
(B) a revelation of a surprising piece of evidence
(C) an attack on the credibility of reputable scientists
(D) evidence of the innate skepticism of professional physicists
(E) support for a position outlined by Ronald Mallett

17. In line 36, the word "swamped" most nearly means

(A) drenched
(B) invaded
(C) submerged
(D) slowed
(E) overwhelmed

18. The author of Passage 1 refers to "horse-drawn carriages" (lines 40-41) in order to

(A) criticize the primitive methods of transportation used by our ancestors
(B) highlight the need for additional research
(C) underscore the rate of scientific progress
(D) demonstrate the superiority of contemporary science
(E) draw attention to the dangers of modern technology

19. The argument outlined in lines 38-45 ("On a . . . ancestors") depends most directly on which of the following assumptions?

(A) Scientists will require thousands of years to develop time travel devices.
(B) Scientists will eventually solve all problems known to man.
(C) Travelers from the future would be unwilling to share their technology with us.
(D) Travelers from the future would be noticeable to contemporary humans.
(E) Travelers from the future would inevitably use technology for hostile purposes.

20. The author of Passage 2 would most likely characterize the Chronological Protection Conjecture as

(A) misunderstood
(B) perplexing
(C) controversial
(D) convoluted
(E) inaccurate

21. Both Stephen Hawking and the author of Passage 1 would agree that

(A) Einstein's Theory of Relativity demonstrates that time travel is impossible
(B) the Chronological Protection Conjecture is considered a controversial theory
(C) scientists should focus on problems in the present rather than seek to travel through time
(D) time travel in one direction may be theoretically possible
(E) time travel remains unlikely as long as science is publicly funded

22. How would Carl Sagan (line 57, Passage 2) most likely respond to the statement by the author of Passage 1 about "hordes of time travelers" (line 46) ?

(A) The issue of time travel requires further study.
(B) The concept of time travel raises serious moral issues.
(C) Time travelers are invisible because they come from another dimension.
(D) Opponents of time travel have ignored crucial evidence.
(E) The laws of the universe defy all logic.

GO ON TO THE NEXT PAGE ⟩

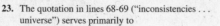
23. The quotation in lines 68-69 ("inconsistencies . . . universe") serves primarily to

- (A) offer an aside
- (B) summarize a difficulty
- (C) pose a riddle
- (D) provide concrete evidence
- (E) question a belief

24. In line 84, "noting" most nearly means

- (A) asserting
- (B) writing
- (C) perceiving
- (D) distinguishing
- (E) recording

STOP

**If you finish before time is called, you may check your work on this section only.
Do not turn to any other section in the test.**

NO TEST MATERIAL ON THIS PAGE.

SECTION 5
Time — 25 minutes
35 Questions

Turn to Section 5 of your answer sheet to answer the questions in this section.

Directions: For each question in this section, select the best answer from among the choices given and fill in the corresponding circle on the answer sheet.

The following sentences test correctness and effectiveness of expression. Part of each sentence or the entire sentence is underlined; beneath each sentence are five ways of phrasing the underlined material. Choice A repeats the original phrasing; the other four choices are different. If you think the original phrasing produces a better sentence than any of the alternatives, select choice A; if not, select one of the other choices.

In making your selection, follow the requirements of standard written English; that is, pay attention to grammar, choice of words, sentence construction, and punctuation. Your selection should result in the most effective sentence—clear and precise, without awkwardness or ambiguity.

EXAMPLE:

Bobby Flay baked his first cake <u>and he was thirteen years old then</u>.

(A) and he was thirteen years old then
(B) when he was thirteen
(C) at age thirteen years old
(D) upon the reaching of thirteen years
(E) at the time when he was thirteen

Ⓐ●ⒸⒹⒺ

1. <u>To arrest and imprison petty criminals</u> undeniably improved the vitality of each city neighborhood.

(A) To arrest and imprison petty criminals
(B) The arrest and imprisonment of petty criminals
(C) Having arrested and imprisoned petty criminals,
(D) Petty criminals, as a result of having been arrested and imprisoned,
(E) The petty criminals, by being arresting and imprisoned,

2. <u>Mark's brother received athletic scholarship offers from all the colleges he applied to, being the national fencing champion.</u>

(A) Mark's brother received athletic scholarship offers from all the colleges he applied to, being the national fencing champion.
(B) Mark's brother received athletic scholarship offers from all the colleges he applied to, and he was the national fencing champion.
(C) Mark's brother, who as the national fencing champion received athletic scholarship offers from all the colleges he applied to.
(D) Being Mark's brother, the national fencing champion received athletic scholarship offers from all the colleges he applied to.
(E) Mark's brother, the national fencing champion, received athletic scholarship offers from all the colleges he applied to.

3. Houses in parts of California are frequently destroyed by earthquakes, mudslides and <u>brushfires, because of this fact, many residents pay large premiums for homeowner's insurance.</u>

(A) brushfires, because of this fact, many residents pay large premiums for homeowner's insurance
(B) brushfires, with many residents therefore paying large premiums for homeowner's insurance
(C) brushfires, many residents pay large premiums for homeowner's insurance as a result
(D) brushfires; and many residents pay large premiums for homeowner's insurance
(E) brushfires; therefore, many residents pay large premiums for homeowner's insurance

4. The sun-ripened fruits from small orchards on rural farms are popularly used for making both <u>fresh pies but delicious</u> tarts.

(A) fresh pies but delicious
(B) fresh pies or delicious
(C) delicious but fresh pies and
(D) fresh pies and delicious
(E) fresh pies being like delicious

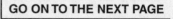

GO ON TO THE NEXT PAGE

5. Fearful of the dangerous by-products from combustion engines and factories in urban areas, <u>ecologists suggest that riding bikes, subways, and public buses will</u> help decrease pollution.

(A) ecologists suggest that riding bikes, subways, and public buses will
(B) riding bikes, subways, and public buses, this is what ecologists suggest will
(C) and with suggestions from ecologists that riding bikes, subways, and public buses will
(D) suggestions from ecologists concerning the riding of bikes, subways, and public buses will
(E) ecologists suggesting that riding bikes, subways, and public buses would

6. In her biography of Abraham Lincoln, Goodwin succeeds in her intention not only to illustrate her historical subject <u>and establishing that</u> his leadership was remarkable.

(A) and establishing that
(B) while establishing that
(C) but also to establish that
(D) but also her establishment of how
(E) and also to establish how

7. Rachel Carson, the author of the controversial book *Silent Spring*, <u>was a supporter of environmental protection, a defender of animal conservation, and an opponent of</u> pesticide usage.

(A) was a supporter of environmental protection, a defender of animal conservation, and an opponent of
(B) was a supporter of environmental protection, a defender of animal conservation, and opposing
(C) was a supporter of environmental protection, defended animal conservation, and an opponent of
(D) was a supporter of environmental protection, a defender of animal conservation, and she opposed
(E) was a supporter of environmental protection, a defender of animal conservation, opposing

8. The school's Honor Society accepts students from various majors <u>having earned</u> excellent grades in all their first-year coursework.

(A) having earned
(B) who have earned
(C) for earning
(D) to be earning
(E) and they earned

9. <u>Working in the rafters, the rehearsal came to an abrupt end when a stagehand dropped a heavy camera;</u> thankfully, no one was injured.

(A) Working in the rafters, the rehearsal came to an abrupt end when a stagehand dropped a heavy camera
(B) Working in the rafters, a heavy camera was dropped by a stagehand, abruptly ending all rehearsal
(C) Abruptly ending all rehearsal, a stagehand dropped a heavy camera working in the rafters
(D) The rehearsal came to an abrupt end when a stagehand working in the rafters dropped a heavy camera
(E) When working in the rafters, a heavy camera dropped by the stagehand abruptly ended all rehearsal

10. We have come to acknowledge that history teaches important lessons <u>which, if they are ignored, you put everyone in jeopardy</u>.

(A) which, if they are ignored, you put everyone in jeopardy
(B) and if you ignore them you put everyone in jeopardy
(C) and ignoring it will be perilous
(D) and it puts everyone in jeopardy to ignore them
(E) that we ignore at our own peril

11. The school board's ideas for reforming the curriculum were offered <u>more as general guidelines than as</u> precise prescriptions for change.

(A) more as general guidelines than as
(B) as general guidelines more than
(C) more for general guidelines than
(D) for general guidelines more than as
(E) as more general guidelines than

GO ON TO THE NEXT PAGE

The following sentences test your ability to recognize grammar and usage errors. Each sentence contains either a single error or no error at all. No sentence contains more than one error. The error, if there is one, is underlined and lettered. If the sentence contains an error, select the one underlined part that must be changed to make the sentence correct. If the sentence is correct, select choice E. In choosing answers, follow the requirements of standard written English.

EXAMPLE:

The other players and her significantly improved
    A   B   C

the game plan created by the coaches. No error
           D   E

Ⓐ ● Ⓒ Ⓓ Ⓔ

12. Prior to the invention of the printing press in the 1400s, the

only way to produce duplicates of books has been to
       A   B   C

have copies handwritten by professional scribes. No error
         D   E

13. The least effective supervisors make their subordinates
       A   B

feel worthless and inadequate; as a result they

often find that their subordinates deliberately refuse to
   C   D

comply with directives and requests. No error
                         E

14. During her term at Trinity University studying music
    A

composition, Julia becoming known for her tendency
              B

to incorporate both traditional instruments and industrial
  C

machinery in her remakes of 1980s rock songs. No error
         D   E

15. Trailing behind the marching band, the art club's float
    A

was the most brightest painted display in the parade.
  B   C   D

No error
E

16. While the speaker showed us her research on
   A

contemporary Chinese architecture, she illustrated

different artistic elements using drawings of her
                         B

own favorite designs influenced by Chinese structures,
   C

giving you a clear understanding of the lecture. No error
   D   E

17. One of the most famous plays from ancient Greece
  A

are The Clouds, a satirical and unusually critical
 B   C

comedy about the teaching styles found in Athens at the
                      D

time. No error
     E

18. An early advocate to the woman's suffrage movement,
       A

Victoria Woodhull was a candidate for President,
            B

although when she tried to vote, election officials would
            C

not accept her ballot. No error
    D   E

19. The city park bounded by North Street, South Street,
        A

First Avenue, and Second Avenue contain a garden and a
                 B

pea patch communally tended by local residents.
       C   D

No error
E

GO ON TO THE NEXT PAGE

20. For most of her life, Janet has saved money carefully, but
    A

    now that her savings are becoming increasingly plentiful
    B   C

    bankers are encouraging her to invest it. No error
                                          D   E

21. At a time when knowledge of the Maori warrior
            A

    tradition appears on the brink to vanishing, the
             B   C

    contemporary media publications in New Zealand are

    making a valiant attempt to preserve this cultural
                     D

    heritage. No error
              E

22. While visiting New York, the tourist group thought that
    A   B

    the city's smog problem was worse than Los Angeles.
                            C   D

    No error
    E

23. Dr. Cartwright smugly revealed his department's latest
                    A   B

    product, a medication that cures the common cold when
            C

    taking a pill. No error
    D   E

24. As interns, young students work not for companies of
    A   B

    their own choosing but rather for companies chosen by
    C   D

    their professors. No error
                     E

25. Even though the weather was abysmal, Anika arrived
                             A

    twenty minutes early for her class since she had
                        B

    ran quickly all the way from the parking lot. No error
    C   D   E

26. Daily requests for interviews with the mayor of Chicago
                                  A

    number more than twice that of the governor of
    B   C   D

    Illinois. No error
              E

27. To claim that an advertisement persuades whomever one
                                                     A

    wants it to persuade is often discounting the intelligence
    B   C

    and even the aptitude of an audience. No error
        D   E

28. Overuse of chemical fertilizers on farm crops

    both destroys many beneficial organisms in the soil
    A   B

    and weakens the crop's resistance to ever more virulent
        C   D

    diseases. No error
              E

29. Between the two major techniques for culturing bacteria,
    A

    the streaking method tends to be the one preferred by
                        B   C

    scientists because it is the most effective. No error
                               D   E

GO ON TO THE NEXT PAGE

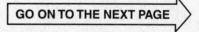

Directions: The following passage is an early draft of an essay. Some parts of the passage need to be rewritten.

Read the passage and select the best answers for the questions that follow. Some questions are about particular sentences or parts of sentences and ask you to improve sentence structure or word choice. Other questions ask you to consider organization and development. In choosing answers, follow the requirements of standard written English.

Questions 30-35 are based on the following passage.

(1) After eating gelato in Florence, Italy, I was amazed at how different it was from the kind sold in America. (2) Gelato is Italian ice cream, but it is smoother and fluffier than ours. (3) Some American cities sell gelato at shops also called *gelaterias,* and some ice cream manufacturers produce processed gelato. (4) Neither product tastes like Italian gelato. (5) I craved the flavors and texture of the Italian version I had experienced. (6) I decided to make my own gelato.

(7) I discovered that gelato is very, very hard to make as good as they do in Italy. (8) First, it needs to have some air by churning it into liquid to make it fluffy, but too much air will make it too fluffy. (9) American stores and manufacturers add things like emulsifiers to keep the gelato fluffy for an unnaturally long time. (10) Gelato in Italy is made and eaten on the same day so the texture does not need artificial and chemical preservatives.

(11) Flavors of American versions of gelato were bland in comparison. (12) American producers find it easier to use frozen canned or otherwise preserved fruits, but highly processed fruits and other ingredients lose a lot of flavor. (13) Italian producers purchase just enough fresh fruit to make the day's batch of gelato. (14) In conclusion, gelato does not work in America because its nature prevents it from mass production. (15) Good gelato must be created correctly, in the Italian way, in small batches and using the freshest ingredients.

30. In context, which of the following is best placed at the beginning of sentence 4 (reproduced below) ?

    Neither product tastes like Italian gelato.

    (A) However,
    (B) Consequently,
    (C) Additionally,
    (D) Subsequently,
    (E) And,

31. In context, which of the following is the best version of sentences 5 and 6 (reproduced below) ?

    I craved the flavors and texture of the Italian version. I decided to make my own gelato.

    (A) In order to make my own gelato I experienced the flavors and texture of the Italian version I craved.
    (B) The flavors and textures differ, and I craved the Italian version, so I attempted to create my own gelato.
    (C) Because I craved the flavors and textures of the Italian version, I decided to make my own gelato.
    (D) Since the flavors and textures differ, I craved the Italian version, I decided to make my own gelato.
    (E) I decided that my own gelato would be made with the flavors and textures of the Italian version because I craved it.

32. In context, which is the best version of the underlined portion of sentence 7 (reproduced below) ?

    I discovered that gelato is very, very hard to make as good as they do in Italy.

    (A) (as it is now)
    (B) gelato is very hard to make, it is better
    (C) because gelato is harder to make as good as it is
    (D) it is very difficult to make gelato as good as the kind found
    (E) it is more difficult to make gelato as good as they do

33. In context, which of the following is the best revision of sentence 8 (reproduced below) ?

    First, it needs to have some air by churning it into liquid to make it fluffy, but too much air will make it too fluffy.

    (A) The fluffy texture of gelato is achieved by carefully churning milk or water to ensure the perfect quantity of air is added to the liquid.
    (B) To make gelato fluffy, one must churn air into a liquid such as milk or water, and watch the texture so that not too much air is churned in.
    (C) Starting with a liquid, such as milk or water, it is churned carefully to add the air that makes it fluffy, though too much air is a bad thing.
    (D) Milk or water plus air transforms the liquid into gelato; one must add the proper amount of air for a fluffy consistency.
    (E) One can churn air into liquid for fluffy gelato; be careful about excess air which makes the gelato overly fluffy.

GO ON TO THE NEXT PAGE ⟩

34. In sentence 9, "things" is best replaced by

(A) stuff
(B) ingredients
(C) processes
(D) objects
(E) manufacturers

35. In context, which of the following is the best revision of sentence 14 (reproduced below) ?

In conclusion, gelato does not work in America because its nature prevents it from mass production.

(A) (As it is now)
(B) Since gelato does not work in America because its nature prevents it from mass production.
(C) However, gelato is not possible in America because its nature makes it difficult to mass-produce.
(D) Simply put, American manufacturers cannot make authentic-tasting gelato because by its nature it is difficult to mass produce.
(E) Being that American manufacturers cannot make authentic-tasting gelato because by nature it is difficult to mass-produce.

STOP

**If you finish before time is called, you may check your work on this section only.
Do not turn to any other section in the test.**

SECTION 6
Time — 25 minutes
18 Questions

Turn to Section 6 of your answer sheet to answer the questions in this section.

Directions: This section contains two types of questions. You have 25 minutes to complete both types. For questions 1-8, solve each problem and decide which is the best of the choices given. Fill in the corresponding circle on the answer sheet. You may use any available space for scratchwork.

Notes

1. The use of a calculator is permitted.

2. All numbers used are real numbers.

3. Figures that accompany problems in this test are intended to provide information useful in solving the problems. They are drawn as accurately as possible EXCEPT when it is stated in a specific problem that the figure is not drawn to scale. All figures lie in a plane unless otherwise indicated.

4. Unless otherwise specified, the domain of any function f is assumed to be the set of all real numbers x for which $f(x)$ is a real number.

Reference Information

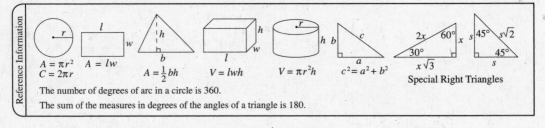

$A = \pi r^2$
$C = 2\pi r$

$A = lw$

$A = \frac{1}{2}bh$

$V = lwh$

$V = \pi r^2 h$

$c^2 = a^2 + b^2$

Special Right Triangles

The number of degrees of arc in a circle is 360.

The sum of the measures in degrees of the angles of a triangle is 180.

1. If one angle in a right triangle is 20, which of the following is the degree measure of another angle in the triangle?

   (A) 30
   (B) 40
   (C) 50
   (D) 60
   (E) 70

2. If $7y = 3$, what is the value of $\frac{21y}{9}$?

   (A) $\frac{3}{7}$
   (B) 1
   (C) $\frac{7}{3}$
   (D) $\frac{14}{3}$
   (E) 9

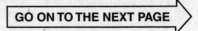
GO ON TO THE NEXT PAGE

NUMBER OF PARKING VIOLATIONS BY YEAR AND MONTH

Month	2007	2008
August	35	30
September	46	51
October	25	30
November	10	15
December	19	39

3. According to the information given in the table above, what was the overall increase from 2007 to 2008 in the number of parking violations for August through December?

(A) 20
(B) 25
(C) 30
(D) 35
(E) 40

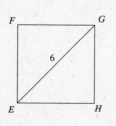

4. In the figure above, *EFGH* is a square. What is the length of side $\overline{EF}$?

(A) 2
(B) $2\sqrt{2}$ (approximately 2.83)
(C) 3
(D) $3\sqrt{2}$ (approximately 4.24)
(E) $3\sqrt{3}$ (approximately 5.20)

5. Which of the following is NOT a possible value of $2 - x$, if x is a one-digit integer?

(A) −8
(B) −6
(C) −4
(D) −2
(E) 2

6. If $a^x = 4$ and $a^c = 64$, what is the value of a^{x-c} ?

(A) −60

(B) −16

(C) $\dfrac{1}{16}$

(D) 16

(E) 32

GO ON TO THE NEXT PAGE

7. Zenia drew a route on a map, starting with a 32 centimeter line from her home due north to Anne's home. She continued the route with a 44 centimeter line due south to Beth's home, a 33 centimeter line due west to Caleb's home, and a 28 centimeter line due east to Damon's home. What is the distance on the map, in centimeters, from Damon's home to Zenia's home?

(A)   5
(B)   12
(C)   13
(D)   33
(E)   55

8. If 60 percent of Jared's jigsaw puzzles have 50 pieces each and 40 percent of his jigsaw puzzles have 30 pieces each, what is the average (arithmetic mean) number of pieces per puzzle?

(A)   36
(B)   38
(C)   40
(D)   42
(E)   44

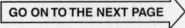

GO ON TO THE NEXT PAGE

Directions: For Student-Produced Response questions 9-18, use the grids at the bottom of the answer sheet page on which you have answered questions 1-8.

Each of the remaining 10 questions requires you to solve the problem and enter your answer by marking the circles in the special grid, as shown in the examples below. You may use any available space for scratch work.

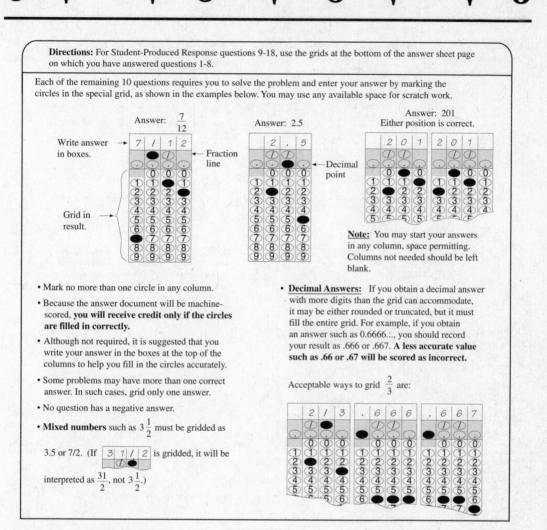

Answer: $\frac{7}{12}$

Write answer in boxes. → Fraction line

Grid in result. →

Answer: 2.5 ← Decimal point

Answer: 201
Either position is correct.

Note: You may start your answers in any column, space permitting. Columns not needed should be left blank.

• Mark no more than one circle in any column.

• Because the answer document will be machine-scored, **you will receive credit only if the circles are filled in correctly.**

• Although not required, it is suggested that you write your answer in the boxes at the top of the columns to help you fill in the circles accurately.

• Some problems may have more than one correct answer. In such cases, grid only one answer.

• No question has a negative answer.

• **Mixed numbers** such as $3\frac{1}{2}$ must be gridded as 3.5 or 7/2. (If [3 1 / 2] is gridded, it will be interpreted as $\frac{31}{2}$, not $3\frac{1}{2}$.)

• **Decimal Answers:** If you obtain a decimal answer with more digits than the grid can accommodate, it may be either rounded or truncated, but it must fill the entire grid. For example, if you obtain an answer such as 0.6666..., you should record your result as .666 or .667. **A less accurate value such as .66 or .67 will be scored as incorrect.**

Acceptable ways to grid $\frac{2}{3}$ are:

9. Belinda can bike 10 miles in 3 hours. At this rate, how many miles can she bike in 4 hours?

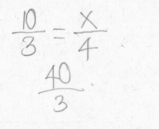

$$\frac{10}{3} = \frac{x}{4}$$

$$\frac{40}{3}$$

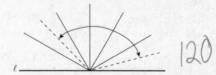

120

10. In the figure above, line ℓ is intersected by five line segments, creating six angles with equal measures. If the dotted segments bisect two of those angles, what is the measure of the angle indicated by the arrow? (Disregard the degree symbol when gridding your answer.)

GO ON TO THE NEXT PAGE ▷

11. If $2,500 < x + 1,300 < 5,200$, and x is an integer, what is the greatest possible value of x ?

3,899

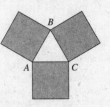

12. In the figure above, ABC is an equilateral triangle formed by the edges of three squares. If triangle ABC has a perimeter of 15, what is the total area of the shaded regions?

75

Number of Hours Spent on Email

13. Plotted on the graph above are the results of a survey in which 17 office workers were asked how many hours a day they spent composing email and attending meetings. Each dot reflects one office worker. The median number of hours spent composing emails is how much less than the median number of hours spent attending meetings?

2

14. In a class of 330 students, there are 60 more girls than boys. How many girls are there in the class?

195

GO ON TO THE NEXT PAGE ⇨

15. Maria has 74 pebbles that she wants to divide into 25 piles. If the tenth pile is to have more pebbles than any other pile, what is the least number of pebbles Maria can put into the tenth pile?

4

16. If $2452 = 60q + 52r$, and q and r are positive integers, what is one possible value for $q + r$?

41, 43, 45, 47

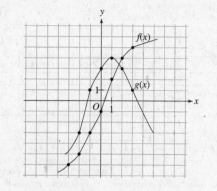

17. Portions of the graphs of functions $f(x)$ and $g(x)$ are shown in the figure above. If $h(x)$ is defined by $h(x) = f(2x) + 2g(x)$ for all values of x, what is the value of $h(1)$?

12

18. In the xy plane, lines a and c intersect at the point with coordinates $(n, \frac{7}{2})$. If the equation of line a is $y = \frac{1}{2}x + 5$, and the equation of line c is $y = \frac{1}{3}x + b$, what is the value of b ?

4.5

STOP

If you finish before time is called, you may check your work on this section only.
Do not turn to any other section in the test.

SECTION 7
Time — 25 minutes
24 Questions

Turn to Section 7 of your answer sheet to answer the questions in this section.

Directions: For each question in this section, select the best answer from among the choices given and fill in the corresponding circle on the answer sheet.

Each sentence below has one or two blanks, each blank indicating that something has been omitted. Beneath the sentence are five words or sets of words labeled A through E. Choose the word or set of words that, when inserted in the sentence, <u>best</u> fits the meaning of the sentence as a whole.

Example:

Desiring to ------- his taunting friends, Mitch gave them taffy in hopes it would keep their mouths shut.

(A) eliminate   (B) satisfy   (C) overcome
  (D) ridicule   (E) silence

Ⓐ Ⓑ Ⓒ Ⓓ ●

---

1. Once viewed as ------- , the dream of cars that produce no harmful pollutants may soon be ------- now that prototypes have been built that emit only water vapor.

   (A) fundamental . . imagined
   (B) quixotic . . achieved
   (C) hypothetical . . deluded
   (D) inescapable . . realized
   (E) conclusive . . mysterious

2. Reviewers noted that the autobiography was exceptionally ------- due to the writer's truthful and revealing descriptions of her life.

   (A) candid   (B) didactic   (C) comprehensive
     (D) baroque   (E) languid

3. Some people who are ------- appear to be aloof when in reality they are merely shy.

   (A) belligerent   (B) pliant   (C) timorous
     (D) conspicuous   (E) avuncular

4. Glowing with joy and delight, Laura was positively ------- on her graduation day.

   (A) rapturous   (B) assiduous   (C) nihilistic
     (D) intractable   (E) phlegmatic

5. Conservationists are contemplating a plan to remove the broken crates, washed-up cargo, and other ------- left over from the shipwreck.

   (A) raiment   (B) detritus   (C) periphery
     (D) desolation   (E) trajectory

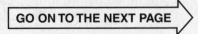
GO ON TO THE NEXT PAGE

> **Directions:** Each passage below is followed by questions based on its content. Answer the questions on the basis of what is <u>stated</u> or <u>implied</u> in each passage and in any introductory material that may be provided.

Questions 6-9 are based on the following passages.

Passage 1

Charles Ives, the iconoclastic American composer who mixed everything from religious hymns to brass band marches to classical music into his symphonies, would have *Line* been right at home in the musical culture of contemporary
5 America. Our musical tastes prove us to be robust explorers, unconstrained by tradition. We mix and match musical styles rather than preserve the preferences of our parents and grandparents. America has no single dominant musical culture. What characterizes our musical taste is how we listen,
10 not what we listen to. As listeners, we commonly amalgamate a wide range of musical styles into our own personal "soundtracks." The whole world's music is our music.

Passage 2

Music is often viewed as one of the most salient indicators of cultural identity. As a little boy, my entire musical universe
15 consisted of Chinese classical music. I thought all kids grew up learning to play instruments such as the Erhu (a two-stringed fiddle) and the Xindi (a bamboo flute). After we immigrated to America, my ideas about music were turned upside down. In school, my classmates seemed to be
20 conversant in every conceivable musical genre. Their tastes rubbed off on me, and I became interested in a broad range of different styles. By the time I graduated from high school, I was as likely to listen to hip-hop or rock as to traditional Chinese music.

6. Which of the following best describes how the two passages differ in their discussions of music?

(A) Passage 1 lists several popular types of music, whereas passage 2 focuses on types that are rarely heard.

(B) Passage 1 suggests that a person's upbringing determines listening habits, whereas Passage 2 implies that listening habits are largely self-determined.

(C) Passage 1 offers a historical analysis of music, whereas Passage 2 presents an abstract theory of music.

(D) Passage 1 emphasizes aspects of music that are common to all cultures, whereas Passage 2 contrasts the music of different cultures.

(E) Passage 1 remarks on a culture's general attitude toward music, whereas Passage 2 discusses the listening habits of a certain individual.

7. The author of Passage 1 would most likely describe the listening habits discussed in the last sentence of Passage 2 (lines 22-24) as

(A) surprisingly bold
(B) regrettably conservative
(C) embarrassingly pretentious
(D) characteristically American
(E) overly tolerant

8. Unlike the author of Passage 1, the author of Passage 2 makes significant use of

(A) literary metaphors
(B) personal experience
(C) historical analysis
(D) direct quotation
(E) hypothetical scenarios

9. Which of the following best describes the relationship between the two passages?

(A) Passage 1 discusses musical styles that are criticized in Passage 2.
(B) Passage 1 provides a broader context for the experiences described in Passage 2.
(C) Passage 1 provides a personal interpretation of the thesis put forth in Passage 2.
(D) Passage 2 cites examples referred to in Passage 1 to correct a common misconception.
(E) Passage 2 raises objections that are resolved in Passage 1.

GO ON TO THE NEXT PAGE

Questions 10-16 are based on the following passage.

The following passage is excerpted from a novel written in 1909. Dr. Karl Hubers, a main character, is a world-famous scientist.

He was one of the men who go before. Out in the great field of knowledge's unsurveyed territory he worked—a blazer of the trail, a voice crying from the wilderness: "I
Line have opened up another few feet. You can come now a little
5 farther." Then the crowd would come in and take possession, soon to become accustomed to the ground, forgetting that only a little while before it had been impassable, scarcely thinking of the little body of men who had opened the way for them. And only the little band itself would ever know how
10 stony that path, how deep the ditches, how thick and thorny the underbrush. "Why this couldn't have been so bad," the crowd said, after it had flocked in - "strange it should have taken so long!"

At the time of his falling in love, Dr. Karl Hubers
15 was thirty-nine years old. He had worked in European laboratories, notably the Pasteur Institute of Paris, and among men of his kind was regarded as one to be reckoned with. Then the president of a great university had spied Karl Hubers, working away over there in Europe. The president
20 had a genius for perceiving when a man stood on the verge of great celebrity, and so he cried out now: "Come over and do some teaching for us! We will give you just as good a laboratory as you have there and plenty of time for your own work." Now, while he would be glad enough to have Dr.
25 Hubers do the teaching, what he wanted most of all was to possess him, so that in the day of victory that young giant of a university would rise up and proclaim: "See! We have done it!" And Dr. Hubers, lured by the promise of time and facility for his own work, liking what he knew of the young
30 university, had come over and established himself in Chicago.

Generations before, his ancestors in Europe had swept things before them with a mighty hand. With defeat and renunciation they did not reckon. If they loved a woman, they picked her up and took her away. And civilisation has not
35 quite washed the blood of those men from the earth. Europe gave to Karl Hubers something more than a scholar's mind. At any rate, he did a very unapproved and most uncivilised thing. When he fell in love and decided he wanted to marry Ernestine Stanley, he asked for his year's leave of absence
40 before he went to find out whether Miss Stanley was kindly disposed to the idea of marrying him. Now why he did that, it is not possible to state, but the thing proving him quite hopeless as a civilised product is that it never struck him that there was anything so very peculiar in his order of procedure.
45 His assistants had to do a great deal of reminding after he came back that week, and they never knew until afterwards that his abstraction was caused by something quite different from germs. They thought—unknowing assistants—that he was on a new trail, and judged from the expression of his face
50 that it was going to prove most productive.

10. Which of the following most resembles the actions of "the crowd" (line 5) ?

(A) A climber who attempts to reach the top of a mountain is forced to stop because of the obstacles in his path
(B) A star athlete who is expected to lead his team suffers a career-ending injury in the first game of the season
(C) A son who inherits a business that his father started is unappreciative of the difficulties that the father faced
(D) A worker who attempts to unionize a group of factory laborers is abruptly fired by his manager
(E) A composer who writes strikingly original music refuses to compromise for the sake of popularity

11. According to the passage, which of the following best describes what the president of the university "wanted most of all" (line 25) ?

(A) To have physical control over Dr. Hubers
(B) To claim credit for Dr. Hubers' achievements
(C) To facilitate Dr. Hubers' spiritual development
(D) To have Dr. Hubers work as an instructor at the university
(E) To make Dr. Hubers feel indebted to him

12. Lines 35-36 ("Europe gave . . . mind") most directly suggest that Dr. Hubers possesses which of the following qualities?

(A) intelligence
(B) brutality
(C) absent-mindedness
(D) cleanliness
(E) impulsiveness

GO ON TO THE NEXT PAGE

13. In line 41, the word "disposed" most nearly means

(A) inclined
(B) rejected
(C) dispensed
(D) conditioned
(E) equipped

14. The author uses the phrase "quite hopeless" (lines 42-43) in order to

(A) emphasize the unlikelihood of Miss Stanley returning his affections
(B) evoke sympathy for Dr. Hubers' unfortunate predicament
(C) suggest that Dr. Hubers is oblivious to social conventions
(D) indicate that Dr. Hubers is accustomed to living in the wilderness
(E) criticize Dr. Hubers for his overly clinical view of marriage

15. The description in lines 45-48 ("His assistants . . . germs") primarily suggests that Dr. Hubers

(A) was too great a thinker to be concerned with trivial details
(B) had discovered a revolutionary cure for a disease
(C) was afflicted by a condition that caused temporary loss of memory
(D) was distracted by concerns unrelated to his work
(E) had never been able to function without the help of others

16. In context, the phrase "unknowing assistants" (line 48) serves to suggest that

(A) a character was predictable
(B) an impression was mistaken
(C) an employee was less than qualified
(D) a reputation was exaggerated
(E) an attitude was upsetting

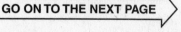

GO ON TO THE NEXT PAGE

Questions 17-24 are based on the following passage.

The following passage considers the reliability of eyewitness testimony in criminal trials and discusses how individual and cultural factors can color visual perception.

Western juries have traditionally found eyewitness testimony to be the most convincing evidence in criminal trials. Seeing is believing, as the saying goes. In numerous
Line cases, when witnesses pointed to the defendant, his or her fate
5 was sealed. But how reliable is eyewitness testimony? Recent cases have suggested that despite our best intentions, we may unwittingly distort what we perceive.

Artists and psychologists have long known that "seeing" is not a simple matter of recording visual input. People
10 perceive the exterior world through a complex matrix of cultural expectations, personality traits, moods, and life experiences. For example, researchers tested the cultural influence on perception by showing a set of optical illusions to various groups, and found that different groups responded
15 in divergent ways. Accustomed to and inundated by perpendicular structures, Western Europeans succumbed easily to illusions based on rectangular lines. On the other hand, the Zulu people of South Africa, whose environment had been comprised almost entirely of circular forms (round
20 houses, doors, etc.) did not fall prey to those linear illusions.

Cultural expectations also influence the selectivity of our seeing. The amount of visual information that exists far exceeds our ability to process it, so we must filter that sensory input into recognizable images. In looking at a face, we do
25 not see elongated ovals set in complex shadows and shading, we see eyes. And that filtering process is informed by what we perceive to be significant, which is influenced by cultural norms. Some cultures may emphasize differences in hair color or texture, others the shape of a nose or mouth, still others the
30 set of the eyes.

But it is not only group expectations that color what we see; personality and mood fluctuation can also alter our perceptions. Orderly minds that shun ambiguity will see an off-center image as firmly fixed in the center. The
35 same photograph of four young men allows for shifting interpretations based on our current feelings: a mood of happiness reveals boys enjoying a relaxing day, while anxiety changes the picture to students worrying about exams.

In addition, numerous prosaic factors affect our ability
40 to record an image accurately. Duration of the encounter, proximity to the subject, lighting, and angle all affect our ability to see, and even stress may further undermine the accuracy of our perceptions.

What will this mean for criminal trials? Juries often have
45 been reluctant to convict without eyewitness identification. Blood samples, fingerprints, and the like frequently require understanding of complex scientific technicalities and do not resonate as deeply with juries as does testimony. But as confidence in eyewitness testimony wanes, such
50 circumstantial evidence may someday replace visual identification as the lynchpin of criminal trials.

17. The primary purpose of the passage is to
(A) raise concerns about the reliability of a type of evidence
(B) examine the role of culture in influencing perception
(C) question the reliability of juries in criminal trials
(D) shed light on the differences between perception and reality
(E) offer solutions to the problem of cultural bias

18. The "saying" in line 3 primarily serves to
(A) emphasize an accepted point of view
(B) weaken an opposing position
(C) define a controversial term
(D) explain an apparent contradiction
(E) voice a long-held concern

19. The author refers to "Western Europeans" and the "Zulu" (lines 16-18) in order to suggest that
(A) no two people ever see the same thing
(B) it is often difficult for two people of different backgrounds to agree
(C) cultural differences may affect what one perceives
(D) one's perception is entirely dependent upon one's culture
(E) people from certain cultures may be easily deceived

20. In line 31, "color" most nearly means
(A) modify
(B) brighten
(C) disguise
(D) excuse
(E) adorn

21. The discussion of the "photograph of four young men" (line 35) most directly demonstrates
(A) the psychological need to conform
(B) a link between emotion and perception
(C) the longing for a forgotten childhood
(D) a discrepancy between fiction and reality
(E) the importance of friendship

GO ON TO THE NEXT PAGE ➡

22. The author's mention of "numerous prosaic factors" (line 39) primarily suggests that perception

(A) frequently leads people to make accusations regarding events that did not occur
(B) may sometimes be used to intentionally deceive those on juries
(C) is often hindered by the way the brain interprets images and colors
(D) may be affected by circumstances unrelated to the viewer's mental state
(E) is often a cause of anxiety in eyewitness testimony for civil and criminal trials

23. The author suggests that "blood samples" and "fingerprints" (line 46) are examples of evidence that

(A) can be interpreted only by trained scientists
(B) may be responsible for the conviction of innocent people
(C) are considered infallible by law enforcement officials
(D) may be seen as less convincing than eyewitness accounts
(E) will result in the elimination of eyewitness testimony from trials

24. Lines 49-51 ("But as . . . trials") primarily serve to

(A) offer support for a previous claim
(B) propose a hypothetical outcome
(C) change the focus of the discussion to an unrelated situation
(D) acknowledge a flaw in an influential study
(E) suggest an area for further research

STOP

**If you finish before time is called, you may check your work on this section only.
Do not turn to any other section in the test.**

SECTION 8
Time — 20 minutes
19 Questions

Turn to Section 8 of your answer sheet to answer the questions in this section.

Directions: For each question in this section, select the best answer from among the choices given and fill in the corresponding circle on the answer sheet.

Each sentence below has one or two blanks, each blank indicating that something has been omitted. Beneath the sentence are five words or sets of words labeled A through E. Choose the word or set of words that, when inserted in the sentence, best fits the meaning of the sentence as a whole.

Example:

Desiring to ------- his taunting friends, Mitch gave them taffy in hopes it would keep their mouths shut.

(A) eliminate   (B) satisfy   (C) overcome
    (D) ridicule   (E) silence

Ⓐ Ⓑ Ⓒ Ⓓ ●

1. After her grandchildren spent hours begging her to make cookies for them, Genevieve finally gave in as a result of the children's ------- .

    (A) merriment   (B) persistence   (C) generosity
        (D) friendliness   (E) hostility

2. Plentiful rainfall is essential to the ------- of fruit trees; if the weather is too dry, their health will be -------.

    (A) soundness . . reiterated
    (B) success . . ensured
    (C) finesse . . belittled
    (D) tenacity . . converged
    (E) survival . . compromised

3. Arsenic, best known as a lethal poison, is surprisingly effective at ------- a variety of diseases, a paradox that illustrates that even the most hazardous substances may have ------- effects.

    (A) infecting . . restorative
    (B) curing . . devastating
    (C) diagnosing . . reciprocal
    (D) treating . . beneficial
    (E) spreading . . salutary

4. Andy is ------- in good times and bad: he is confidently optimistic and virtually impossible to discourage.

    (A) morose   (B) facetious   (C) obdurate
        (D) sanguine   (E) controvertible

5. It was clear that the children were ------- at the end of the trip; with droopy eyes and frequent yawning, they began to doze off on the way home.

    (A) vertiginous   (B) inconsolable   (C) sedulous
        (D) somnolent   (E) fractious

6. Although winning large sums often changes one's attitude toward money, the most ------- skinflint is unlikely to shed a ------- entrenched over a lifetime and live opulently.

    (A) inveterate . . disposition
    (B) gracious . . habit
    (C) chronic . . collaboration
    (D) cantankerous . . dilemma
    (E) benevolent . . personality

GO ON TO THE NEXT PAGE

Questions 7-19 are based on the following passage.

The following passage relates some conclusions the author draws after listening to a lecture by a college professor.

Several weeks ago, when the weather was still fine, I decided to eat my lunch on the upper quad, an expanse of lawn stretching across the north end of campus and hedged
Line in by ancient pine trees on one side and university buildings
5 on the other. Depositing my brown paper lunch bag on the grass beside me, I munched in silence, watching the trees ripple in the wind and musing over the latest in a series of "controversial" symposiums I had attended that morning. The speaker, an antiquated professor in suspenders and a
10 mismatched cardigan, had delivered an earnest diatribe against modern tools of convenience like electronic mail and instant messaging programs. I thought his speech was interesting, but altogether too romantic.

My solitude was broken by two girls, deep in conversation,
15 who approached from behind and sat down on the grass about ten feet to my left. I stared hard at my peanut butter sandwich, trying to not eavesdrop, but their stream of chatter intrigued me. They interrupted each other frequently, paused at the same awkward moments, and responded to each
20 other's statements as if neither one heard what the other said. Confused, I stole a glance at them out of the corner of my eye. I could tell that they were college students by their style of dress and the heavy backpacks sinking into the grass beside them. Their body language and proximity also indicated that
25 they were friends. Instead of talking to each other, however, each one was having a separate dialogue on her cell phone.

As I considered this peculiar scene, this morning's bleary-eyed lecturer again intruded into my thoughts. His point in the symposium was that, aside from the disastrous
30 effects of emails and chatting on the spelling, grammar, and punctuation of the English language, these modern conveniences also considerably affect our personal lives. Before the advent of electronic mail, people wrote letters. Although writing out words by hand posed an inconvenience,
35 it also conferred certain important advantages. The writer had time to think about his message, about how he could best phrase it in order to help his reader understand him, about how he could convey his emotions without the use of dancing and flashing smiley-face icons. When he finished
40 his letter, he had created a permanent work of art to which a hurriedly typed email or abbreviated chat room conversation could never compare. The temporary, impersonal nature of computers, Professor Spectacles concluded, is gradually rendering our lives equally temporary and impersonal.

45 And what about cell phones? I thought. I have attended classes where students, instead of turning off their cell phones for the duration of the lecture, leave the classroom to take calls without the slightest hint of embarrassment. I have sat in movie theaters and ground my teeth in frustration at the
50 person behind me who can't wait until the movie is over to give his colleague a scene-by-scene replay. And then I watched each girl next to me spend her lunch hour talking to someone else instead of her friend. Like the rest of the world, these two pay a significant price for the benefits of
55 convenience and the added safety of being in constant contact with the world. When they have a cell phone, they are never alone, but then again, *they are never alone.*

They may not recognize it, but those girls, like most of us, could use a moment of solitude. Cell phones make it so easy
60 to reach out and touch someone that they have us confused into thinking that being alone is the same thing as being lonely. It's all right to disconnect from the world every once in a while; in fact, I feel certain that our sanity and identity as humans necessitates it. And I'm starting to think that maybe
65 the Whimsical Professor ranting about his "technological opiates" is not so romantic after all.

7. The sentence in which "controversial" (lines 5-8) appears indicates that the narrator considers the word to be

(A) a metaphor
(B) a prediction
(C) an impression
(D) an overstatement
(E) an epithet

8. In lines 9-10, the narrator mentions "suspenders and a mismatched cardigan" primarily in order to

(A) point out that college professors are often underpaid
(B) portray the speaker as somewhat eccentric
(C) criticize the speaker's lack of fashion sense
(D) examine the relationship between clothing and technology
(E) praise the speaker for his refusal to conform to society

9. Lines 14-20 suggest that the narrator viewed the conversation between the two girls as

(A) refined
(B) insignificant
(C) disjointed
(D) hostile
(E) tedious

GO ON TO THE NEXT PAGE ➡

10. In line 21, "stole" most nearly means

   (A) visited
   (B) borrowed
   (C) appropriated
   (D) illustrated
   (E) hazarded

11. The passage as a whole suggests that the narrator regards the conversation between the two girls as

   (A) a situation that causes the narrator to reflect on an opinion expressed in the previous paragraph
   (B) a typical conversation between two college students
   (C) the reasons that modern modes of communication are necessary
   (D) an incident that resulted in a confrontation between two students
   (E) the narrator's annoyance with inconsiderate students

12. The narrator's reference to "smiley-face icons" (line 39) most directly suggests

   (A) nostalgia for an easier way of life
   (B) skepticism about certain modes of communication
   (C) annoyance at the insensitivity of modern writers
   (D) confusion over the complexities of modern conveniences
   (E) appreciation for the expressive possibilities of email

13. Which of the following examples, if true, would best illustrate the symposium speaker's reasoning as described in the third paragraph?

   (A) A newlywed couple sends copies of a generic thank-you card from an Internet site to wedding guests.
   (B) A high school student uses a graphing program for her algebra homework.
   (C) A former high school class president uses the Internet to locate and invite members of the class to a reunion.
   (D) A publisher utilizes an editing program to proofread texts before they are printed.
   (E) A hostess uses her computer to design and print nameplates for all her party guests.

14. The narrator suggests that the "person" (line 50) is

   (A) impetuous
   (B) languid
   (C) tactless
   (D) demonstrative
   (E) taciturn

15. The author would most likely define the "significant price" (line 54) as the

   (A) costs that must be shouldered by people of all nations
   (B) charges that result from excessive cell phone use
   (C) difficulty of experiencing a certain amount of privacy
   (D) satisfaction that comes from close personal relationships
   (E) insecurity caused by modern communication devices

16. In line 57, the author italicizes the words "they are never alone" primarily to

   (A) draw attention to a social problem
   (B) indicate that the phrase is a translation
   (C) suggest that the phrase is a metaphor
   (D) imply an alternate meaning of the phrase
   (E) point out that the phrase is an exaggeration

17. In context, the reference to the "Whimsical Professor" in line 65 suggests that the narrator was experiencing

   (A) a sensation of regret
   (B) an unforeseen difficulty
   (C) a moment of solitude
   (D) a feeling of loneliness
   (E) a change of heart

18. In the context of the passage, which piece of technology would the narrator disapprove of most?

   (A) A wristwatch that automatically updates the time with a global server
   (B) A portable gaming device featuring realistic graphics
   (C) A device allowing the user to chat with other people at any time
   (D) An earpiece that automatically translates languages to English
   (E) A digital book reader with a large, bulky screen

19. The primary purpose of the passage is to

   (A) criticize an expert
   (B) evaluate an argument
   (C) describe a conversation
   (D) relate an anecdote
   (E) defend a technology

STOP

**If you finish before time is called, you may check your work on this section only.
Do not turn to any other section in the test.**

NO TEST MATERIAL ON THIS PAGE.

SECTION 9
Time — 20 minutes
16 Questions

Turn to Section 9 of your answer sheet to answer the questions in this section.

Directions: For this section, solve each problem and decide which is the best of the choices given. Fill in the corresponding circle on the answer sheet. You may use any available space for scratchwork.

Notes

1. The use of a calculator is permitted.

2. All numbers used are real numbers.

3. Figures that accompany problems in this test are intended to provide information useful in solving the problems. They are drawn as accurately as possible EXCEPT when it is stated in a specific problem that the figure is not drawn to scale. All figures lie in a plane unless otherwise indicated.

4. Unless otherwise specified, the domain of any function f is assumed to be the set of all real numbers x for which $f(x)$ is a real number.

Reference Information

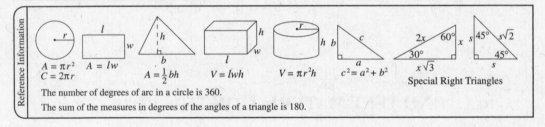

$A = \pi r^2$ $A = lw$ $A = \frac{1}{2}bh$ $V = lwh$ $V = \pi r^2 h$ $c^2 = a^2 + b^2$

Special Right Triangles

The number of degrees of arc in a circle is 360.
The sum of the measures in degrees of the angles of a triangle is 180.

1. Which of the following represents "the square of the sum of a and b" ?

   (A) $a^2 + b^2$
   (B) $(a + b)^2$
   (C) $a^2 + b$
   (D) $2a + 2b$
   (E) $a + b^2$

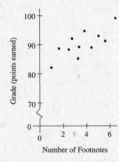

2. Eleven students were instructed to write an essay. The scatterplot above shows the grade and the number of footnotes in each essay. Which of the following is true regarding the line of best fit?

   (A) Its slope is negative.
   (B) Its slope is positive.
   (C) It goes through the point $(0, t)$, where $t \le 0$.
   (D) It goes through the point $(s, 0)$, where $s \ge 0$.
   (E) It goes through the point $(0, 0)$.

GO ON TO THE NEXT PAGE

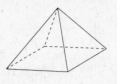

3. The pyramid shown above has a square base with an area of 100 square feet. If each edge from the top of the pyramid to a corner of the base is 13 feet long, what is the sum of the lengths of the 8 edges of the pyramid?

(A) 92
(B) 96
(C) 100
(D) 104
(E) 108

4. Selena has two types of records, worth a total of $41.75. Of her 25 records, b records are worth $1.25 each and the remaining d records are worth $2.30 each. Selena has no other types of records. Which of the following sets of equations can be solved to determine how many of each record type Selena has?

(A) $b + d = 41.75$
$3.55(b + d) = 25$
(B) $3.55(b + d) = 41.75$
$1.25(b + d) = 2.30$
(C) $3.55(b + d) = 41.75$
$1.25b + 2.30d = 25$
(D) $b + d = 25$
$2.30b + 1.25d = 41.75$
(E) $b + d = 25$
$1.25b + 2.30d = 41.75$

5. Eva and Magnus took a road trip and shared the driving. Eva drove four times as many miles as Magnus drove. What percent of the total miles of the trip did Eva drive?

(A) 70%
(B) 75%
(C) 80%
(D) 85%
(E) 90%

6. Cathy's average rate during the Boston Marathon was 10 minutes a mile for the first b hours where $b < 4$. In terms of b, how many more miles does Cathy have to run to complete the 26-mile race?

(A) $26 - 6b$

(B) $26 - 600b$

(C) $6b - 26$

(D) $26 - \dfrac{6}{b}$

(E) $\dfrac{26 - b}{6}$

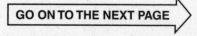
GO ON TO THE NEXT PAGE

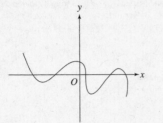

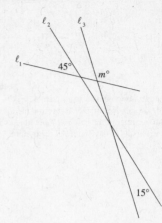

7. What is the total number of x- and y-intercepts contained in the graph that would result from reflecting the graph above about the x-axis?

(A) Three
(B) Four
(C) Five
(D) Six
(E) Seven

9. Three lines, ℓ_1, ℓ_2, and ℓ_3 intersect as shown. What is the value of m ?

(A) 115
(B) 120
(C) 125
(D) 130
(E) 145

8. If $w + x = 5$ and $y + z = 6$, what is the value of $wy + xz + wz + xy$?

(A) 11
(B) 22
(C) 30
(D) 41
(E) 60

$$a^3 \times a^6 = a^c$$

$$\frac{\left(b^5\right)^d}{b^d} = b^{40}$$

10. In the equations above, $a > 1$ and $b > 1$. What is the sum of c and d ?

(A) 8
(B) 9
(C) 15
(D) 17
(E) 19

GO ON TO THE NEXT PAGE

11. If $a + b - c = d + 6$, $c - b = 8$, and $3a = 2 - d$, what is the value of a ?

(A) 2
(B) 4
(C) 8
(D) 12
(E) 16

12. If $\dfrac{z}{3} - \dfrac{5}{6} = \left| \dfrac{z}{3} - \dfrac{5}{6} \right|$, what is the least possible integer value of z ?

(A) −3
(B) 0
(C) 2
(D) 3
(E) 6

13. The number represented by $\dfrac{1}{x}$ has a tens digit larger than its units digit. If the tens digit of $\dfrac{1}{x}$ is odd, what is the greatest possible value of x ?

(A) 0.010204. . .
(B) 0.027027 . . .
(C) 0.03333333 . . .
(D) 0.09090909 . . .
(E) 0.1

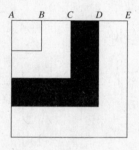

Note: Figure not drawn to scale.

14. In the figure above, four squares share a vertex at point A. If B is the midpoint of $\overline{AC}$, C is the midpoint of $\overline{AD}$, and D is the midpoint of $\overline{AE}$, what fractional part of the largest square is shaded?

(A) $\dfrac{1}{16}$

(B) $\dfrac{1}{8}$

(C) $\dfrac{3}{16}$

(D) $\dfrac{1}{4}$

(E) $\dfrac{5}{16}$

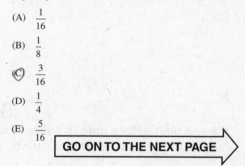

GO ON TO THE NEXT PAGE

Practice Test 1 | 63

$$\frac{5}{\sqrt{x-3}} = 3$$

15. For $x > 3$, which of the following equations is equivalent to the equation above?

(A) $5 = 3(x-3)$
(B) $3 = 9(x-3)$
(C) $25 = 3(x-9)$
(D) $25 = 9(x-3)$
(E) $25 = 3(x-3)$

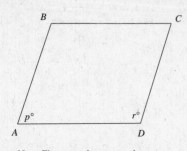

Note: Figure not drawn to scale.

16. In the figure above, $AB \parallel CD$ and $AD \parallel BC$. If $p = 5r$, what is the value of p ?

(A) 15
(B) 30
(C) 75
(D) 90
(E) 150

STOP

If you finish before time is called, you may check your work on this section only.
Do not turn to any other section in the test.

NO TEST MATERIAL ON THIS PAGE.

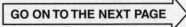
SECTION 10
Time — 10 minutes
14 Questions

Turn to Section 10 of your answer sheet to answer the questions in this section.

Directions: For each question in this section, select the best answer from among the choices given and fill in the corresponding circle on the answer sheet.

The following sentences test correctness and effectiveness of expression. Part of each sentence or the entire sentence is underlined; beneath each sentence are five ways of phrasing the underlined material. Choice A repeats the original phrasing; the other four choices are different. If you think the original phrasing produces a better sentence than any of the alternatives, select choice A; if not, select one of the other choices.

In making your selection, follow the requirements of standard written English; that is, pay attention to grammar, choice of words, sentence construction, and punctuation. Your selection should result in the most effective sentence—clear and precise, without awkwardness or ambiguity.

EXAMPLE:

Bobby Flay baked his first cake <u>and he was thirteen years old then</u>.

(A) and he was thirteen years old then
(B) when he was thirteen
(C) at age thirteen years old
(D) upon the reaching of thirteen years
(E) at the time when he was thirteen

Ⓐ ● Ⓒ Ⓓ Ⓔ

1. <u>The International Students' Club sponsoring bake sales last month</u> in order to raise funds for foreign exchange students to visit their families during the holidays.

(A) The International Students' Club sponsoring bake sales last month
(B) The International Students' Club would sponsor bake sales last month
(C) Sponsoring bake sales last month, the International Students' Club
(D) The International Students' Club sponsored bake sales last month
(E) Bake sales sponsored last month by the International Students' Club

2. <u>As an area that is a habitat for 40,000 varieties of plants, the Amazon Rainforest is growing</u> across 1.7 billion acres in the center of South America.

(A) As an area that is a habitat for 40,000 varieties of plants, the Amazon Rainforest is growing
(B) An area that is a habitat for 40,000 varieties of plants, the growth of the Amazon Rain forest
(C) A habitat for 40,000 varieties of plants, the Amazon Rainforest grows
(D) It is a habitat for 40,000 varieties of plants but the Amazon Rainforest also grows
(E) A habitat for 40,000 varieties of plants, the Amazon Rainforest, growing

3. Albert Einstein, who won a Nobel prize for physics, <u>dedicated the last years of his life and searched</u> for a unified field theory.

(A) dedicated the last years of his life and searched
(B) dedicated the last years of his life having searched
(C) having dedicated the last years of his life doing his searching
(D) dedicated the last years of his life to searching
(E) dedicating the last years of his life searching

4. <u>The Beatles, remembered for their groundbreaking music, which</u> dramatically affected the new, burgeoning teen culture of the band's biggest fans.

(A) The Beatles, remembered for their groundbreaking music, which
(B) The Beatles are remembered for their groundbreaking music, it
(C) The Beatles are remembered for their groundbreaking music, which
(D) The Beatles, with their groundbreaking music that
(E) The Beatles, their groundbreaking music is remembered to have

GO ON TO THE NEXT PAGE

5. Mastering the dozens of recipes for stocks and sauces found in many French cookbooks <u>are essential for young cooks when they work</u> in four-star kitchens.

(A) are essential for young cooks when they work
(B) is essential for young cooks working
(C) is the essential thing young cooks make when they work
(D) for young working cooks, are essential
(E) and which are essential for young cooks who work

6. The manager's directions for the project described how to organize the team, <u>meeting the deadline, and satisfying the client</u>.

(A) meeting the deadline, and satisfying the client
(B) both meeting the deadline, and satisfying the client
(C) with meeting the deadline and then satisfying the client
(D) meet and satisfy the deadline and the client
(E) meet the deadline, and satisfy the client

7. In the mid-nineteenth century, English novelists and political theorists described cities full of workers <u>experiencing a world of misery and struggling</u> against extreme poverty for their survival.

(A) experiencing a world of misery and struggling
(B) experiencing a world of misery, and they struggle
(C) who were experiencing a world of misery, to struggle
(D) who experienced a world of misery, then they struggled
(E) they experienced a world of misery to struggle

8. Most troublesome of the anthracnose fungi, *Discula destructiva*, if untreated, kills its host tree <u>gradually, and they are also known to cause</u> symptoms that resemble those of other diseases.

(A) gradually, and they are also known to cause
(B) gradually, and it is known that they cause
(C) gradually and is also known to cause
(D) gradually also causing their
(E) gradually, in addition, it causes its

9. The reason Mark Twain's writings utilize satire to address social questions is <u>that satire can both entertain readers and provoke</u> thought and controversy.

(A) that satire can both entertain readers and provoke
(B) it both entertained readers and it could provoke
(C) because satire entertain readers and provoke
(D) because of it entertaining readers and provoking
(E) that of entertaining readers and provoking

10. The admissions officers reported that applying for scholarships and other types of financial aid <u>neither increase or decrease</u> a student's chance of being accepted into the program.

(A) neither increase or decrease
(B) neither increase nor decrease
(C) neither increases nor decreases
(D) do not increase or decrease
(E) does nor increase or decreases

11. <u>Since they are instructed to avoid controversial statement-making</u>, political speeches are usually bland and innocuous.

(A) Since they are instructed to avoid controversial statement making
(B) Being instructed to avoid making controversial statements
(C) Based on instructions to speechwriters to avoid making controversial statements
(D) Advising speechwriters to avoid making controversial statements
(E) Because speechwriters are instructed to avoid making controversial statements

12. Playwrights convey the range of human emotions <u>by combining the comedic with the tragedy</u> in their plays.

(A) by combining the comedic with the tragedy
(B) by combining the comedic with the tragic
(C) in a combining of comedy with the tragic
(D) when their combining comedy with the tragic
(E) through combinations of comedy and tragic

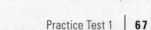

GO ON TO THE NEXT PAGE

13. The school's stringent dress codes and guidelines for proper conduct <u>were not impulsive but a need</u> to prevent lewd and offensive behavior from distracting the student population.

   (A) were not impulsive but a need
   (B) were not impulsive but needed
   (C) were not because of impulse, it needed
   (D) resulted not from impulse, but it needed
   (E) resulted not from impulse but from a need

14. Despite its efficient and widespread use in America, the synthetic pesticide DDT was <u>banned: its effects were</u> found to be extremely dangerous for humans and the environment.

   (A) banned: its effects were
   (B) banned, its effects were
   (C) banned; its effects being
   (D) banned; its effects were being
   (E) banned, yet its effects were

STOP

**If you finish before time is called, you may check your work on this section only.
Do not turn to any other section in the test.**

Chapter 4
Practice Test 1
Answers and
Explanations

PRACTICE TEST 1: ANSWER KEY

2 Math	4 Reading	5 Writing	6 Math	7 Reading	8 Reading	9 Math	10 Writing
1. C	1. C	1. B	1. E	1. B	1. B	1. B	1. D
2. E	2. D	2. E	2. B	2. A	2. E	2. B	2. C
3. C	3. B	3. E	3. C	3. C	3. D	3. A	3. D
4. B	4. C	4. D	4. D	4. A	4. D	4. E	4. C
5. B	5. B	5. A	5. A	5. B	5. D	5. C	5. B
6. D	6. B	6. C	6. C	6. E	6. A	6. A	6. E
7. D	7. A	7. A	7. C	7. D	7. D	7. D	7. A
8. A	8. E	8. B	8. D	8. B	8. B	8. C	8. C
9. D	9. A	9. D	9. $\frac{40}{3}$ or 13.3	9. B	9. C	9. B	9. A
10. C	10. E	10. E		10. C	10. E	10. E	10. C
11. C	11. B	11. A	10. 120	11. B	11. A	11. B	11. E
12. D	12. E	12. C	11. 3,899	12. E	12. B	12. D	12. B
13. D	13. C	13. E	12. 75	13. A	13. A	13. E	13. E
14. E	14. D	14. B	13. 2	14. C	14. C	14. C	14. A
15. E	15. E	15. C	14. 195	15. D	15. C	15. D	
16. E	16. A	16. D	15. 4	16. B	16. D	16. E	
17. D	17. E	17. B	16. 41, 43, 45,	17. A	17. E		
18. A	18. C	18. A	47	18. A	18. C		
19. C	19. D	19. B	17. 12	19. C	19. B		
20. A	20. C	20. D	18. $\frac{9}{2}$ or 4.5	20. A			
	21. D	21. C		21. B			
	22. A	22. D		22. D			
	23. E	23. D		23. D			
	24. A	24. E		24. B			
		25. C					
		26. D					
		27. C					
		28. E					
		29. D					
		30. A					
		31. C					
		32. D					
		33. A					
		34. B					
		35. D					

EXPLANATIONS

Section 2

1. **C** Start by finding the weight of each individual item. Each water container weighs 25 pounds. Food: $\frac{400}{8}$ = 50, so each sack of food weighs 50 pounds. Blankets: $\frac{360}{120}$ = 3, so each blanket weighs 3 pounds. Now multiply each of these weights by the number of those items loaded onto the truck. Water: 25 × 5 = 125, so Leah loads 125 pounds of water onto the truck. Food: 50 × 3 = 150 pounds of food. Blankets: 3 × 40 = 120 pounds of blankets. Add these for the total weight of the cargo: 125 + 150 + 120 = 395, answer (C)

2. **E** Draw segment $\overline{PQ}$ and Plug In the information from the question. $3m$ is half of the total length, which is therefore $6m$, answer (E). We can Plug In our own number for m as well: if $m = 2$, then $\overline{FQ}$ is 6 and the whole length of $\overline{PQ}$ is 12. Among the answers, only (E) gives 12 when $m = 2$. The result is (A) if $\overline{FQ}$ is divided rather than multiplied by 2, while (B) is the length of $\overline{PF}$.

3. **C** On the number line, the space between the 96 and the 97 is divided into 5 equal parts. The first tick mark is equal to 96.2, the second equals 96.4, the third equals 96.6, the fourth equals 96.8. Since we are looking for which point is equal to 96.7, we need the one that is between the third and fourth lines after 96, which is where point C is located.

4. **B** In January, Jacksonville Tax Service spent $200 on office supplies and spent $400 on supplies in May. This is double what it was in January, so (B) 2 is the correct answer.

5. **B** It costs $10 to buy a hand-stitched bag and $.50 for each polished stone, represented by p. So in dollars, each polished stone would cost $.5p$ or $\frac{1}{2}p$. The stones are going into 2 bags that cost $20 together, so the total cost for the bag of polished stones would be $20 + \frac{1}{2}p$, as in (B). We can also replace the variable with a number. If $p = 4$, the stones would cost $2, for a total of $22 with the bag. Only (B) gives an answer of $22 when the p is replaced with a 4 in the answer choices. (A) gives $28, (C) gives $42, (D) gives $60, and (E) gives $40.

6. **D** Five of the numbers are greater than –2, and there are a total of 8 numbers, so the correct fraction is (D) $\frac{5}{8}$. The answer in (E) incorrectly includes –2; (A) is the probability that the number would be less than –2; (B) is the probability that the number is –2 or less.

7. **D** Translate the question into math. Three times a number is the same as $3x$. That number subtracted from 12 is the same as $12 - x$. So $3x = 12 - x$. Now solve: Add x to each side: $4x = 12$, and $x = 3$. The answer is (D).

8.   A   Begin by finding how much water is left in the pond at the end of the seventh week. Half of the water evaporates each week, which means that there's half as much water left at the end of each week. There are 2,400 gallons at the end of the third week, so there are 1,200 gallons in the pond at the end of the fourth week, 600 gallons at the end of the fifth week, 300 gallons at the end of the sixth week, and 150 gallons at the end of the seventh week. To find how much more water was in the pond in the third week, subtract this from the 2,400 gallons from the third week: 2,400 − 150 = 2,250, answer (A).

9.   D   Because AB is a radius of the circle, use the area formula, πr^2, to find that the area of the whole circle is 36π. The question states that the arc is $\dfrac{1}{9}$ of the circumference so the sector is $\dfrac{1}{9}$ of the total area. $\dfrac{36\pi}{9}$ gives the area of the sector, 4π (D).

10. C   Because all the answer choices have the value −2 on the left, $4t + 1$ in the middle, and 2 on the right, all we need to do is focus on the inequality signs. We can eliminate (E) off the bat, because it is saying that −2 is greater than 2. On the number line, a hollow dot indicates that the number is **not** included in the range of values, so for the first inequality symbol in each number sentence, eliminate the answers that have a ≤ rather than <. (A) and (B) are out. A solid dot indicates that the number is included and should be represented by ≤, so eliminate (D). The correct answer is (C).

11. C   Only in (C) is a positive y guaranteed a negative x and vice-versa. Start by drawing the lines in the answer choices. (A) is a horizontal line in which all the y values are −2. When the x value is also negative, the

product of the coordinates is positive. (B) is a vertical line in which all the x values are –2. When the y value is also negative, the product of the coordinates is positive. To disprove (D) use the equation to find points on the line. Using $x = 2$ and $x = -2$, gives coordinate pairs (2, –6) and (–2, 2), which if connected cut through the portion of the coordinate plane where x and y are both negative, thus giving a positive product. (E) can be disproved because if $x = -2$ in the equation, the y value is –6, which gives a positive product.

12. **D** Collect like terms by getting all the variables onto one side: $100 = x^2 + 2xy + y^2$. The right side of the equation is a commonly used quadratic equation: $x^2 + 2xy + y^2 = (x + y)^2$. Use this to factor the right side of the equation and get $(x + y)^2 = 100$, as seen in (D).

13. **D** To prove the statement false, we need to find a number in which the sum of the digits is odd, but p is even (opposite of *must be odd*). Eliminate (A), (C), and (E) because they are odd and we are looking for an even number. (D) is correct because the sum of the digits in 1,020 is odd, but the number itself is even. The sum of the digits in (B) is even, and therefore does not prove the statement false.

14. **E** One way to solve this is to use each answer as the area of the square and see if the surrounding rectangles can be made to have sides that are all integers. Eliminate (A) and (B) because the area of the square cannot be larger than the area of one of the rectangles. In (C) the short side of rectangles A and B is 5 and the long side is 6, but this leaves only 1 unit, which cannot be split into two integers. In (D), an area of 16 means the short side of rectangles A and B is 4, but the long side of would have to be 7.5, which cannot be split into two integers. Only (E) works: rectangles A and B would have dimensions of 3×10, leaving 7 units for sides of the surrounding rectangles. 7 can be split into 1 and 6, 2 and 5, or 3 and 4.

15. **E** We can find the answer by replacing b and h with real numbers. Let's say $b = 3$ and $h = 4$. Since the area of a triangle is $\frac{1}{2}$ base times height, the area of triangle A is $\frac{1}{2} \times 3 \times 4 = 6$. The area of the triangle is x, so $x = 6$. Now find the area of the rectangle, where $b = 3$ and $h = 4$: each quantity is doubled, so the rectangle is 6 by 8. The area of a rectangle is length times width, so the area of rectangle B is 48. Choice (E) represents 48 when $x = 6$. To solve this question algebraically, use the triangle area formula, $A = \frac{1}{2}bh$, to find the area of triangle A: $x = \frac{1}{2}bh$. The area of rectangle B (length × width) is $2b \times 2h$, or $4bh$. Since $4bh$ is $8 \times \frac{1}{2}bh$, the area of rectangle B is $8x$, as seen in (E). Watch out for (B); that's the area of a triangle with those dimensions.

16. **E** Plug In a value for a. Let's say $a = 16$; therefore, $a^{\frac{1}{2}}$ is $16^{\frac{1}{2}}$, or 4. So the equation is now $4 = b^2$, which means that $b = 2$. The question asks for the value of a^2, which would be 16^2, or 256. Find the values in the answer choices for when $b = 2$. Choice (E) gives 2^8, which is 256. To solve this question algebraically, first find a^2, which results from raising $a^{\frac{1}{2}}$ to the fourth power. When we raise a number with an exponent to another power, we multiply the exponents. So $\left(a^{\frac{1}{2}} \right)^4 = a^{\frac{4}{2}} = a^2$. Now do the same on the other side of the equal sign for b^2: $\left(b^2 \right)^4 = b^8$, the answer in (E).

17. D We can determine how many different meals Shawn can make by multiplying the number of pastas, sauces, and toppings; the product is the number of meals Shawn can make. Since Shawn can make 30 different meals, the number of sauces available to Shawn must be a factor of 30. Only choice (D) gives a number that is not a factor of 30. For example, choice (C) is incorrect because Shawn could have 3 sauces available. He could also have, say, 2 types of pasta and 5 types of toppings; the product of 2, 3, and 5 is 30. Choice (D) is correct because he can't have 4 choices of sauces to make 30 different meals. If the product of the number of pastas, sauces (4), and toppings is 30, then the product of the number of pastas and toppings is $\frac{30}{4}$, and there's no number of pastas and toppings that, when multiplied, will give you $\frac{30}{4}$.

18. A This question is most easily answered using the group formula: group 1 + group 2 − both + neither = total number. In this case, we don't need the "neither" portion. We know that the number of appetizers is 7 more than the number of deserts, and that half of the entire class made both dishes. This gives us $d + (d + 7) - 25 = 50$. Solving the equation gives $d = 34$, but that is the number of everyone who made a dessert, not those who made *only* dessert. Subtract the "both" number from this to get $34 - 25 = 9$, answer (A). (B) is the number of students who made only an appetizer, (C) is the number of students who made both dishes, (D) is the total number of desserts made and (E) is the total number of appetizers made.

19.   **C**   To find the sides of the triangle, find the x- and y-intercepts of the function. To find the y-intercept, substitute 0 for all the x-values: $y = 3x^2 - 8x + 4 = 3(0) - 8(0) + 4 = 4$.   Thus,   the   side MN in the figure has a measure of 4. To find the x-intercept, set $y = 0$: $0 = 3x^2 - 8x + 4 = (3x - 2)(x - 2)$.   The x-intercept,   therefore,   has two values: $x = \dfrac{2}{3}$ and $x = 2$. Note, however, that the point N on the figure is the x-intercept farther from the origin, so N must be the x-intercept given by the point (2, 0). Accordingly, the length of side LM is 2. To find the area of this triangle, use the area formula $A = \dfrac{1}{2}bh = \dfrac{1}{2}(2)(4) = 4$, answer (C).

20.   **A**   The easiest way to work this question is to Plug In numbers for the variables. Since b is in both equations, let's say b = 2. Then solve for a and c. $2a = 3(2)$, so a = 3. $\frac{1}{3}c$ = $6(2^2)$ + 2, so c = 78. The question asks for c, so look for an answer that equals 78. Remember that a = 3.

Choice (A) is equal to 78, so that's the answer. Choice (B) is equal to 84, (C) is 114, (D) is 168, and (E) is 174, so they're all wrong. To work the question algebraically, solve for b in the first equation by dividing both sides by 3 to get $\frac{2a}{3} = b$. Now, to solve for c, factor the second equation to get $\frac{1}{3}c$ = $(2b)(3b)$ + 2. Substitute for $2b$ and $3b$, using the value of b from the first equation, to get $\frac{1}{3}c = \left(2 \times \frac{2a}{3}\right)(2a) + 2$.

Now collect like terms and simplify the equation: $\frac{1}{3}c = \left(\frac{4a}{3}\right)(2a) + 2$, $\frac{1}{3}c = \frac{8a^2}{3} + 2$, and multiply both sides by 3 to get $c = 8a^2 + 6$, answer (A).

Section 4

1. **C** Since we know that the *witness's testimony* was *rambling and incoherent*, we want something that means "rambling." (C), *disjointed*, means "not connected," or "out of order," which matches what we know about the witness's testimony.

2. **D** Most of the words (except *recommendations*) work for the first blank, so focus on the second blank. There is a time trigger in the sentence: a *recent addition* will *soon* change something about the funds. The new *members* don't care about *fundraising* but throw *expensive parties*. A good word for the second blank is "gone." Only (D) *exhausted* is anything like "gone."

3. **B** The clue for the first blank is that *he did not take a stand on any issue*. His speeches must mean something like "not taking a position." This eliminates choices (C), (D), and (E). If he is *misleading* or *vague*, how do voters feel about his *position on topics*? The word *uncertain* (B) fits the sentence better than *assured*.

4. **C** For the first blank we need a word for something that would *support his theory*, such as "proof." Both (C) *substantiation* and (E) *verification* could mean "proof." A clue for the second blank, *nonetheless, he was surprised*, lets us know that the *claim was rejected* because of his lack of *support*. So the second blank must mean or be something "unsupported" or "unproven." (A) *hearsay* is close, because gossip is often not substantiated; (C) *fallacy* means "an erroneous or false idea" that would be unable to be proven. (E) *treachery* has to do with dishonesty, but *treachery* is a more serious type of betrayal than the sentence calls for. Only (C) matches both blanks.

5. **B** *Although* indicates that the blank is the opposite of *respectful. Impugned,* which means "attacked," is the only word that fits. The correct answer is (B).

6. **B** In the sentence, *straightforward descriptions* is opposite of *technical jargon,* and that these *books help beginners* tells us the book has no *technical jargon.* The first blank should mean *without* when combined with *of.* Both (B) and (D) work for the first blank. The second blank is a verb that means "teach" or "provide" *new knowledge…to beginners.* (B), (C), and maybe (A) could work in the second blank; eliminate (D) and (E); (B) is the only one that matches in both blanks.

7. **A** The word *because* tells us we're looking for a synonym for *pampered and spoiled.* Only *cosseted* fits. The correct answer is (A).

8. **E** So Greg *carefully accumulated money,* which means the blank must mean that *Greg was extremely* "good at saving money for the future." (A) *reticent* means that Greg wouldn't talk much, which doesn't work. (B) *assiduous* means that he pays careful attention to detail, which isn't the same as saving money. (C) *fallible* means he can makes mistakes, which isn't supported by the sentence, and (D) *clairvoyant* means that he can see the future. So (E), the only answer left, is correct. *Provident* means "frugal" or "saves money for a rainy day."

9. **A** The author of the passage brings up the victim in order to show a time when the National Parks had to pay a huge lawsuit because they didn't have enough warning signs. (A), *support a previous claim,* matches up with this: he had previously claimed that the signs were there to *protect the parks from unnecessary litigation,* and the reference to the victim gives an example of the unnecessary litigation the Parks are trying to avoid.

10. **E** Whittlesey compares the National Parks to Central Park, commenting that it would be ridiculous to put up as many warning signs in Central Park as the National Park is required to put up. He is not a fan of the ruling. (E), *sarcastic*, means he is making fun of it, which is exactly what he is doing.

11. **B** The passage states that *unlike traditional journalists, gonzo journalists use the power of both emotions and personal experience*, meaning that traditional journalists normally do not use emotions or personal experience—they remain objective in their writings. (B), *neutral*, comes closest to meaning "objective." (A), (C), and (D) are not synonyms for objective and (E), *subjective*, is the opposite of objective.

12. **E** The author mentions that gonzo journalism is different in many ways from standard journalistic writing: it can be sarcastic, emotional, rough, or personal. The only answer that matches this is (E), *its unconventionality*. (C) is wrong because although it mentions editing, it is not the focus of the passage. (D) is wrong because the passage states that gonzo journalism is different because of how it is written, not what is written about.

13. **C** The author of Passage 1 clearly argues one position: that time travel is unlikely. The author of Passage 2, on the other hand, has no position; he simply presents three opinions, ranging from skeptical (Stephen Hawking) to noncommittal (Carl Sagan) to optimistic (Ronald Mallett). (A), (B), (D), and (E) all mention things that are contradicted by the passages.

14. **D** The author brings up *contraptions* to show that in science fiction, time travel is easy. This contrasts sharply with the view he expresses in the next sentence. (D) paraphrases this contrast nicely. (A) contradicts the author's point of view, while (B), (C), and (E) are not mentioned in the passage.

15. E The "celebrity scientists" mentioned in the passage have postulated or hypothesized about the existence of wormholes, warp drives, and other theoretical constructs that might make time travel a reality. So the correct answer should be about someone who is thinking of a way to make time travel real. Only Ronald Mallett, at the end of Passage 2, does this, so answer (E) is correct. H.G. Wells and the science fiction fans (C) in Passage 1, are certainly fascinated by time travel, but they are not doing anything to make time travel a reality.

16. A The author of Passage 2 begins by acknowledging the importance of the Conjecture, but then notes that *Not everyone...is convinced* (line 57). He then goes on to outline two positions that differ, in varying degrees, with Hawking's Conjecture. Thus, he would regard the claim by the author of Passage 1 as *an oversimplification of a complex issue*, as in (A). (B), (C), and (D) are not mentioned in Passage 2, while (E) contradicts the passage.

17. E The passage mentions *hordes of time travelers,* suggesting *overwhelmed,* (E). (A) and (C) are the overly literal traps, (D) doesn't make sense, and (B) is extreme; they're *time-tourists,* so they're not coming to attack us!

18. C The author states that *the pace of technological advancement has been dramatic,* and then illustrates his point with an example: *In less than a hundred years, we have gone from horse-drawn carriages to walking on the moon.* (C) is a nice paraphrase of the author's point. The other answers are not indicated in the passage.

19. D The *argument* is stated as *if time travel were possible, wouldn't we be swamped with visitors from the future?* But, we would know if we were *swamped* only if we could see the visitors from the future. What if they are invisible? The author doesn't consider this possibility, because he is assuming that we would be able to see or somehow *notice* these visitors, as described in (D).

20. **C** After noting that Stephen Hawking's opinion *carries a great deal of weight*, the author states that the Conjecture *has caused many a professional scientist to dismiss the whole concept*. The next paragraph begins, *Not everyone, however, is convinced.* The passage as a whole shows two opposing reactions to the *Chronological Protection Conjecture*, thus showing the concept to be *controversial*, (C).

21. **D** The author of Passage 1 states *I agree...that Einstein's Theory of Relativity ought to make some form of limited travel to the future possible.* The author of Passage 2 states *Stephen Hawking's "Chronological Protection Conjecture,"...allow[s] for the possibility of time travel to the future.* These two statements support choice (D). (A) is false, while (B), (C), and (E) are not indicated in the passage.

22. **A** The statement about *hordes of time travelers* shows that the author of Passage 1 doesn't believe that time travel is possible. How would Sagan respond to this? We don't have to read his mind; we just have to know what he's already said which is that he *prefer[s] to "withhold judgment until there is better evidence."* (A) paraphrases this nicely.

23. **E** The quote is clearly used to throw into doubt the *Grandfather Paradox*, which (as we learned in Passage 1) claims that the universe must obey the laws of causality. (E) summarizes the purpose of the statement accurately.

24. **A** The word *noting* in the passage means something like "saying" or "stating an opinion." The colleague is stating his opinion as to the likelihood of time travel. The only answer that matches with this is (A), *asserting*, which means "to state an opinion."

Section 5

1. **B**   As written, the sentence has no subject: *to arrest and imprison* are verbs, so eliminate (A). (B) fixes this problem with nouns *the arrest and imprisonment*. (D) and (E) change the meaning to state that the *petty criminals* themselves *improve the vitality*, rather than their arrest and imprisonment. (C) is an incomplete sentence.

2. **E**   (A) and (D) use the unnecessary verb form *being* to modify *Mark's brother*. (C) is a sentence fragment. (B) changes the meaning of the sentence: the fact that he is *the national fencing champion* is not a new point, it is the reason for the scholarship. (E) keeps *the national fencing champion* as a modifier and places it closest to the person it is modifying.

3. **E**   (A), (C), and (D) contain incorrect punctuation: two independent clauses cannot be joined by a comma and a dependent clause cannot follow a semicolon. (B) changes the meaning of the original sentence by adding *with*. (E) fixes the comma splice and keeps the original meaning.

4. **D**   The conjunction *both* requires "and" between the conjoined elements. The absence of "and" from (A), (B), and (E) is reason enough to eliminate them. (C) lacks parallel structure, making (D) the better choice.

5. **A**   The sentence is correct as written. (C) and (E) are sentence fragments. (D) has a misplaced modifier. In (B) the comma between two independent clauses creates a comma splice. (A) has the verbs in the proper tense and has the modified noun, *ecologists*, right next to its modifier.

6. **C**   The sentence as written has an idiom error: the correct form is *not only… but also*. Eliminate (A), (B), and (E). The original sentence also has a parallelism error in *to illustrate…establishing*. Only (C) has the correct idiom and parallel structure.

7. **A** (A) contains all nouns—*a supporter, a defender, an opponent*—in parallel form. (B), (C), (D), and (E) all contain parallelism errors because they each change one of these to a gerund, such as *opposing* in (B) and (E) or a verb, such as *defended* in (C) and *opposed* in (D).

8. **B** (A) and (D) have incorrect verb tenses. (C) changes the meaning of the sentence with an unnecessary preposition and (E) adds an unnecessary conjunction. (B) uses the correct verb tense and the correct pronoun to start a modifying clause.

9. **D** As written the sentence has a misplaced modifier: *the rehearsal* could not have *been working in the rafters*. Nor could *a heavy camera* (B), (C), and (E). The only sentence that correctly identifies the stagehand as the one working in the rafters is (D).

10. **E** The sentence as written switches the pronoun from *We* to *you*, as does answer (B). The pronoun *it* in (C) does not agree with *lessons* in the non-underlined portion of the sentence. In (D) it is not clear what *it* refers to. (E) has pronouns that agree with the rest of the sentence (*we, our*) and eliminates unnecessary wordiness.

11. **A** This sentence is correct as written. The word *more* is appropriate because two things are being compared. The idiom *more…than* is correct, as is the parallel use of *as* after each word to go along with *offered*.

12. **C** The correct choice is (C) because of a verb tense error. The modifying phrase refers to a time in the past, so the main verb must be in the past tense. Since *has been* is in the present perfect tense, it is incorrect.

13. **E** There is no error in the sentence. (B) is the correct possessive pronoun to use with the plural noun *supervisors*. (C) has the correct plural form of the verb, since the subject of *find* is they.

14. **B** The correct choice is (B) because of a verb tense error. The verb *becoming* should be "became." As it stands, without the verb form the sentence is a fragment.

15. **C** The correct choice is (C) because *most brightest* is redundant. The correct phrasing would be *most brightly painted*.

16. **D** There is a pronoun error in answer choice (D). The pronoun *you* does not match *us*, causing an agreement error. It might be tempting to choose (C) because *own favorite* sounds weird, but that phrase does not break a grammar rule.

17. **B** The correct choice is (B) because of a subject-verb agreement error. The subject of the sentence is *one of the most famous plays* which refers to *The Clouds*. Since the subject is singular, the verb should be as well.

18. **A** Answer (A) contains an idiom error. *Advocate to* should be *advocate of*. Be sure to go through each answer choice carefully with grammar rules for each part of speech in mind when trying to spot an error.

19. **B** Choice (B) includes an agreement error. The subject of the sentence is *city park* which is singular, so the verb should be *contains* in order to agree. Choice (A) is an example of the way ETS will throw in uncommon usage which may sound wrong but doesn't break a rule.

20. **D** There is a pronoun error in choice (D). Remember, any time a pronoun is underlined, check that it agrees with the subject. In this case, *savings* is plural and the pronoun *it* is singular.

21. **C** Answer (C) contains an idiom error. The correct phrase is *brink of* not *brink to*. Remember that most idiom errors can be spotted by the misuse of a preposition, so when prepositions are underlined, always check for idioms.

22. **D** The correct choice is (D) because of a comparison error. The sentence is comparing New York City's smog problem to the actual city of Los Angeles instead of comparing it to Los Angeles' smog problem.

23. **D** This sentence contains a misplaced modifier in answer (D). As written, it sounds as if the *medication* takes the pill, which is not the intended meaning of the sentence.

24. **E** There is no error in this sentence. Don't rely on what the sentence "sounds" like when trying to find an error.

25. **C** Answer (C) contains a verb error. *Had ran* is incorrect; it would be correct as *had run*. When two things both start and stop in the past, we need the past perfect tense, which uses the helping verb *had* and the present tense of the verb.

26. **D** Choice (D) contains an agreement error. The subject is *requests*, which is plural, so the pronoun that replaces it should be *those* rather than *that*. Answer (C) might be tempting, since using *number* as a verb is slightly uncommon; however, it is grammatical, so (C) can't be correct.

27. **C** Answer (C) contains a parallelism error; the tense is inconsistent with that of the rest of the sentence. *Discounting* does not match *to claim*. To be parallel, (C) should read "to discount."

28. **E** There is no error in this sentence, so (E) is correct. There are some phrases like *ever more virulent* or *both destroys* that may sound awkward, but there are no grammar rules broken in this sentence.

29. **D** The correct choice is (D) because of a comparison error. The superlative *most* can be used only when comparing more than two things. When comparing only two things, "more" must be used.

30. **A** (B), (C), (D), and (E) suggest that sentence 4 stems from the prior sentences as a natural conclusion. However, sentence 4 opposes the previous sentences, so (A), *However,* is the best option. Understanding this sentence requires understanding these transition words.

31. **C** (A) is awkward and questionable in meaning. (B) is close, but does not flow very well due to the short phrases separated by commas. (D) creates a comma splice by having two complete phrases connected by a comma. (E) is passive and has the ambiguous pronoun *it*. This leaves only (C) as the correct answer.

32. **D** As written, the sentence has an ambiguous pronoun, *they,* and the sentence is made awkward by the repeated *very* and the phrase *make as good*. (B) creates a comma splice by joining two complete sentences with a comma. (C) creates an incomplete sentence by starting a phrase with the word *because* without providing the result. (E) does not clear up the ambiguous pronoun, and adds an extra comparison with *more*. (D) is the clearest form of the sentence.

33. **A** (B) is awkward and wordy. (C) is awkward: The sentence would not need the unclear pronoun *it* if *liquid* were the subject, rather than *Starting with a liquid*. (D) leaves out the churning process, and is not as clear as (A) about how the air is added to the liquid. In (E), the person speaking changes halfway through the sentence; the first clause is in the third person and the second clause is in the second person command form. The end of (E) in unnecessarily repetitive.

34. **B** (A) does not clarify the sentence at all; (B) is a better choice. (C), (D), and (E) aren't things that could be added to the gelato, so (B) is indeed the correct answer.

35. **D** In the original sentence, *In conclusion* is a stiff and obvious way of presenting a point, and the awkward phrase *gelato does not work in America because its nature prevents it from mass production* is unclear about who or what *prevents it*. Choice (B) becomes a sentence fragment when *Since*, a word that introduces a dependent clause, replaces *In conclusion*. The awkward phrase is replaced by a somewhat less awkward one in (C), but the word *However* incorrectly indicates a change of direction in the sentence or a contrast to the previous idea. Both (D) and (E) replace the awkward phrase with clearer ones, however, (E) introduces the sentence with *Being that*, which makes the sentence a fragment, leaving (D) as the correct answer.

Section 6

1. **E** The sum of the measures of the angles of a triangle must be 180 degrees. The question gives us two angles: 90 degrees (it's a right triangle) and 20 degrees. $180 - 90 - 20 = 70$, the measure of the third angle. (E) is correct.

2. **B** Although we can solve for y and plug that value into the fraction, it is easier to change the equation to match the fraction. You may notice that 21 is 3×7 and 9 is 3×3. So, multiply both sides of $7y = 3$ by 3, to get $21y = 9$ and then divide both sides by 9 to see that $\frac{21y}{9} = 1$, answer (B). (A) gives the value of y. Answer choice (C) is the reciprocal of y.

3. **C** Add the two columns and subtract: The total number of parking violations for 2007 is 135. The total for 2008 is 165. So, they increase from 135 to 165, which is 30, (C).

4. **D** As the diagonal of the square, $\overline{EG}$ divides the square into two 45-45-90-degree triangles. In such a triangle, the legs have length s and the hypotenuse has length $s\sqrt{2}$. In ΔEFG, the hypotenuse is 6, which means that $s\sqrt{2}=6$. To find the length of the sides, solve for s:

$s=\dfrac{6}{\sqrt{2}}=\dfrac{6\sqrt{2}}{\sqrt{2}\sqrt{2}}=\dfrac{6\sqrt{2}}{2}=3\sqrt{2}$, answer (D).

5. **A** The easiest way to find out which answer choice is NOT equal to $2-x$ is to try each answer, and eliminate the ones that do work. If $2-x=-8$, is there a one-digit integer we could Plug In for x that would work? To make the equation work, x would have to be 10, which isn't a one-digit integer, so (A) does not work. All the other answers do work: for (B), x would be 8, for (C) x would be 6, for (D) x would be 4, and for (E) x would be 0.

6. **C** This could be solved using $a=2$ or $a=4$, and either way (C) $\dfrac{1}{16}$ is the correct answer. If $a=4$, then $x=1$ and $c=3$. This gives $ax^{-c}=4^{-2}$. A negative exponent means that we put the expression (without the negative sign) as the denominator of a fraction with 1 as the numerator. $\dfrac{1}{4^{2}}=\dfrac{1}{16}$, making (C) the correct answer.

7. **C** Draw this one out. Because Anne's, Zenia's, and Beth's all lie in that order on a vertical line with a length of 44, and we know the length between and Anne's and Zenia's is 32, the length between Zenia's and Beth's is 12. Moving due west from Beth's creates a right angle. Caleb's, Damon's, and Beth's all lie on the horizontal line in that order. The length between Caleb's and Beth's is 33, so subtract the length between Caleb's and Damon's to see that

the length between Damon's and Beth's is 5. Now we have a right triangle with legs of 5 and 12. Use the Pythagorean theorem or remember the 5-12-13 triplet to find that the diagonal distance between Damon's and Zenia's home is 13, (C).

8. **D** Since the problem never indicates how many jigsaw puzzles Jared has, we can make up our own number. Assuming Jared has 10 puzzles, 6 puzzles have 50 pieces and 4 puzzles have 30 pieces. The average is $\dfrac{\text{total number of pieces}}{\text{total number of puzzles}} = \dfrac{6(50) + 4(30)}{10} = 42$, answer (D). Choice (B) mixes up the percentages. Choice (C) ignores the percentages and just finds the average of 50 and 30 pieces.

9. $\dfrac{40}{3}$ **or 13.3**

First, find the rate given: $\dfrac{10 \text{ miles}}{3 \text{ hours}} = 3.33$ mph; then find the miles covered in four hours: 3.33 mph × 4 hours = 13.3 miles.

10. **120** To find the measure of each individual angle, remember that we're really just dealing with a straight line, and that 6 equal angles form that line. There are 180° in a straight line, therefore $6x = 180°$ and each individual angle (x in this case) is 30°. If two angles are "bisected," that simply means they are split in half, so any bisected 30° angle will be split into two 15° angles. To find the measure of the angle indicated by the arrow, count the smaller angles contained therein. There are three 30° angles and two 15° angles, so 30 + 30 + 30 + 15 + 15 = 120.

11. **3,899**

First, find the range of x by subtracting 1,300 from all parts of the inequality: $1,200 < x < 3,900$. In this case, the largest possible value for x is 3,899, because x must be an integer *less than* (NOT *less than or equal to*) 3,900.

12. **75** Since the perimeter of the equilateral triangle is 15, each side is 5. That means each side of the three squares is 5. Area of a square is side squared, so the area of each square is 25. The total area of the three squares is 75.

13. **2** The median is the middle number when all the items in a list are organized in ascending order. List out the numbers: 5 people spent one hour on email, so 1, 1, 1, 1, 1 are our first five numbers. 5 spent two hours on email, so we add 2, 2, 2, 2, 2. Continuing on, the full list is 1 1 1 1 1 2 2 2 2 2 3 3 4 4 4 5 5. The median here is 2. Do the same thing for Meeting Attendance, and we get a list of 1 1 2 2 2 2 3 3 4 4 4 4 5 5 5 5 6. The median for this list is 4, so the difference between the medians is 2.

14. **195** Set a variable g for girls, and translate the information in the problem into an equation: $g + (g - 60) = 330$. Therefore, $2g - 60 = 330$; $2g = 390$; and $g = 195$.

15. **4** One pile of 4 pebbles will leave 70 pebbles to divide among the remaining 24 piles, which we can do with a combination of piles of 1, 2, and/or 3 pebbles. 3 couldn't be the biggest pile because we would need more than one pile of 3 to get to 74 in only 25 piles. This question hinges upon the fact that we can't have fractional pebbles, and that we're allowed only one pile of the highest number.

16. **41, 43, 45, and 47**
    The easiest way to answer this question is to make a guess as to what the numbers might be and check to make sure it works with the information in the question. The 52 in 2,452 and $52r$ reveals an opportunity to break 2,452 into 2,400 + 52, which are individually multiples of 60 and 52, respectively. The equation will look like this: $2{,}400 + 52 = 60q + 52r$. We can then determine possible values for q and r by creating two equations: $2{,}400 = 60q$ and $52 = 52r$. In this case, $q = 40$ and $r = 1$. Remember, we need to find only one answer for a question that asks for "one possible value."

17. **12** The first step is to simplify the expression into $h(1) = f(2) + 2 \times g(1)$. Next, use the graphs to determine the values of $f(2)$ and $g(1)$. The value of $f(2)$ is 4, and the value of $g(1)$ is 4, which yields $h(1) = 4 + 2 \times 4$, which equals 12.

18. $\dfrac{9}{2}$ **or 4.5**

    Solve for n in the equation for line a by replacing x with n and y with $\dfrac{7}{2}$; $n = -3$. Since the point of intersection is now $(-3, \dfrac{7}{2})$ we can use those two values in the second equation to find b by replacing x with -3 and y with $\dfrac{7}{2}$ to give us $\dfrac{7}{2} = \dfrac{1}{3} \times (-3) + b$, solving for $b = \dfrac{9}{2}$.

Section 7

1. **B** Start with the second blank. The phrase *now that prototypes have been built that emit only water vapor* tells us that the *dream* is likely to come true. A good word for the second blank is something like "reality." Therefore, eliminate (A), (C), and (E). Now tackle the first blank. The

word *once* tells us that the first blank is opposed in meaning to the second blank, so eliminate (D). The first blank should mean something like "unrealistic," which is a synonym for *quixotic* (B).

2. **A** We know that the autobiography was *truthful* and *revealing*. (A), *candid*, matches this description. (B), *didactic*, means "instructive," which doesn't match with what we know about the autobiography. (C) means "overly sentimental," (D) means "extravagant or complex," and (E) means "immature," none of which works.

3. **C** The *people* are not *aloof*; they are *merely shy*. So we need a synonym for *shy*. *Timorous*, which means nervous or timid, is the only word that matches. The correct answer is (C).

4. **A** Laura was *Glowing with joy and delight*—so that is what the blank means. We want something positive. We can eliminate (C) because it is negative. While (A) and (B) are both positive, (A) means "happy" while (B) means "hard working." (A) *rapturous* is the best choice for the blank.

5. **B** We know that the conservationists are trying to remove all those *broken crates* and *washed up junk* from the shipwreck so the blank must mean something like "garbage leftover from a shipwreck." (B), *detritus*, means this. The other tough word here is (A), *raiment*, which means clothing.

6. **E** Process of Elimination is a good strategy for this question. Eliminate (A) because *popular* is not an apt description of the types listed in Passage 1, and we don't know if the types listed in Passage 2 are *rarely heard*. Eliminate (B) because it directly contradicts the passage; we *mix and match musical styles rather than preserve the preferences of our parents and grandparents*. Get rid of (C) because there's neither a *historical analysis* in Passage 1, nor an *abstract theory* in Passage 2. Eliminate (D)

because Passage 1 discusses only American culture, not *all cultures*. (E) nicely summarizes a difference between the two passages.

7. **D** The author of Passage 1 states that we *mix and match musical styles rather than preserve the preferences of our parents and grandparents.* Therefore, he or she would describe the listening habits as typical of an American, which is a good match for (D).

8. **B** The author of Passage 2 discusses his or her own experiences, whereas Passage 1 is entirely in the third person. Therefore, Passage 2 makes significant use of *personal experience*, (B).

9. **B** Process of Elimination is a good strategy for this question. Eliminate (A) because Passage 2 doesn't *criticize*. (B) sounds good. (C) is a trap because it switches the order of the passages. (D) doesn't work because there's no attempt to *correct a common misconception*. Eliminate (E) because there are no *objections* and no *resolving*. (B) is indeed the correct answer.

10. **C** This question asks us to draw an analogy between the actions of the crowd and the situations in the answer choices. Begin by describing the crowd in general terms. The crowd *come(s) in and take(s) possession* after someone else has *opened the way*; they also don't appreciate how tough it was for the persons who paved the way, as shown by the statements *Why this couldn't have been so bad,…strange it should have taken so long!* Of the answer choices, only (C) is similar to the crowd.

11. **B** The president knew that Dr. Hubers *stood on the verge of great celebrity*, meaning he was going to do great things. The president also promised him *just as good a laboratory as you have there and plenty of time for your own work.* Why? Because he wanted to be able to *rise up and proclaim: "See! We have done it!"* In other words, *claim credit for Dr. Hubers' achievements* (B). (A) and (C) are traps that exploit the literal

meaning of *possess*. (D) is NOT what he *wanted most of all,* and (E) is not indicated.

12. **E** The beginning of the paragraph describes Dr. Hubers' ancestors and suggests that Dr. Hubers retained certain of their characteristics. And what were these characteristics? The phrase *If they loved a woman, they picked her up and took her away* indicates *impulsiveness* (E). (B) is close, but there is no evidence of *brutality*—it's a little too strong. (A) and (C) may be characteristics of Dr. Hubers, but not the ones asked about in this question. (D) is never indicated in the passage.

13. **A** Go back to the passage and come up with a word to replace *disposed* based on the context of the sentence. Something like "willing" or "receptive" fits the meaning well. Only *inclined* (A) is a good match. Don't go for the primary meaning of the word in these questions; (C) is a blatant trap answer.

14. **C** The author states that what made Hubers *quite hopeless as a civilised product* was that *it never struck him that there was anything so very peculiar* with his taking a year off to get married before he had even asked Miss Stanley to marry him. The author's not talking about Miss Stanley, so we can remove (A). He's not trying to make us feel bad for Hubers, so we can remove (B). (C) matches up with Hubers' *very un-approved and most uncivilised thing* of neglecting to get Miss Stanley's opinion before taking action. (D) is not mentioned at all, so eliminate it. (E) is wrong because the passage doesn't state that Hubers has an *overly clinical view of marriage.*

15. **D** The phrase *His assistants had to do a great deal of reminding after he came back that week* tells us that Dr. Hubers was *distracted,* and from the previous paragraph we know it was because he proposed to Miss Stanley, so his distraction was *unrelated to his work.* (D) does a good

job of paraphrasing this point. The other answers are not indicated in the passage.

16. **B** The assistants believed Dr. Hubers was distracted because *he was on a new trail,* when actually he was distracted by his relationship with Miss Stanley (as explained in the previous paragraph). Thus, their *impression was mistaken* (B).

17. **A** The purpose of the passage is to show how eyewitness testimony is not always reliable, which matches (A). (B) is too narrow; it applies only to the second and third paragraphs. (C) is not mentioned in the passage, and (D) and (E) are too sweeping (and also are not supported by the passage).

18. **A** The author of the passage explains that juries have traditionally found eyewitness testimony to be the most convincing evidence and that, after all, seeing is believing. So the author uses the saying to *emphasize an accepted point of view,* (A).

19. **C** Western Europeans and the Zulu are used as examples of how, when shown the same images, *different groups responded in divergent ways.* (C) summarizes this point succinctly. (A) and (D) are too extreme, while (B) and (E) are not supported by the passage.

20. **A** The clue to the meaning of *color* is the following phrase: *personality and mood fluctuation can also alter our perceptions.* Substitute *alter* for *color* and then eliminate any choices that don't match. (A) *modify* is closest to "alter."

21. **B** The *photograph of four young men* is used by the author to show that happy people believe the photograph is of four happy kids, but people who are anxious assume those in the photo are anxious. So the author is showing how the viewer's emotion can change their perception, answer choice (B).

22. D The *numerous prosaic factors* mentioned include ordinary things that can affect the accuracy of perception such as *duration of the encounter, proximity to the subject, lighting, and angle*. So the author is saying that it's not just the mental things he has mentioned previously that can affect the accuracy of perception. (D) mentions these *circumstances unrelated to the viewer's mental state*.

23. D The author states that *[blood samples* and *fingerprints] do not resonate as deeply with juries as does testimony*. (D) paraphrases this sentence nicely. (A), (C), and (E) are all too absolute, while (B) is not indicated in the passage.

24. B The author concludes the passage by saying that, because of the problems with eyewitness testimony, it may no longer be as important as things like blood samples and fingerprints. The author is not supporting a previous claim, but making a new one so (A) is out. (B) is exactly what the author is doing: saying what could happen in the future. Choice (C) is wrong because he is not talking about *an unrelated situation*. (D) is wrong because he does not mention any study in this paragraph. (E) is incorrect because he is not telling anyone what should be studied.

Section 8

1. B The clue is that they *spent hours begging*. So the blank must mean continuing to do something. The closest word in the choices is *persistence*, (B). Choice (C) may be appealing, but it is the grandmother who is generous, not the *grandchildren*.

2. E We know we are worried about the trees' *health* from the last half of the sentence. Recycle that clue for the first blank. Keep (A), (B), (E),

and maybe (D). The second blank should be negative; (A), (B), and (D) don't match because their words for the second blank are neutral. *Compromised* may not seem negative, but it has a secondary definition that works. (E) is the best answer.

3. **D** *Surprisingly* indicates that the first blank contradicts *lethal poison*, so eliminate (A) and (E), and note that (C) is weak. We now know we're looking for a positive word for the second blank, so eliminate (B) and (C). The correct answer is (D).

4. **D** The semicolon indicates that we're looking for a synonym for *confidently optimistic*. Only *sanguine* matches. The correct answer is (D).

5. **D** The clue is that the children had *droopy eyes and frequent yawning*. The semicolon serves as a same direction trigger, which tells us we can recycle the clue. The blank must mean "sleepy." The only word that means "sleepy" is *somnolent,* (D). Although *sedulous* sounds close to "sedated," it does not mean tired.

6. **A** The second part of the sentence tells us that the *skinflint is unlikely to* do something. That "something" is in the first part of the sentence: *changes one's attitude.* A good word for the second blank is a synonym for *attitude.* (A), (E), and maybe (B) work. The clue for the first blank is [*attitude*] *entrenched over a lifetime*, so we're looking for something that means "habitual." Answers (A) and (C) both work for the first blank, but only (A) fits in both blanks.

7. **D** The quotes around *"controversial,"* and his description of the speaker indicate that the author does not think that the symposiums were particularly controversial. So calling it controversial is *an overstatement,* (D).

8.   **B**   We know that the speaker is opposed to *modern conveniences*, which makes him rather unusual, especially in front of a group of college students. The author mentions his wardrobe, which is also clearly out of step with the times, to accentuate the impression that the speaker is a little unusual. (B) *eccentric* captures this "unusualness" best. (C) is too much of a stretch; the author doesn't really *criticize*, and anyway that's not *why* he mentions the speaker's apparel. (E) is off because he's not praising the professor at this point. (A) and (D) are not supported by the passage.

9.   **C**   The author notes that the girls interrupted each other frequently, paused at the same awkward moments, and responded to each other's statements as if neither one heard what the other said. The word *disjointed* (C) sums this up accurately. The conversation might be *insignificant* (B), but it doesn't say so in the passage.

10.   **E**   Go back to the passage and come up with a word to replace *stole* based on the context of the sentence. To "steal" a glance means to glance quickly to avoid the glance being noticed by its subject. "Risked" would be a good choice because he runs the risk of being caught looking. Only *hazarded* is a good match—hazard means "take a chance; risk." (B) and (C) are traps based on the usual meanings of the word, while (A) and (D) don't fit at all.

11.   **A**   Why does the author tell the story about the girls? He's just told us about the symposium speaker's point, which is that the speaker is *against modern tools of convenience*. The narrator felt the *speech* was *altogether too romantic*. Observing the girls' conversations led him to reconsider or *reflect*, as in (A). By the end of the passage, the narrator feels the professors' speech was *not so romantic after all*.

12. **B** The reference to *smiley-faced icons* is used to show that old-fashioned letter writing had *certain important advantages* over modern ways of communication. Thus, the reference expresses *skepticism about certain modes of communication*. Although the narrator does seem *nostalgic* for the old days, there's nothing about an *easier way of life*, so (A) can't work. (C) is too sweeping; the narrator is not discussing *modern writers*. (D) is not indicated in the passage, and (E) directly contradicts the passage.

13. **A** The symposium speaker's reasoning is that *The temporary, impersonal nature of computers,…is gradually rendering our lives equally temporary and impersonal.* In the answers, (A) is an example of a newlywed couple using technology to make communication more impersonal. None of the other answers use technology in a way that could be called impersonal.

14. **C** The person in the movie theater was clearly not thinking about anyone else around him. So he was *tactless*, "unthinking or careless," answer (C). If he were *impetuous* (A), he would be suddenly energetic or impulsive. If he were *languid* (B), he would be tired and unmoving. The person in the theater was not necessarily *demonstrative* (D); he just talked a lot. To be demonstrative is to openly demonstrate one's emotions. He also wasn't *taciturn*, (E), which means not talkative.

15. **C** The author states that the *significant price* is that the girls *are never alone,* and elaborates by noting that the girls *could use a moment of solitude.* Thus, they have *difficulty experiencing a certain amount of privacy.* (A) and (B) are overly literal traps—we're not talking about a monetary price. (D) contradicts the passage, while (E) is not supported.

16. **D** The first time the narrator states *they are never alone*, he uses the phrase to show that the girls never have to be out of touch. But the second iteration, in italics, is used to show that the girls are unable to experience solitude. Thus, the italics are used to *imply an alternate meaning of the phrase*. Though (A) is true, it's no reason to use italics, and (B), (C), and (E) are not supported.

17. **E** The last sentence makes it clear that the narrator is now in sympathy with the professor. Whereas previously, he thought the professor was out of touch, he now feels that the professor had a valid point. The narrator therefore had *a change of heart* (E). (A) refers to the situation caused by modern technology. There is no *unforeseen difficulty* as mentioned in (B). (C) is mentioned in the paragraph, but as a quality that *the girls* lack. (D) is also mentioned, but not as something that the narrator is experiencing.

18. **C** The narrator's biggest problem with technology is when it doesn't allow a person to disconnect from the world. (C) would keep everyone in constant contact, which is what the narrator warns about in his discussion of cell phones.

19. **B** The narrator starts out unconvinced by the speaker, but by the end of the passage, after considering the argument carefully, he's in agreement. Thus, he *evaluates an argument*. He doesn't primarily *criticize*, so eliminate (A). (C) and (D) deal with the second paragraph only, so they're too specific. (E) is not supported by the passage.

Section 9

1. **B** Start with the sum of *a* and *b*: *a* + *b*. The square of this would be $(a + b)^2$, making (B) the correct answer. (A) is "the sum of the squares of *a* and *b*."

2. **B** The line of best fit is a straight line that best approximates the data. If you draw a line to approximate the trend in the scatterplot, you see that as the number of citations increases, the grade increases. This means that the line of best fit has a positive slope: choice (B). Choice (A) indicates that as citations increase, grade decreases. Choice (C) says the line of best fit has a negative y-intercept, but the line in the graph has a positive y-intercept. Choice (D) says line of best fit has a positive x-intercept; if this line continued in both directions, it would have a negative x-intercept. Choice (E) says the line of best fit passes through the origin, but you already know that the line has a positive y-intercept.

3. **A** Since the base is square, and the area is 100, each edge must be 10. Because there are 4 edges along the square base, multiply 4 by 10 to get 40, the total length of the base edges. There are four edges from the top of the pyramid to a corner and each is 13 feet, so $4 \times 13 = 52$, the total length of those four edges. Add 40 and 52 to get 92, (A) the total length of all 8 edges of the pyramid.

4. **E** Do not solve the equation sets, as the question does not seek the actual values of b and d. Deal with the number of albums first. Because b and d represent the number of each type of album and there are a total of 25 albums, $b + d = 25$. Eliminate (A), (B), and (C). Now address the value. The b albums cost \$1.25 each and the d albums cost \$2.30 each; the grand total is \$41.75. Answer choice (E) reflects this equation. If you picked (D), you reversed the costs of b and d.

5. **C** Since we have a ratio, but no real numbers, let's make up some distances. Let's say that Magnus drove 10 miles. This means that Eva drove 4 times as many miles, so Eva drove 40 miles. The trip was therefore 50 miles altogether. Eva drove 40 miles out of 50 total miles, which is 80%.

6. **A** Make up a number for b. Suppose $b = 2$, which means that Cathy runs for 2 hours at 10 minutes per mile. First, convert 2 hours to 120 minutes and then set up as a proportion to find how many miles she travels. So, $\dfrac{10 \text{ min}}{1 \text{ mile}} = \dfrac{120 \text{ min}}{x \text{ miles}}$. Cross-multiply to get $10x = 120$ or $x = 12$ miles. Now, $26 - 12 = 14$ miles left. Replace b with 2 in the answer choices, and the one that gives 14 is the correct answer. To also solve this algebraically, if Cathy runs a mile in 10 minutes, she runs 6 miles per hour for b hours. So for the first b hours she runs $6b$ miles. Subtract this from 26 to get the distance remaining after b hours: $26 - 6b$, as in (A).

7. **D** In the image, the graph hits the x- and y- axes six times. The reflected version of the graph would be a mirror image graph, such that the curves are shifted to the opposite sides of the x-axis. Thus, the new graph will have exactly the same number of intercept points: (D) Six. If you picked (C), you counted only the x-intercept points.

8. **C** One easy way to work this problem is to Plug In numbers for the variables. Since $w + x = 5$, make $w = 2$ and $x = 3$ and since $y + z = 6$, make $y = 1$ and $z = 5$. Now use the values to find the products being added together: $wy = 2$, $xz = 15$, $wz = 10$, $xy = 3$. $2 + 15 + 10 + 3 = 30$, answer (C). We can solve it algebraically by putting the terms $w + x$ and $y + z$ into parentheses and using FOIL; you get $wy + wz + xy + xz$, which is slightly different from the order of the pairs listed in the question, but the pairs are the same ones and adding in any order gives the same answer. Since you know the value of the expressions in the parentheses, just multiply those numbers: $(w + x)(y + z) = (5)(6) = 30$, answer (C).

9. B The three lines form a triangle, and each of the degree measurements given are vertical angles of the triangle. Therefore, the three angles of the triangle are, 45°, 15°, and $m°$. $45 + 15 + m = 180$, and $m = 120$. The answer is (B).

10. E When you multiply numbers with the same bases, you add the exponents. This means this first equation can be simplified to $a^9 = a^c$; therefore, $c = 9$. When you raise a number with an exponent to another power, you multiply the exponents, so the top half of the second equation becomes b^{5d} and the second equation becomes $\dfrac{b^{5d}}{b^d} = b^{40}$. When you divide numbers with the same bases, you subtract the exponents; therefore, the second equation becomes $b^{4d} = b^{40}$ and $4d = 40$, so $d = 10$.

Then add c and d to get the answer seen in (E): $9 + 10 = 19$.

11. B Stack the three equations and add, like this:

$$
\begin{array}{rcl}
a + b - c = & d + 6 \\
-b + c = & 8 \\
+\ 3a \qquad\quad = & -d + 2 \\
\hline
4a \qquad\qquad = & 16
\end{array}
$$

On the left side of the equation, $a + 3a$ is $4a$, $b + (-b)$ is 0, and $-c + c$ is 0, so the sum of the left sides of the equations is $4a$. The sum of the right sides of the equations is 16 (the b's, c's, and d's cancel out). So $4a = 16$; therefore, $a = 4$, as in (B).

12.   **D**   Try out the answer choices in the question and see which is the smallest value for z that makes the equation true. Answer choices (A), (B), and (C) create a negative number on the left side of the equation and a positive number on the right side. With (D) and (E), both sides of the equation are positive, and since 3 is smaller than 6, the correct answer is (D).

13.   **E**   Begin with the description of $\frac{1}{x}$: its tens digit is odd and larger than its units digit. 10 fits the description and is an easy number to work with. So say $\frac{1}{x}$ is 10 and solve for x: $\frac{1}{x}=10$, so $1 = 10x$, and $x = \frac{1}{10}$. In decimals, this is 0.1, so choice (E) works. Since the question asks for the largest possible value and this is the biggest number in the answers, you've found the credited response. If 0.1 weren't the biggest number you could try another number, like 31. If $\frac{1}{x}$ were 31, then $x = \frac{1}{31} = 0.0322580...$ and you could continue trying numbers until you found the biggest number that worked. Plug In The Answers. (B) gives 37 and (D) gives 11, in conflict with the description that $\frac{1}{x}$ should give a number with a tens digit larger than the units digit. All of the numbers in the answer choices are possible values of x in that they give you numbers with a larger, odd tens digit, but (E) has the greatest value of x. Be careful! (A) gives the largest value in the list for $\frac{1}{x}$ not x.

14.   C   Since there are no values for the lengths in the figure, let's say AB is 1. And since B, C, and D are the midpoints mentioned in the question, $AC = 2$, $AD = 4$, and $AE = 8$. Find the area of the shaded region by subtracting the areas of the squares with sides $\overline{AD}$ and $\overline{AC}$. The area of a square is the length of the side of the square raised to the second power, so the area of the square with side $\overline{AD}$ is 16 and the area of the square with side $\overline{AC}$ is 4; therefore the area of the shaded region is $16 - 4 = 12$. To find the answer, you'll need the area of the largest square. Its side has length 8, so its area is 64. The fractional part that is shaded is the area of the shaded region divided by the area of the large square: $\dfrac{12}{64} = \dfrac{3}{16}$, the fraction in (C).

15.   D   To find an equivalent equation, simplify. One clue is that none of the answers has a root, go get rid of that by squaring both sides of the equation, which gives $\dfrac{25}{x-3} = 9$. None of the answers has a fraction, so get rid of that by multiplying both sides of the equation by the denominator, which gives $25 = 9(x - 3)$, which is seen in answer (D).

16.   E   When a line passes through two parallel lines, all the small angles are the same, all the big angles are the same, and any big angle plus any small angle adds up to 180. So, $p + r = 180$. Replace p with $5r$, such that $5r + r = 180$. Thus, r is 30, and $5r$ is 150, which is the value of p, making (E) the correct choice. If you picked (B) you stopped solving when you found the value of r, not p. If you picked (A) or (C), you mistakenly solved for $p + r = 90$.

Section 10

1. **D** (A), (C), and (E) are sentence fragments because of incorrect verb forms and structures. (B) contains a verb tense error: *would* cannot be used with *last month*. (D) has the proper form of the verb to agree with the event occurring *last month*.

2. **C** The sentence as written is passive and wordy. (B) has a misplaced modifier: *An area* cannot describe *the growth*. (C) removes the passive voice from the phrase, "As an area…plants." (D) has an unnecessary *also* that does not link two ideas. (E) is an incomplete sentence.

3. **D** The original sentence contains a verb error. The verb *dedicated* requires a prepositional phrase or a verb phrase to follow it. This eliminates (A). (B) and (E) introduce verb tense errors. (C) has a wordy and awkward construction. (D) has the necessary prepositional phrase *to searching* and correct verb tense.

4. **C** The sentence as written lacks a verb; both (B) and (C) fix that problem by making *The Beatles* the subject and *are* the verb of the sentence. (B), however, contains a comma splice, leaving only (C).

5. **B** This sentence has a subject-verb agreement error. The subject *Mastering*—a gerund that is used as a noun for the process or action—is singular. Eliminate (A), (D), and (E) for using the plural verb. (C) is wordier and doesn't make sense: *Mastering* isn't something that *young cooks make*. Only (B) is grammatically correct.

6. **E** The list of actions in the sentence as written is not parallel. The verbs must all have the same form as *organize*. (D) and (E) both use *meet* and *satisfy* but (D) changes the meaning by separating the verbs from their objects, leaving (E) as the correct answer choice.

7.   A   The sentence is correct as written. (B) is not parallel. (C) changes the meaning of the sentence, indicating that *novelists and political theorists* wrote in order *to struggle*. (D) changes the meaning of the sentence. (E) creates a run-on sentence and changes the meaning.

8.   C   The sentence as written has an agreement problem: *they* does not agree with the singular *Discula destructiva,* so eliminate (A). (B) and (D) also have agreement problems. (E) creates a comma splice.

9.   A   The sentence is correct as written. (B) is not parallel; (C) and (D) have redundant use of *because* following *The reason,* which requires *that*. The "ing" words in (E) together are plural, and do not agree with *is* in the non-underlined part.

10. C   The correct idiom is *neither...nor*. The sentence as written use *or*. The phrase *applying for* is a singular subject, and so needs verbs *increases* and *decreases*. Only (C) has the correct idiom and verb structure.

11. E   In the sentence as written, *they* is an ambiguous pronoun. (B) and (D) have misplaced modifiers: *speeches* cannot be *instructed to avoid* something nor can they advise *speechwriters*. (C) is wordy and awkward. (E) correctly sets up a cause for the effect given in the non-underlined portion of the sentence.

12. B   The sentence as written compares an adjective (*comedic*) and a noun (*tragedy*). Eliminate (A). All the other answers use *tragic,* so compare the rest of the choices, looking for other errors. The correct answer will match comedic with tragic. (B) adds no additional errors. The phrase *in a combining of* in (C) is awkward and ungrammatical. (D) is incomplete due to the addition of *when* and (E) mismatches *comedy* and *tragic*.

13.   **E**   (A) and (B) contain adjective errors: the subject of the sentence, the *dress codes*, cannot be described as *impulsive*, only the reason for establishing them can be. (C) creates a comma splice. (D) creates a parallelism error. (E) is parallel and corrects the adjective error.

14.   **A**   (A) correctly joins two independent clauses with a colon. (B) creates a comma splice error. (C) incorrectly joins a dependent clause to an independent clause with a semicolon. (D) introduces the unnecessary verb *being*, and (E) uses the redundant conjunction *yet*.

SAT SCORING WORKSHEET
For directions on how to score your SAT practice test, see pages 5–7.

SAT Writing Section

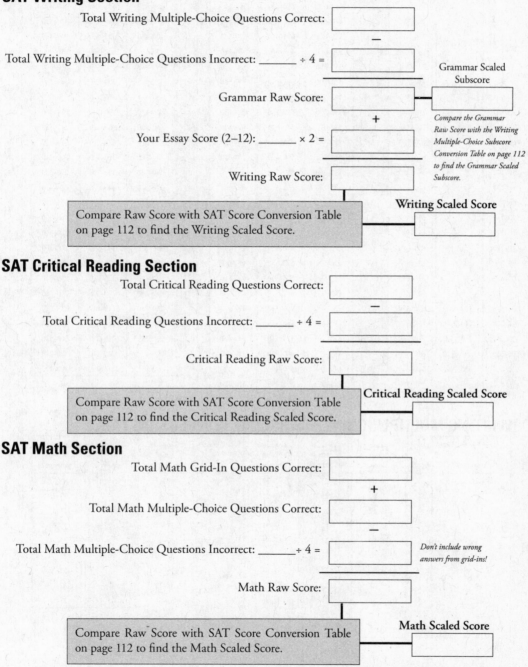

Total Writing Multiple-Choice Questions Correct:

−

Total Writing Multiple-Choice Questions Incorrect: _____ ÷ 4 =

Grammar Raw Score:

Grammar Scaled Subscore

+

Compare the Grammar Raw Score with the Writing Multiple-Choice Subscore Conversion Table on page 112 to find the Grammar Scaled Subscore.

Your Essay Score (2–12): _____ × 2 =

Writing Raw Score:

Compare Raw Score with SAT Score Conversion Table on page 112 to find the Writing Scaled Score.

Writing Scaled Score

SAT Critical Reading Section

Total Critical Reading Questions Correct:

−

Total Critical Reading Questions Incorrect: _____ ÷ 4 =

Critical Reading Raw Score:

Critical Reading Scaled Score

Compare Raw Score with SAT Score Conversion Table on page 112 to find the Critical Reading Scaled Score.

SAT Math Section

Total Math Grid-In Questions Correct:

+

Total Math Multiple-Choice Questions Correct:

−

Total Math Multiple-Choice Questions Incorrect: _____ ÷ 4 =

Don't include wrong answers from grid-ins!

Math Raw Score:

Compare Raw Score with SAT Score Conversion Table on page 112 to find the Math Scaled Score.

Math Scaled Score

SAT SCORE CONVERSION TABLE

Raw Score	Reading Scaled Score	Math Scaled Score	Writing Scaled Score	Raw Score	Reading Scaled Score	Math Scaled Score	Writing Scaled Score	Raw Score	Reading Scaled Score	Math Scaled Score	Writing Scaled Score
73			800	47	580–620	650–690	540–580	21	410–450	440–480	380–420
72			780–800	46	570–610	640–680	530–570	20	410–450	430–470	370–410
71			770–800	45	570–610	630–670	520–560	19	400–440	420–460	360–400
70			750–790	44	560–600	620–660	520–560	18	390–430	420–460	350–390
69			740–780	43	550–590	610–650	510–550	17	390–430	410–450	350–390
68			730–770	42	550–590	600–640	500–540	16	380–420	400–440	340–380
67	800		720–760	41	540–580	600–640	500–540	15	370–410	390–430	330–370
66	780–800		710–750	40	530–570	590–630	490–530	14	370–410	390–430	320–360
65	770–800		700–740	39	530–570	580–620	480–520	13	360–400	380–420	310–350
64	760–800		690–730	38	520–560	570–610	480–520	12	350–390	370–410	310–350
63	750–790		680–720	37	510–550	560–600	470–510	11	340–380	360–400	300–340
62	730–770		680–720	36	510–550	550–590	460–500	10	330–370	350–390	290–330
61	710–750		670–710	35	500–540	550–590	460–500	9	330–370	340–380	280–320
60	700–740		660–700	34	500–540	540–580	450–490	8	320–360	330–370	270–310
59	690–730		650–690	33	490–530	530–570	440–480	7	310–350	320–360	260–300
58	680–720		640–680	32	480–520	520–560	430–470	6	300–340	310–350	260–300
57	670–710		630–670	31	480–520	510–550	430–470	5	290–330	300–340	260–300
56	660–700		620–660	30	470–510	510–550	420–460	4	280–320	290–330	250–290
55	650–690		610–650	29	460–500	500–540	420–460	3	270–310	270–310	250–290
54	640–680	800	600–640	28	460–500	490–530	410–450	2	250–290	260–300	240–280
53	630–670	760–800	590–630	27	450–490	480–520	400–440	1	240–280	240–280	230–270
52	620–660	740–780	580–620	26	450–490	480–520	400–440	0	220–260	230–270	220–260
51	610–650	710–750	570–610	25	440–480	470–510	390–430	−1	200–220	210–250	200–220
50	600–640	690–730	560–600	24	430–470	460–500	390–430	−2	200–220	200–210	200–220
49	600–640	670–710	560–600	23	430–470	450–490	380–420	−3	200	200	200–220
48	590–630	660–700	550–590	22	420–460	450–490	380–420				

WRITING MULTIPLE-CHOICE SUBSCORE CONVERSION TABLE

Grammar Raw Score	Grammar Scaled Subscore	Grammar Raw Score	Grammar Scaled Subscore	Grammar Raw Score	Grammar Scaled Subscore	Grammar Raw Score	Grammar Scaled Subscore	Grammar Raw Score	Grammar Scaled Subscore
49	78–80	38	60–64	27	49–53	16	40–44	5	30–34
48	77–80	37	59–63	26	48–52	15	39–43	4	28–32
47	74–78	36	58–62	25	48–52	14	38–42	3	27–31
46	72–76	35	57–61	24	47–51	13	38–42	2	25–29
45	70–74	34	56–60	23	46–50	12	37–41	1	24–28
44	68–72	33	55–59	22	45–49	11	36–40	0	22–26
43	66–70	32	54–58	21	44–48	10	35–39	−1	20–22
42	65–69	31	53–57	20	43–47	9	34–38	−2	20–22
41	64–68	30	52–56	19	42–46	8	33–37	−3	20–22
40	62–66	29	51–55	18	42–46	7	32–36		
39	61–65	28	50–54	17	41–45	6	31–35		

Chapter 5
Practice Test 2

THIS PAGE INTENTIONALLY LEFT BLANK

SECTION 1

○ I prefer NOT to grant the College Board the right to use, reproduce, or publish my essay for any purpose beyond the assessment of my writing skills, even though my name will not be used in any way in conjunction with my essay. I understand that I am free to mark this circle with no effect on my score.

IMPORTANT: **USE A NO. 2 PENCIL. DO NOT WRITE OUTSIDE THE BORDER!**
Words written outside the essay box or written in ink **WILL NOT APPEAR** in the copy sent to be scored and your score will be affected.

Begin your essay on this page. If you need more space, continue on the next page.

Continue on the next page, if necessary.

Continuation of ESSAY Section 1 from previous page. Write below only if you need more space.
IMPORTANT: DO NOT START on this page—if you do, your essay may appear blank and your score may be affected.

PLEASE DO NOT WRITE IN THIS AREA

SERIAL #

COMPLETE MARK ● 　EXAMPLES OF INCOMPLETE MARKS Ⓐ Ⓑ Ⓓ Ⓐ Ⓑ Ⓓ

You must use a No. 2 pencil and marks must be complete. Do not use a mechanical pencil. It is very important that you fill in the entire circle darkly and completely. If you change your responses, erase as completely as possible. Incomplete marks or erasures may affect your score.

SECTION 2

1 Ⓐ Ⓑ Ⓒ Ⓓ Ⓔ	11 Ⓐ Ⓑ Ⓒ Ⓓ Ⓔ	21 Ⓐ Ⓑ Ⓒ Ⓓ Ⓔ	31 Ⓐ Ⓑ Ⓒ Ⓓ Ⓔ
2 Ⓐ Ⓑ Ⓒ Ⓓ Ⓔ	12 Ⓐ Ⓑ Ⓒ Ⓓ Ⓔ	22 Ⓐ Ⓑ Ⓒ Ⓓ Ⓔ	32 Ⓐ Ⓑ Ⓒ Ⓓ Ⓔ
3 Ⓐ Ⓑ Ⓒ Ⓓ Ⓔ	13 Ⓐ Ⓑ Ⓒ Ⓓ Ⓔ	23 Ⓐ Ⓑ Ⓒ Ⓓ Ⓔ	33 Ⓐ Ⓑ Ⓒ Ⓓ Ⓔ
4 Ⓐ Ⓑ Ⓒ Ⓓ Ⓔ	14 Ⓐ Ⓑ Ⓒ Ⓓ Ⓔ	24 Ⓐ Ⓑ Ⓒ Ⓓ Ⓔ	34 Ⓐ Ⓑ Ⓒ Ⓓ Ⓔ
5 Ⓐ Ⓑ Ⓒ Ⓓ Ⓔ	15 Ⓐ Ⓑ Ⓒ Ⓓ Ⓔ	25 Ⓐ Ⓑ Ⓒ Ⓓ Ⓔ	35 Ⓐ Ⓑ Ⓒ Ⓓ Ⓔ
6 Ⓐ Ⓑ Ⓒ Ⓓ Ⓔ	16 Ⓐ Ⓑ Ⓒ Ⓓ Ⓔ	26 Ⓐ Ⓑ Ⓒ Ⓓ Ⓔ	36 Ⓐ Ⓑ Ⓒ Ⓓ Ⓔ
7 Ⓐ Ⓑ Ⓒ Ⓓ Ⓔ	17 Ⓐ Ⓑ Ⓒ Ⓓ Ⓔ	27 Ⓐ Ⓑ Ⓒ Ⓓ Ⓔ	37 Ⓐ Ⓑ Ⓒ Ⓓ Ⓔ
8 Ⓐ Ⓑ Ⓒ Ⓓ Ⓔ	18 Ⓐ Ⓑ Ⓒ Ⓓ Ⓔ	28 Ⓐ Ⓑ Ⓒ Ⓓ Ⓔ	38 Ⓐ Ⓑ Ⓒ Ⓓ Ⓔ
9 Ⓐ Ⓑ Ⓒ Ⓓ Ⓔ	19 Ⓐ Ⓑ Ⓒ Ⓓ Ⓔ	29 Ⓐ Ⓑ Ⓒ Ⓓ Ⓔ	39 Ⓐ Ⓑ Ⓒ Ⓓ Ⓔ
10 Ⓐ Ⓑ Ⓒ Ⓓ Ⓔ	20 Ⓐ Ⓑ Ⓒ Ⓓ Ⓔ	30 Ⓐ Ⓑ Ⓒ Ⓓ Ⓔ	40 Ⓐ Ⓑ Ⓒ Ⓓ Ⓔ

SECTION 3

1 Ⓐ Ⓑ Ⓒ Ⓓ Ⓔ	11 Ⓐ Ⓑ Ⓒ Ⓓ Ⓔ	21 Ⓐ Ⓑ Ⓒ Ⓓ Ⓔ	31 Ⓐ Ⓑ Ⓒ Ⓓ Ⓔ
2 Ⓐ Ⓑ Ⓒ Ⓓ Ⓔ	12 Ⓐ Ⓑ Ⓒ Ⓓ Ⓔ	22 Ⓐ Ⓑ Ⓒ Ⓓ Ⓔ	32 Ⓐ Ⓑ Ⓒ Ⓓ Ⓔ
3 Ⓐ Ⓑ Ⓒ Ⓓ Ⓔ	13 Ⓐ Ⓑ Ⓒ Ⓓ Ⓔ	23 Ⓐ Ⓑ Ⓒ Ⓓ Ⓔ	33 Ⓐ Ⓑ Ⓒ Ⓓ Ⓔ
4 Ⓐ Ⓑ Ⓒ Ⓓ Ⓔ	14 Ⓐ Ⓑ Ⓒ Ⓓ Ⓔ	24 Ⓐ Ⓑ Ⓒ Ⓓ Ⓔ	34 Ⓐ Ⓑ Ⓒ Ⓓ Ⓔ
5 Ⓐ Ⓑ Ⓒ Ⓓ Ⓔ	15 Ⓐ Ⓑ Ⓒ Ⓓ Ⓔ	25 Ⓐ Ⓑ Ⓒ Ⓓ Ⓔ	35 Ⓐ Ⓑ Ⓒ Ⓓ Ⓔ
6 Ⓐ Ⓑ Ⓒ Ⓓ Ⓔ	16 Ⓐ Ⓑ Ⓒ Ⓓ Ⓔ	26 Ⓐ Ⓑ Ⓒ Ⓓ Ⓔ	36 Ⓐ Ⓑ Ⓒ Ⓓ Ⓔ
7 Ⓐ Ⓑ Ⓒ Ⓓ Ⓔ	17 Ⓐ Ⓑ Ⓒ Ⓓ Ⓔ	27 Ⓐ Ⓑ Ⓒ Ⓓ Ⓔ	37 Ⓐ Ⓑ Ⓒ Ⓓ Ⓔ
8 Ⓐ Ⓑ Ⓒ Ⓓ Ⓔ	18 Ⓐ Ⓑ Ⓒ Ⓓ Ⓔ	28 Ⓐ Ⓑ Ⓒ Ⓓ Ⓔ	38 Ⓐ Ⓑ Ⓒ Ⓓ Ⓔ
9 Ⓐ Ⓑ Ⓒ Ⓓ Ⓔ	19 Ⓐ Ⓑ Ⓒ Ⓓ Ⓔ	29 Ⓐ Ⓑ Ⓒ Ⓓ Ⓔ	39 Ⓐ Ⓑ Ⓒ Ⓓ Ⓔ
10 Ⓐ Ⓑ Ⓒ Ⓓ Ⓔ	20 Ⓐ Ⓑ Ⓒ Ⓓ Ⓔ	30 Ⓐ Ⓑ Ⓒ Ⓓ Ⓔ	40 Ⓐ Ⓑ Ⓒ Ⓓ Ⓔ

CAUTION Grid answers in the section below for SECTION 2 or SECTION 3 only if directed to do so in your test book.

Student-Produced Responses ONLY ANSWERS THAT ARE GRIDDED WILL BE SCORED. YOU WILL NOT RECEIVE CREDIT FOR ANYTHING WRITTEN IN THE BOXES.

Quality Assurance Mark ●

9　10　11　12　13

14　15　16　17　18

COMPLETE MARK ● EXAMPLES OF INCOMPLETE MARKS Ⓐ Ⓑ ⊖ Ⓓ / ⊘ ⊘ ⦿

You must use a No. 2 pencil and marks must be complete. Do not use a mechanical pencil. It is very important that you fill in the entire circle darkly and completely. If you change your responses, erase as completely as possible. Incomplete marks or erasures may affect your score.

SECTION 4

1 Ⓐ Ⓑ Ⓒ Ⓓ Ⓔ   11 Ⓐ Ⓑ Ⓒ Ⓓ Ⓔ   21 Ⓐ Ⓑ Ⓒ Ⓓ Ⓔ   31 Ⓐ Ⓑ Ⓒ Ⓓ Ⓔ
2 Ⓐ Ⓑ Ⓒ Ⓓ Ⓔ   12 Ⓐ Ⓑ Ⓒ Ⓓ Ⓔ   22 Ⓐ Ⓑ Ⓒ Ⓓ Ⓔ   32 Ⓐ Ⓑ Ⓒ Ⓓ Ⓔ
3 Ⓐ Ⓑ Ⓒ Ⓓ Ⓔ   13 Ⓐ Ⓑ Ⓒ Ⓓ Ⓔ   23 Ⓐ Ⓑ Ⓒ Ⓓ Ⓔ   33 Ⓐ Ⓑ Ⓒ Ⓓ Ⓔ
4 Ⓐ Ⓑ Ⓒ Ⓓ Ⓔ   14 Ⓐ Ⓑ Ⓒ Ⓓ Ⓔ   24 Ⓐ Ⓑ Ⓒ Ⓓ Ⓔ   34 Ⓐ Ⓑ Ⓒ Ⓓ Ⓔ
5 Ⓐ Ⓑ Ⓒ Ⓓ Ⓔ   15 Ⓐ Ⓑ Ⓒ Ⓓ Ⓔ   25 Ⓐ Ⓑ Ⓒ Ⓓ Ⓔ   35 Ⓐ Ⓑ Ⓒ Ⓓ Ⓔ
6 Ⓐ Ⓑ Ⓒ Ⓓ Ⓔ   16 Ⓐ Ⓑ Ⓒ Ⓓ Ⓔ   26 Ⓐ Ⓑ Ⓒ Ⓓ Ⓔ   36 Ⓐ Ⓑ Ⓒ Ⓓ Ⓔ
7 Ⓐ Ⓑ Ⓒ Ⓓ Ⓔ   17 Ⓐ Ⓑ Ⓒ Ⓓ Ⓔ   27 Ⓐ Ⓑ Ⓒ Ⓓ Ⓔ   37 Ⓐ Ⓑ Ⓒ Ⓓ Ⓔ
8 Ⓐ Ⓑ Ⓒ Ⓓ Ⓔ   18 Ⓐ Ⓑ Ⓒ Ⓓ Ⓔ   28 Ⓐ Ⓑ Ⓒ Ⓓ Ⓔ   38 Ⓐ Ⓑ Ⓒ Ⓓ Ⓔ
9 Ⓐ Ⓑ Ⓒ Ⓓ Ⓔ   19 Ⓐ Ⓑ Ⓒ Ⓓ Ⓔ   29 Ⓐ Ⓑ Ⓒ Ⓓ Ⓔ   39 Ⓐ Ⓑ Ⓒ Ⓓ Ⓔ
10 Ⓐ Ⓑ Ⓒ Ⓓ Ⓔ 20 Ⓐ Ⓑ Ⓒ Ⓓ Ⓔ   30 Ⓐ Ⓑ Ⓒ Ⓓ Ⓔ   40 Ⓐ Ⓑ Ⓒ Ⓓ Ⓔ

SECTION 5

1 Ⓐ Ⓑ Ⓒ Ⓓ Ⓔ   11 Ⓐ Ⓑ Ⓒ Ⓓ Ⓔ   21 Ⓐ Ⓑ Ⓒ Ⓓ Ⓔ   31 Ⓐ Ⓑ Ⓒ Ⓓ Ⓔ
2 Ⓐ Ⓑ Ⓒ Ⓓ Ⓔ   12 Ⓐ Ⓑ Ⓒ Ⓓ Ⓔ   22 Ⓐ Ⓑ Ⓒ Ⓓ Ⓔ   32 Ⓐ Ⓑ Ⓒ Ⓓ Ⓔ
3 Ⓐ Ⓑ Ⓒ Ⓓ Ⓔ   13 Ⓐ Ⓑ Ⓒ Ⓓ Ⓔ   23 Ⓐ Ⓑ Ⓒ Ⓓ Ⓔ   33 Ⓐ Ⓑ Ⓒ Ⓓ Ⓔ
4 Ⓐ Ⓑ Ⓒ Ⓓ Ⓔ   14 Ⓐ Ⓑ Ⓒ Ⓓ Ⓔ   24 Ⓐ Ⓑ Ⓒ Ⓓ Ⓔ   34 Ⓐ Ⓑ Ⓒ Ⓓ Ⓔ
5 Ⓐ Ⓑ Ⓒ Ⓓ Ⓔ   15 Ⓐ Ⓑ Ⓒ Ⓓ Ⓔ   25 Ⓐ Ⓑ Ⓒ Ⓓ Ⓔ   35 Ⓐ Ⓑ Ⓒ Ⓓ Ⓔ
6 Ⓐ Ⓑ Ⓒ Ⓓ Ⓔ   16 Ⓐ Ⓑ Ⓒ Ⓓ Ⓔ   26 Ⓐ Ⓑ Ⓒ Ⓓ Ⓔ   36 Ⓐ Ⓑ Ⓒ Ⓓ Ⓔ
7 Ⓐ Ⓑ Ⓒ Ⓓ Ⓔ   17 Ⓐ Ⓑ Ⓒ Ⓓ Ⓔ   27 Ⓐ Ⓑ Ⓒ Ⓓ Ⓔ   37 Ⓐ Ⓑ Ⓒ Ⓓ Ⓔ
8 Ⓐ Ⓑ Ⓒ Ⓓ Ⓔ   18 Ⓐ Ⓑ Ⓒ Ⓓ Ⓔ   28 Ⓐ Ⓑ Ⓒ Ⓓ Ⓔ   38 Ⓐ Ⓑ Ⓒ Ⓓ Ⓔ
9 Ⓐ Ⓑ Ⓒ Ⓓ Ⓔ   19 Ⓐ Ⓑ Ⓒ Ⓓ Ⓔ   29 Ⓐ Ⓑ Ⓒ Ⓓ Ⓔ   39 Ⓐ Ⓑ Ⓒ Ⓓ Ⓔ
10 Ⓐ Ⓑ Ⓒ Ⓓ Ⓔ 20 Ⓐ Ⓑ Ⓒ Ⓓ Ⓔ   30 Ⓐ Ⓑ Ⓒ Ⓓ Ⓔ   40 Ⓐ Ⓑ Ⓒ Ⓓ Ⓔ

CAUTION Grid answers in the section below for SECTION 4 or SECTION 5 only if directed to do so in your test book.

Student-Produced Responses

ONLY ANSWERS THAT ARE GRIDDED WILL BE SCORED. YOU WILL NOT RECEIVE CREDIT FOR ANYTHING WRITTEN IN THE BOXES.

Quality
● Assurance Mark

9 10 11 12 13

Each grid contains:
⊘ ⊘ ⊘
. . . .
⓪ ⓪ ⓪
① ① ① ①
② ② ② ②
③ ③ ③ ③
④ ④ ④ ④
⑤ ⑤ ⑤ ⑤
⑥ ⑥ ⑥ ⑥
⑦ ⑦ ⑦ ⑦
⑧ ⑧ ⑧ ⑧
⑨ ⑨ ⑨ ⑨

14 15 16 17 18

Each grid contains:
⊘ ⊘ ⊘
. . . .
⓪ ⓪ ⓪
① ① ① ①
② ② ② ②
③ ③ ③ ③
④ ④ ④ ④
⑤ ⑤ ⑤ ⑤
⑥ ⑥ ⑥ ⑥
⑦ ⑦ ⑦ ⑦
⑧ ⑧ ⑧ ⑧
⑨ ⑨ ⑨ ⑨

COMPLETE MARK ●

EXAMPLES OF INCOMPLETE MARKS Ⓐ Ⓑ ⊕ Ⓛ ⊘ ⊗ ⊜

You must use a No. 2 pencil and marks must be complete. Do not use a mechanical pencil. *It is very important that you fill in the entire circle darkly and completely. If you change your responses, erase as completely as possible. Incomplete marks or erasures may affect your score.*

SECTION 6

1 Ⓐ Ⓑ Ⓒ Ⓓ Ⓔ	11 Ⓐ Ⓑ Ⓒ Ⓓ Ⓔ	21 Ⓐ Ⓑ Ⓒ Ⓓ Ⓔ	31 Ⓐ Ⓑ Ⓒ Ⓓ Ⓔ
2 Ⓐ Ⓑ Ⓒ Ⓓ Ⓔ	12 Ⓐ Ⓑ Ⓒ Ⓓ Ⓔ	22 Ⓐ Ⓑ Ⓒ Ⓓ Ⓔ	32 Ⓐ Ⓑ Ⓒ Ⓓ Ⓔ
3 Ⓐ Ⓑ Ⓒ Ⓓ Ⓔ	13 Ⓐ Ⓑ Ⓒ Ⓓ Ⓔ	23 Ⓐ Ⓑ Ⓒ Ⓓ Ⓔ	33 Ⓐ Ⓑ Ⓒ Ⓓ Ⓔ
4 Ⓐ Ⓑ Ⓒ Ⓓ Ⓔ	14 Ⓐ Ⓑ Ⓒ Ⓓ Ⓔ	24 Ⓐ Ⓑ Ⓒ Ⓓ Ⓔ	34 Ⓐ Ⓑ Ⓒ Ⓓ Ⓔ
5 Ⓐ Ⓑ Ⓒ Ⓓ Ⓔ	15 Ⓐ Ⓑ Ⓒ Ⓓ Ⓔ	25 Ⓐ Ⓑ Ⓒ Ⓓ Ⓔ	35 Ⓐ Ⓑ Ⓒ Ⓓ Ⓔ
6 Ⓐ Ⓑ Ⓒ Ⓓ Ⓔ	16 Ⓐ Ⓑ Ⓒ Ⓓ Ⓔ	26 Ⓐ Ⓑ Ⓒ Ⓓ Ⓔ	36 Ⓐ Ⓑ Ⓒ Ⓓ Ⓔ
7 Ⓐ Ⓑ Ⓒ Ⓓ Ⓔ	17 Ⓐ Ⓑ Ⓒ Ⓓ Ⓔ	27 Ⓐ Ⓑ Ⓒ Ⓓ Ⓔ	37 Ⓐ Ⓑ Ⓒ Ⓓ Ⓔ
8 Ⓐ Ⓑ Ⓒ Ⓓ Ⓔ	18 Ⓐ Ⓑ Ⓒ Ⓓ Ⓔ	28 Ⓐ Ⓑ Ⓒ Ⓓ Ⓔ	38 Ⓐ Ⓑ Ⓒ Ⓓ Ⓔ
9 Ⓐ Ⓑ Ⓒ Ⓓ Ⓔ	19 Ⓐ Ⓑ Ⓒ Ⓓ Ⓔ	29 Ⓐ Ⓑ Ⓒ Ⓓ Ⓔ	39 Ⓐ Ⓑ Ⓒ Ⓓ Ⓔ
10 Ⓐ Ⓑ Ⓒ Ⓓ Ⓔ	20 Ⓐ Ⓑ Ⓒ Ⓓ Ⓔ	30 Ⓐ Ⓑ Ⓒ Ⓓ Ⓔ	40 Ⓐ Ⓑ Ⓒ Ⓓ Ⓔ

SECTION 7

1 Ⓐ Ⓑ Ⓒ Ⓓ Ⓔ	11 Ⓐ Ⓑ Ⓒ Ⓓ Ⓔ	21 Ⓐ Ⓑ Ⓒ Ⓓ Ⓔ	31 Ⓐ Ⓑ Ⓒ Ⓓ Ⓔ
2 Ⓐ Ⓑ Ⓒ Ⓓ Ⓔ	12 Ⓐ Ⓑ Ⓒ Ⓓ Ⓔ	22 Ⓐ Ⓑ Ⓒ Ⓓ Ⓔ	32 Ⓐ Ⓑ Ⓒ Ⓓ Ⓔ
3 Ⓐ Ⓑ Ⓒ Ⓓ Ⓔ	13 Ⓐ Ⓑ Ⓒ Ⓓ Ⓔ	23 Ⓐ Ⓑ Ⓒ Ⓓ Ⓔ	33 Ⓐ Ⓑ Ⓒ Ⓓ Ⓔ
4 Ⓐ Ⓑ Ⓒ Ⓓ Ⓔ	14 Ⓐ Ⓑ Ⓒ Ⓓ Ⓔ	24 Ⓐ Ⓑ Ⓒ Ⓓ Ⓔ	34 Ⓐ Ⓑ Ⓒ Ⓓ Ⓔ
5 Ⓐ Ⓑ Ⓒ Ⓓ Ⓔ	15 Ⓐ Ⓑ Ⓒ Ⓓ Ⓔ	25 Ⓐ Ⓑ Ⓒ Ⓓ Ⓔ	35 Ⓐ Ⓑ Ⓒ Ⓓ Ⓔ
6 Ⓐ Ⓑ Ⓒ Ⓓ Ⓔ	16 Ⓐ Ⓑ Ⓒ Ⓓ Ⓔ	26 Ⓐ Ⓑ Ⓒ Ⓓ Ⓔ	36 Ⓐ Ⓑ Ⓒ Ⓓ Ⓔ
7 Ⓐ Ⓑ Ⓒ Ⓓ Ⓔ	17 Ⓐ Ⓑ Ⓒ Ⓓ Ⓔ	27 Ⓐ Ⓑ Ⓒ Ⓓ Ⓔ	37 Ⓐ Ⓑ Ⓒ Ⓓ Ⓔ
8 Ⓐ Ⓑ Ⓒ Ⓓ Ⓔ	18 Ⓐ Ⓑ Ⓒ Ⓓ Ⓔ	28 Ⓐ Ⓑ Ⓒ Ⓓ Ⓔ	38 Ⓐ Ⓑ Ⓒ Ⓓ Ⓔ
9 Ⓐ Ⓑ Ⓒ Ⓓ Ⓔ	19 Ⓐ Ⓑ Ⓒ Ⓓ Ⓔ	29 Ⓐ Ⓑ Ⓒ Ⓓ Ⓔ	39 Ⓐ Ⓑ Ⓒ Ⓓ Ⓔ
10 Ⓐ Ⓑ Ⓒ Ⓓ Ⓔ	20 Ⓐ Ⓑ Ⓒ Ⓓ Ⓔ	30 Ⓐ Ⓑ Ⓒ Ⓓ Ⓔ	40 Ⓐ Ⓑ Ⓒ Ⓓ Ⓔ

CAUTION Grid answers in the section below for SECTION 6 or SECTION 7 only if directed to do so in your test book.

Student-Produced Responses

ONLY ANSWERS THAT ARE GRIDDED WILL BE SCORED. YOU WILL NOT RECEIVE CREDIT FOR ANYTHING WRITTEN IN THE BOXES.

Quality Assurance Mark ●

COMPLETE MARK ●   EXAMPLES OF INCOMPLETE MARKS Ⓐ Ⓑ Ⓓ Ⓔ / Ⓐ Ⓑ Ⓓ Ⓔ

You must use a No. 2 pencil and marks must be complete. Do not use a mechanical pencil. It is very important that you fill in the entire circle darkly and completely. If you change your responses, erase as completely as possible. Incomplete marks or erasures may affect your score.

SECTION 8

1 Ⓐ Ⓑ Ⓒ Ⓓ Ⓔ
2 Ⓐ Ⓑ Ⓒ Ⓓ Ⓔ
3 Ⓐ Ⓑ Ⓒ Ⓓ Ⓔ
4 Ⓐ Ⓑ Ⓒ Ⓓ Ⓔ
5 Ⓐ Ⓑ Ⓒ Ⓓ Ⓔ
6 Ⓐ Ⓑ Ⓒ Ⓓ Ⓔ
7 Ⓐ Ⓑ Ⓒ Ⓓ Ⓔ
8 Ⓐ Ⓑ Ⓒ Ⓓ Ⓔ
9 Ⓐ Ⓑ Ⓒ Ⓓ Ⓔ
10 Ⓐ Ⓑ Ⓒ Ⓓ Ⓔ

11 Ⓐ Ⓑ Ⓒ Ⓓ Ⓔ
12 Ⓐ Ⓑ Ⓒ Ⓓ Ⓔ
13 Ⓐ Ⓑ Ⓒ Ⓓ Ⓔ
14 Ⓐ Ⓑ Ⓒ Ⓓ Ⓔ
15 Ⓐ Ⓑ Ⓒ Ⓓ Ⓔ
16 Ⓐ Ⓑ Ⓒ Ⓓ Ⓔ
17 Ⓐ Ⓑ Ⓒ Ⓓ Ⓔ
18 Ⓐ Ⓑ Ⓒ Ⓓ Ⓔ
19 Ⓐ Ⓑ Ⓒ Ⓓ Ⓔ
20 Ⓐ Ⓑ Ⓒ Ⓓ Ⓔ

21 Ⓐ Ⓑ Ⓒ Ⓓ Ⓔ
22 Ⓐ Ⓑ Ⓒ Ⓓ Ⓔ
23 Ⓐ Ⓑ Ⓒ Ⓓ Ⓔ
24 Ⓐ Ⓑ Ⓒ Ⓓ Ⓔ
25 Ⓐ Ⓑ Ⓒ Ⓓ Ⓔ
26 Ⓐ Ⓑ Ⓒ Ⓓ Ⓔ
27 Ⓐ Ⓑ Ⓒ Ⓓ Ⓔ
28 Ⓐ Ⓑ Ⓒ Ⓓ Ⓔ
29 Ⓐ Ⓑ Ⓒ Ⓓ Ⓔ
30 Ⓐ Ⓑ Ⓒ Ⓓ Ⓔ

31 Ⓐ Ⓑ Ⓒ Ⓓ Ⓔ
32 Ⓐ Ⓑ Ⓒ Ⓓ Ⓔ
33 Ⓐ Ⓑ Ⓒ Ⓓ Ⓔ
34 Ⓐ Ⓑ Ⓒ Ⓓ Ⓔ
35 Ⓐ Ⓑ Ⓒ Ⓓ Ⓔ
36 Ⓐ Ⓑ Ⓒ Ⓓ Ⓔ
37 Ⓐ Ⓑ Ⓒ Ⓓ Ⓔ
38 Ⓐ Ⓑ Ⓒ Ⓓ Ⓔ
39 Ⓐ Ⓑ Ⓒ Ⓓ Ⓔ
40 Ⓐ Ⓑ Ⓒ Ⓓ Ⓔ

SECTION 9

1 Ⓐ Ⓑ Ⓒ Ⓓ Ⓔ
2 Ⓐ Ⓑ Ⓒ Ⓓ Ⓔ
3 Ⓐ Ⓑ Ⓒ Ⓓ Ⓔ
4 Ⓐ Ⓑ Ⓒ Ⓓ Ⓔ
5 Ⓐ Ⓑ Ⓒ Ⓓ Ⓔ
6 Ⓐ Ⓑ Ⓒ Ⓓ Ⓔ
7 Ⓐ Ⓑ Ⓒ Ⓓ Ⓔ
8 Ⓐ Ⓑ Ⓒ Ⓓ Ⓔ
9 Ⓐ Ⓑ Ⓒ Ⓓ Ⓔ
10 Ⓐ Ⓑ Ⓒ Ⓓ Ⓔ

11 Ⓐ Ⓑ Ⓒ Ⓓ Ⓔ
12 Ⓐ Ⓑ Ⓒ Ⓓ Ⓔ
13 Ⓐ Ⓑ Ⓒ Ⓓ Ⓔ
14 Ⓐ Ⓑ Ⓒ Ⓓ Ⓔ
15 Ⓐ Ⓑ Ⓒ Ⓓ Ⓔ
16 Ⓐ Ⓑ Ⓒ Ⓓ Ⓔ
17 Ⓐ Ⓑ Ⓒ Ⓓ Ⓔ
18 Ⓐ Ⓑ Ⓒ Ⓓ Ⓔ
19 Ⓐ Ⓑ Ⓒ Ⓓ Ⓔ
20 Ⓐ Ⓑ Ⓒ Ⓓ Ⓔ

21 Ⓐ Ⓑ Ⓒ Ⓓ Ⓔ
22 Ⓐ Ⓑ Ⓒ Ⓓ Ⓔ
23 Ⓐ Ⓑ Ⓒ Ⓓ Ⓔ
24 Ⓐ Ⓑ Ⓒ Ⓓ Ⓔ
25 Ⓐ Ⓑ Ⓒ Ⓓ Ⓔ
26 Ⓐ Ⓑ Ⓒ Ⓓ Ⓔ
27 Ⓐ Ⓑ Ⓒ Ⓓ Ⓔ
28 Ⓐ Ⓑ Ⓒ Ⓓ Ⓔ
29 Ⓐ Ⓑ Ⓒ Ⓓ Ⓔ
30 Ⓐ Ⓑ Ⓒ Ⓓ Ⓔ

31 Ⓐ Ⓑ Ⓒ Ⓓ Ⓔ
32 Ⓐ Ⓑ Ⓒ Ⓓ Ⓔ
33 Ⓐ Ⓑ Ⓒ Ⓓ Ⓔ
34 Ⓐ Ⓑ Ⓒ Ⓓ Ⓔ
35 Ⓐ Ⓑ Ⓒ Ⓓ Ⓔ
36 Ⓐ Ⓑ Ⓒ Ⓓ Ⓔ
37 Ⓐ Ⓑ Ⓒ Ⓓ Ⓔ
38 Ⓐ Ⓑ Ⓒ Ⓓ Ⓔ
39 Ⓐ Ⓑ Ⓒ Ⓓ Ⓔ
40 Ⓐ Ⓑ Ⓒ Ⓓ Ⓔ

SECTION 10

1 Ⓐ Ⓑ Ⓒ Ⓓ Ⓔ
2 Ⓐ Ⓑ Ⓒ Ⓓ Ⓔ
3 Ⓐ Ⓑ Ⓒ Ⓓ Ⓔ
4 Ⓐ Ⓑ Ⓒ Ⓓ Ⓔ
5 Ⓐ Ⓑ Ⓒ Ⓓ Ⓔ
6 Ⓐ Ⓑ Ⓒ Ⓓ Ⓔ
7 Ⓐ Ⓑ Ⓒ Ⓓ Ⓔ
8 Ⓐ Ⓑ Ⓒ Ⓓ Ⓔ
9 Ⓐ Ⓑ Ⓒ Ⓓ Ⓔ
10 Ⓐ Ⓑ Ⓒ Ⓓ Ⓔ

11 Ⓐ Ⓑ Ⓒ Ⓓ Ⓔ
12 Ⓐ Ⓑ Ⓒ Ⓓ Ⓔ
13 Ⓐ Ⓑ Ⓒ Ⓓ Ⓔ
14 Ⓐ Ⓑ Ⓒ Ⓓ Ⓔ
15 Ⓐ Ⓑ Ⓒ Ⓓ Ⓔ
16 Ⓐ Ⓑ Ⓒ Ⓓ Ⓔ
17 Ⓐ Ⓑ Ⓒ Ⓓ Ⓔ
18 Ⓐ Ⓑ Ⓒ Ⓓ Ⓔ
19 Ⓐ Ⓑ Ⓒ Ⓓ Ⓔ
20 Ⓐ Ⓑ Ⓒ Ⓓ Ⓔ

21 Ⓐ Ⓑ Ⓒ Ⓓ Ⓔ
22 Ⓐ Ⓑ Ⓒ Ⓓ Ⓔ
23 Ⓐ Ⓑ Ⓒ Ⓓ Ⓔ
24 Ⓐ Ⓑ Ⓒ Ⓓ Ⓔ
25 Ⓐ Ⓑ Ⓒ Ⓓ Ⓔ
26 Ⓐ Ⓑ Ⓒ Ⓓ Ⓔ
27 Ⓐ Ⓑ Ⓒ Ⓓ Ⓔ
28 Ⓐ Ⓑ Ⓒ Ⓓ Ⓔ
29 Ⓐ Ⓑ Ⓒ Ⓓ Ⓔ
30 Ⓐ Ⓑ Ⓒ Ⓓ Ⓔ

31 Ⓐ Ⓑ Ⓒ Ⓓ Ⓔ
32 Ⓐ Ⓑ Ⓒ Ⓓ Ⓔ
33 Ⓐ Ⓑ Ⓒ Ⓓ Ⓔ
34 Ⓐ Ⓑ Ⓒ Ⓓ Ⓔ
35 Ⓐ Ⓑ Ⓒ Ⓓ Ⓔ
36 Ⓐ Ⓑ Ⓒ Ⓓ Ⓔ
37 Ⓐ Ⓑ Ⓒ Ⓓ Ⓔ
38 Ⓐ Ⓑ Ⓒ Ⓓ Ⓔ
39 Ⓐ Ⓑ Ⓒ Ⓓ Ⓔ
40 Ⓐ Ⓑ Ⓒ Ⓓ Ⓔ

SECTION 1
ESSAY
Time — 25 minutes

Turn to Section 1 of your answer sheet to write your essay.

The essay gives you an opportunity to show how effectively you can develop and express ideas. You should, therefore, take care to develop your point of view, present your ideas logically and clearly, and use language precisely.

Your essay must be written on the lines provided on your answer sheet—you will receive no other paper on which to write. You will have enough space if you write on every line, avoid wide margins, and keep your handwriting to a reasonable size. Remember that people who are not familiar with your handwriting will read what you write. Try to write or print so that what you are writing is legible to those readers.

You have twenty-five minutes to write an essay on the topic assigned below. DO NOT WRITE ON ANOTHER TOPIC. AN OFF-TOPIC ESSAY WILL RECEIVE A SCORE OF ZERO.

Think carefully about the issue presented in the following excerpt and the assignment below.

> Until every soul is freely permitted to investigate every book, creed, and dogma for itself, the world cannot be free. Mankind will be enslaved until there is wisdom enough to allow each man to have his thought and say. It is amazing to me that a difference of opinion upon subjects that we know nothing about should make us hate, persecute, and despise each other.
>
> Adapted from Robert Green Ingersoll

Assignment: Does a lack of knowledge cause conflict? Plan and write an essay in which you develop your point of view on this issue. Support your position with reasoning and examples taken from your reading, studies, experience, and observations.

DO NOT WRITE YOUR ESSAY IN YOUR TEST BOOK. You will receive credit only for what you write on your answer sheet.

BEGIN WRITING YOUR ESSAY IN SECTION 1 OF THE ANSWER SHEET.

S T O P
If you finish before time is called, you may check your work on this section only.
Do not turn to any other section in the test.

SECTION 2
Time — 25 minutes
24 Questions

Turn to Section 2 of your answer sheet to answer the questions in this section.

Directions: For each question in this section, select the best answer from among the choices given and fill in the corresponding circle on the answer sheet.

Each sentence below has one or two blanks, each blank indicating that something has been omitted. Beneath the sentence are five words or sets of words labeled A through E. Choose the word or set of words that, when inserted in the sentence, <u>best</u> fits the meaning of the sentence as a whole.

Example:

Desiring to ------- his taunting friends, Mitch gave them taffy in hopes it would keep their mouths shut.

(A) eliminate   (B) satisfy   (C) overcome
   (D) ridicule   (E) silence

ⒶⒷⒸⒹ●

---

1. Douglas's habit of missing deadlines and finishing projects late has earned him the well-deserved reputation of being -------.

    (A) an authority   (B) a diplomat   (C) an eliminator
       (D) a procrastinator   (E) an altruist

2. Unfortunately, the referee's decision to cancel the game was -------; after about fifteen minutes the rain cleared up and the conditions were ------- for playing.

    (A) varied . . . mandated
    (B) rash . . . implicit
    (C) similar . . . versatile
    (D) premature . . . suitable
    (E) mysterious . . . ensured

3. Most fish can only take in oxygen from the water, so the labyrinth fish must be considered ------- because it is ------- breathing air as well.

    (A) explosive . . aware of
    (B) harsh . . edified by
    (C) insightful . . proficient at
    (D) united . . precluded from
    (E) atypical . . capable of

4. Chronic pain can have ------- effect on sufferers, sapping one's strength and depriving one of energy.

    (A) an evocative   (B) a cathartic   (C) an enervating
       (D) a pejorative   (E) a disingenuous

5. African American artist Romare Bearden had a remarkably ------- set of talents: he was a painter, a composer, and a player in the Negro Baseball League.

    (A) disaffected   (B) eclectic   (C) regressive
       (D) impugned   (E) corresponding

GO ON TO THE NEXT PAGE

Directions: Each passage below is followed by questions based on its content. Answer the questions on the basis of what is <u>stated</u> or <u>implied</u> in each passage and in any introductory material that may be provided.

Questions 6-7 are based on the following passage.

I have always viewed a chairmaker's shop as a place alive with sounds. Curly wood shavings crackle like popcorn under the stomp of heavy work boots. Sharp drawknives sing shrilly
Line as they skate across the surface of rough-sawn spindles.
5 Coarse files cough and wheeze as they scrape away, while the table saw hums contentedly in the center of the room. The true craftsman listens intently to these sounds; one might say that he engages in an ongoing conversation with them. The slightest variation in a tool's familiar tune will cause him to
10 alter his stroke, or pause to sharpen the tool's blade.

6. The author implies that a "true craftsman" is one who

   (A) enjoys conversing with coworkers
   (B) possesses manual dexterity
   (C) appreciates the fine arts
   (D) responds to subtle changes
   (E) accepts occasional imperfections

7. The rhetorical device featured most prominently in the passage is

   (A) metaphorical language
   (B) flashback
   (C) irony
   (D) veiled allusion
   (E) deliberate understatement

Questions 8-9 are based on the following passage.

Theodore Roosevelt, the 26th President of the United States, was fond of the saying "speak softly but carry a big stick." Interestingly, the same president who was renowned
Line for his "big-stick" approach to foreign affairs was awarded a
5 Nobel Peace Prize in 1906 for his diplomatic efforts to bring about an end to the Russo-Japanese war. Roosevelt also had a profound impact on domestic politics: he used his executive authority to break up the monopolies of large companies, curbed the abuse and exploitation of workers in the meat-
10 packing industry, and created the system of national parks long before environmentalism was fashionable.

8. The author would most probably disagree with which of the following statements about Theodore Roosevelt?

   (A) He took no interest in regulating businesses.
   (B) He was an advocate of an assertive foreign policy.
   (C) He sought to protect the rights of employees.
   (D) His interest in preserving open spaces was unusual at the time.
   (E) His efforts to work for peace brought him public recognition.

9. The primary purpose of the passage is to

   (A) trace the history of the United States Presidency
   (B) explain Theodore Roosevelt's interest in foreign affairs
   (C) encourage more people to pursue careers in politics
   (D) summarize a number of Theodore Roosevelt's accomplishments
   (E) provide a character analysis of Theodore Roosevelt

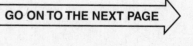

GO ON TO THE NEXT PAGE

Questions 10-15 are based on the following passage.

The following passage is an excerpt from the memoir of a well-known African American singer and community leader. It is set in New York and Philadelphia in the 1920s.

I now had what amounted to a complex about music. Hopes had been raised too high, and when they crashed too low, I could not be objective. Perhaps I had not admitted it
Line to myself, but Town Hall in New York had represented the
5 mainstream of American musical life, and I had plunged into it hoping to become one of the fortunate swimmers.

I kept rehashing the concert in my mind, lingering on some points and thrusting others so thoroughly aside that I do not remember to this day which dress I wore, whether it was
10 the one Mrs. Patterson had made over for me or a special one. I don't remember what financial arrangements were made with the young man who managed the event, but I do know that I received nothing and that he must have lost money. I thought then, and still do, that I might have done better
15 if I had not been told that auditorium was full. If you are sensitive, and I was perhaps too sensitive, a misrepresentation like that can throw you off balance, particularly if you feel that you have a great deal at stake.

I stopped going regularly to Mr. Boghetti's studio. I
20 appeared once in a while, and things must have gone very indifferently. He realized how much the fiasco had shaken me, and he did not make an issue of my irregular attendance.

Mother and I talked about the whole thing, and with her patience and understanding she helped me out of my trouble.
25 I knew that the criticism was right and that I should not have given the critics the opportunity to write as they did. I kept reiterating that I had wanted so very much to sing well enough to please everybody.

"Listen my child," Mother said. "Whatever you do in this
30 world, no matter how good it is, you will never be able to please everybody. All you can strive for is to do the best it is humanly possible for you to do."

As the months went by I was able again to consider singing as a career. "Think about it for a while," Mother
35 advised, "and think of other things you might like to do."

I thought about it. It took a long time before I could confront singing again with enthusiasm, before the old conviction returned that nothing in life could be as important as music.

10. The passage as a whole best supports which explanation of the narrator's "complex about music" (line 1) ?

(A) Her taste in musical styles became more varied as she grew older.
(B) A critical review of a performance caused her to change careers.
(C) Becoming an accomplished singer was not her primary ambition.
(D) A formidable experience led her to question her aspirations.
(E) Performing in Town Hall was the pinnacle of her early musical career.

11. In line 6, "fortunate swimmers" refers to the author's

(A) obsession with music
(B) desire to be a popular singer
(C) confusion about specifics
(D) respect for other famous singers
(E) rapid change of fortune

12. The use of the phrase "thrusting . . . aside" (line 8) conveys a sense of the narrator's

(A) distress
(B) resentment
(C) instability
(D) sentimentality
(E) perseverance

13. According to the passage, the "misrepresentation" (line 16) refers to a discrepancy between

(A) the narrator's actual proficiency at singing and her performance at the Town Hall
(B) the amount of money the narrator was promised and what she received
(C) the stated number of people in the attendance and the actual number
(D) the reaction of the audience to the Town Hall performance and the reviews of it
(E) the narrator's desire to please everybody and her inability to do so

14. The third paragraph (lines 19-22) primarily focuses on

(A) the importance of rehearsals
(B) the kindness of strangers
(C) an observation about motherhood
(D) a return to a musical career
(E) the consequences of a performance

15. In line 26, the narrator's comment about giving critics "the opportunity" suggests that she

(A) acknowledged that the unfavorable reviews were warranted
(B) intended to switch careers from music to journalism
(C) doubted that the critics who reviewed her did so objectively
(D) recognized the influence critics exert on a singer's career
(E) gave generously even when others insulted her

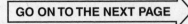

GO ON TO THE NEXT PAGE

Questions 16-24 are based on the following passages.

The following passages, adapted from books published in 2004 and 2008 respectively, discuss an image, known as "The Scream," painted by Norwegian artist Edvard Munch (1863–1944).

Passage 1

Edvard Munch created it at least four times, using whatever materials were handy. He then created a lithographic version, so that he could make limitless clones of the original.
Line After his death, the copies continued. Andy Warhol made silk
5 screened prints of it. Poster companies sold millions of copies of it. It is *The Scream*, one of the most reproduced works of art ever created.

Broad, wide strokes define *The Scream*. A red sky floats oppressively above a dark green and brown bridge. A dark
10 blue river flows from below the bridge, but also seemingly out of the head of the painting's key element: a pale, androgynous human, clad in black, mouth open, hands against his cheeks. The background is vague, and deliberately undefined in such a way that the entire composition seems to squash and
15 dominate the painting's key figure The figure's vague shape, contorted in apparent pain, would later be seen as a signpost for the Expressionist movement to come. And it is crude, seemingly unfinished: exactly as the artist intended.

Of course, then there is the scream itself. Through the
20 stillness of image, we cannot actually know if the main figure is screaming, or merely reacting to, as Munch himself described it, "the infinite scream passing through nature." But the eye invariably falls upon that odd, skull-like face, with its open mouth and eyes round and wide with fear. There are no
25 lines upon the face, just the broad contours of a pallid brown flecked with blue. This is the true power of the painting: in one simple shape, a distorted and oblong head, Munch has captured a raw, gut feeling.

Passage 2

Edvard Munch's *The Scream* is one of those works of
30 art that transcends art itself. Even those who have never placed one foot inside a museum often recognize, and claim an appreciation for, *The Scream*. Simple but surprisingly deep, the painting holds the weight of many differing interpretations. The hopeless struggle of modern man. The
35 realization that we are all ultimately alone. The moment of dread and fear that every person has felt at some point. For some critics, the mere fact that so many people react to *The Scream* in such a primal way justifies the painting's reputation.

40 It is worth pointing out, however, that the initial reaction to Munch's work was less than favorable. Critics tended to either dismiss the crude smears of paint as no better than the aimless "masterpieces" of a bored child, or express mock concern for the emotional well-being of the painter. *The*
45 *Scream* certainly had fans who championed its bleak but direct power, but to most viewers it was simply a poorly-executed painting of a cartoonish mummy in an awkward pose. Munch, however, felt he had stumbled upon a motif that demanded more attention, and began to create prints
50 of *The Scream* in stark black ink. Historian Monica Bohm-Duchen has noted that it was these copies, which in turn were reproduced in several art magazines, that began *The Scream*'s canonization among the Great Works. The effect is almost mathematically direct: as the painting became more
55 accessible, it was more widely admired.

With copies of *The Scream* came variations on *The Scream*. Scholars, such as Leonard Bartin, have pointed out that it has been copied so often because it speaks to an emotion that is common to us all. According to Bartin, if a
60 college student wants to hang a poster in which a cartoonish speech balloon has been superimposed over Munch's masterpiece, it is evidence that *The Scream* is a work of art able to provoke a response, and therefore great. If children want to wear masks that look like the face of the figure in the
65 painting, it is because "something in that face . . . holds us rapt."

The Scream has been reproduced often, true. But these bland, spare reproductions hold no relevance to the actual painting, just as whistling a few notes of a melody from
70 Mozart is not the same as listening to a performance of his *Requiem*. Devoid of context, the central figure is no longer a piece functioning in a larger work of art, he is simply a logo, a brand. It is this logo that adorns coffee cups and movie posters. The simplicity of a logo, the ease at which a
75 simplified version of art can be digested and processed, can quickly allow the watered-down version eclipse the original. Is *The Scream* a great work of art? I will gladly step aside and let the reader judge: but judge the painting itself, and nothing else.

16. Which feature of *The Scream* is mentioned in both passages?

(A) The figure's face
(B) The figure's hands
(C) The composition
(D) The color of the sky
(E) The materials used to create it

GO ON TO THE NEXT PAGE

17. The details described in lines 4-7 of Passage 1 ("After his
    . . . created") would mostly likely be regarded by Monica
    Bohm-Duchen (lines 50-53, Passage 2) as

    (A) incidents that must be considered in any appreciation
        of *The Scream*
    (B) situations that have served to hinder criticism from
        art enthusiasts
    (C) events that may themselves have added to the renown
        of *The Scream*
    (D) facts that have proved troublesome for several art
        historians
    (E) circumstances that have hindered art critics ability to
        judge *The Scream* objectively

18. Both authors would most likely agree that *The Scream*

    (A) is Edvard Munch's masterpiece
    (B) has been copied too many times
    (C) was an artistic breakthrough
    (D) ought to be viewed and analyzed
    (E) takes years of study to understand

19. The quotation from Edvard Munch in line 22 serves
    primarily to

    (A) settle a dispute
    (B) establish a context
    (C) defend a theory
    (D) simplify an interpretation
    (E) downplay a misconception

20. In line 28, "raw" most nearly means

    (A) fresh
    (B) inexperienced
    (C) stark
    (D) exposed
    (E) cruel

21. The quotation marks in line 43 of Passage 2 are used by the
    author primarily to suggest that the critics were

    (A) skeptical of *The Scream*'s aesthetic properties
    (B) interested in the simplicity of *The Scream*'s
        composition
    (C) incorrect in their analysis of *The Scream*
    (D) tired of seeing paintings by children receive praise
    (E) commenting on the connection between mental
        illness and creativity

22. Both the author of Passage 1 and Leonard Bartin (line 57,
    Passage 2) make which of the following points regarding
    The Scream ?

    (A) Its simple shapes make it relatively easy to
        reproduce.
    (B) Its key features are often overlooked in scholarly
        interpretations.
    (C) Its idiosyncrasies are what make it an important
        painting.
    (D) It has inspired several generations of artists.
    (E) It tends to elicit a strong instinctive reaction from
        viewers.

23. The author of Passage 2 mentions "*Mozart's Requiem*"
    primarily in order to

    (A) show that many works of art are often best known in
        shorter versions
    (B) illustrate that a simplified version of a work of art can
        lack crucial elements
    (C) emphasize the universal features those works of art
        share with *The Scream*
    (D) remind readers that works of art can take many
        different forms
    (E) suggest that *The Scream* is also a work of art on a par
        with *Mozart's Requiem*

24. Which of the following statements best characterizes
    the different ways in which the authors of Passage 1 and
    Passage 2 approach *The Scream* ?

    (A) The first focuses on its emotional content, while
        the second argues for a purely intellectual
        interpretation.
    (B) The first stresses its stylistic features, while the
        second emphasizes possible reasons for its cultural
        significance.
    (C) The first references its repercussions in the larger
        world, while the second debates its artistic merits.
    (D) The first speculates about its intended meaning,
        while the second examines the variety of attitudes
        about it.
    (E) The first alludes to its unique place in art history,
        while the second downplays its importance.

STOP

**If you finish before time is called, you may check your work on this section only.
Do not turn to any other section in the test.**

NO TEST MATERIAL ON THIS PAGE.

SECTION 3
Time — 25 minutes
20 Questions

Turn to Section 3 of your answer sheet to answer the questions in this section.

Directions: For this section, solve each problem and decide which is the best of the choices given. Fill in the corresponding circle on the answer sheet. You may use any available space for scratchwork.

Notes

1. The use of a calculator is permitted.

2. All numbers used are real numbers.

3. Figures that accompany problems in this test are intended to provide information useful in solving the problems. They are drawn as accurately as possible EXCEPT when it is stated in a specific problem that the figure is not drawn to scale. All figures lie in a plane unless otherwise indicated.

4. Unless otherwise specified, the domain of any function f is assumed to be the set of all real numbers x for which $f(x)$ is a real number.

Reference Information

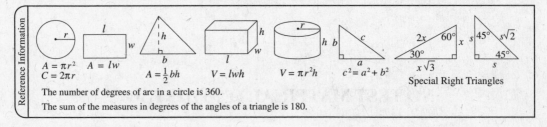

$A = \pi r^2$
$C = 2\pi r$

$A = lw$

$A = \frac{1}{2}bh$

$V = lwh$

$V = \pi r^2 h$

$c^2 = a^2 + b^2$

Special Right Triangles

The number of degrees of arc in a circle is 360.
The sum of the measures in degrees of the angles of a triangle is 180.

1. A snail travels 1 foot in 48 minutes. If the snail travels at a constant rate, how many minutes does it take to travel 1 inch? (1 foot = 12 inches)

   (A) One
   (B) Two
   (C) Three
   (D) Four
   (E) Five

66, 34, 18, m, 6, . . .

2. The first five terms of a sequence are shown above. In this sequence, the first term is 66 and each term after it is 1 more than $\frac{1}{2}$ the previous term. What is the value of m ?

   (A)   9
   (B)   10
   (C)   12
   (D)   13
   (E)   14

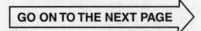
GO ON TO THE NEXT PAGE

3. What is nine times y if 4 more than three times y is equal to 11 ?

(A) $2\frac{1}{3}$

(B) 7

(C) $9\frac{2}{3}$

(D) 14

(E) 21

Questions 4-5 refer to the following graph

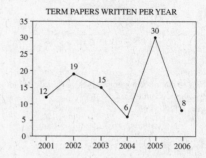

TERM PAPERS WRITTEN PER YEAR

The line graph above shows the number of term papers Joana wrote in each of the years 2001 through 2006.

4. How many more term papers did Joana write in the years 2001 and 2003 combined than she wrote in the year 2002 ?

(A) 6
(B) 8
(C) 10
(D) 12
(E) 14

5. If the data about Joana's term papers were shown in a circle graph, what would be the measure of the central angle of the sector that illustrates the year 2005 ?

(A) 30
(B) 45
(C) 90
(D) 120
(E) 135

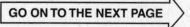

GO ON TO THE NEXT PAGE

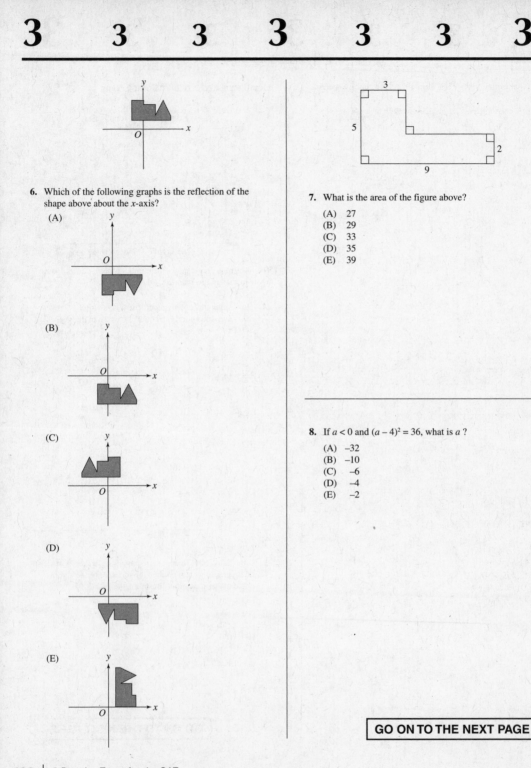

6. Which of the following graphs is the reflection of the shape above about the *x*-axis?

(A)

(B)

(C)

(D)

(E)

7. What is the area of the figure above?

(A) 27
(B) 29
(C) 33
(D) 35
(E) 39

8. If $a < 0$ and $(a - 4)^2 = 36$, what is a ?

(A) −32
(B) −10
(C) −6
(D) −4
(E) −2

GO ON TO THE NEXT PAGE

$$-5p, -3p, p, 3p$$

9. If $p < 0$, which of the numbers above has the least value?

(A) $-5p$
(B) $-3p$
(C) p
(D) $3p$
(E) It cannot be determined from the information given.

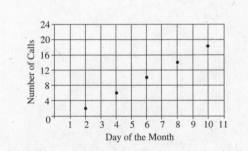

Day of the Month

10. A mechanic created a graph showing the number of calls he received about stalled cars during the first 10 days of January. Let C represent the number of calls he received and D represent the number of the day of the month. Which of the following equations represents the data shown above?

(A) $C = 2$
(B) $C = D - 2$
(C) $C = 2D - 2$
(D) $C = D + 4$
(E) $C = 2D$

$$a = b^2 + b^3$$

11. In the equation above, $b = c^2$ for any integer c. What is a in terms of c ?

(A) c^5
(B) $c^4 + c^9$
(C) $c^4 + c^6$
(D) $c^3 + c^4$
(E) $c^2 + c^3$

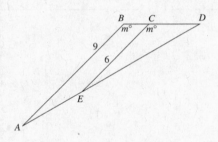

12. In the figure above, what is the ratio of BC to BD ?

(A) 5 to 6
(B) 2 to 3
(C) 1 to 2
(D) 1 to 3
(E) 1 to 6

GO ON TO THE NEXT PAGE

8, 10, x, 12, 8, 10, 8, 10, 10

13. If the set of numbers above has both a median and a single mode of 10, then each of the numbers below could be the value of x EXCEPT

(A) 4
(B) 5
(C) 6
(D) 7
(E) 8

15. If x is directly proportional to $\sqrt{y}$, then y is inversely proportional to

(A) x^2

(B) $\sqrt{x}$

(C) $\dfrac{1}{\sqrt{x}}$

(D) $\dfrac{1}{x}$

(E) $\dfrac{1}{x^2}$

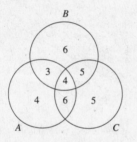

14. The numbers in the Venn diagram indicate the number of elements in sets A, B and C that belong in each region. How many total items are in sets A and C combined?

(A) 41
(B) 37
(C) 33
(D) 27
(E) 10

GO ON TO THE NEXT PAGE

$y = f(x)$

16. The function f is graphed in the xy-plane above. If the function g is defined by $g(x) = |f(x)|$, which of the following is the graph of function g ?

(A)

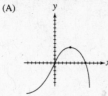

(B)

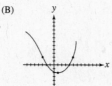

(C)

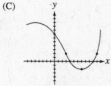

(D)

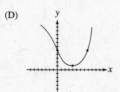

(E)

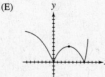

17. The values of x and y are such that $f(x) = f(2y)$ for a certain function f. Which of the following is equivalent to $f(x) + f(x)$?

   I. $2f(2y)$
   II. $f(4y)$
   III. $2[f(y) + f(y)]$

(A) I only
(B) II only
(C) I and III
(D) II and III
(E) I, II, and III

18. A right circular cylinder vase with an inner base radius of 6 inches is filled with water to a height of 20 inches. After a smaller solid right circular cylinder with base radius of 4 inches is then completely submerged in the water, the height of the water is 24 inches. What is the height, in inches, of the smaller cylinder?

(A)   8
(B)   9
(C) 10
(D) 11
(E) 12

GO ON TO THE NEXT PAGE

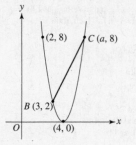

19. Points B and C lie on the parabola above. What is the slope of segment $\overline{BC}$?

(A) 2

(B) $\dfrac{5}{4}$

(C) 1

(D) $\dfrac{4}{5}$

(E) $\dfrac{1}{2}$

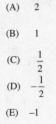

20. In the set of numbers above, there is no mode and the median is x^3. What is one possible value of x ?

(A) 2

(B) 1

(C) $\dfrac{1}{2}$

(D) $-\dfrac{1}{2}$

(E) -1

STOP
**If you finish before time is called, you may check your work on this section only.
Do not turn to any other section in the test.**

NO TEST MATERIAL ON THIS PAGE.

SECTION 5
Time — 25 minutes
24 Questions

Turn to Section 5 of your answer sheet to answer the questions in this section.

Directions: For each question in this section, select the best answer from among the choices given and fill in the corresponding circle on the answer sheet.

Each sentence below has one or two blanks, each blank indicating that something has been omitted. Beneath the sentence are five words or sets of words labeled A through E. Choose the word or set of words that, when inserted in the sentence, best fits the meaning of the sentence as a whole.

Example:

Desiring to ------- his taunting friends, Mitch gave them taffy in hopes it would keep their mouths shut.

(A) eliminate   (B) satisfy   (C) overcome
   (D) ridicule   (E) silence

Ⓐ Ⓑ Ⓒ Ⓓ ●

1. The randomly occurring chemical reactions observed in nature are proof that some reactions can be -------.

   (A) spontaneous   (B) hazardous   (C) experimental
      (D) deliberate   (E) constructive

2. The doctor regarded her patient's condition with -------, but after the surgery the patient ------- and was able to return home much sooner than anticipated.

   (A) hesitation . . benefited
   (B) apprehension . . recuperated
   (C) enthusiasm . . deliberated
   (D) apathy . . installed
   (E) concern . . approved

3. None of the petitioners was able to gather enough signatures in support of keeping the city's nuclear power plant open, an obvious ------- of the community's -------.

   (A) avoidance . . concealment
   (B) experiment . . resistance
   (C) rejection . . sponsorship
   (D) sponsorship . . espousal
   (E) demonstration . . opposition

4. In order to ensure that the children were -------, the school administrators enforced a code of conduct designed to promote ------- behavior among the students.

   (A) balanced . . extreme
   (B) obedient . . tractable
   (C) docile . . prestigious
   (D) studious . . boisterous
   (E) diverse . . spontaneous

5. The article "Tyranny of the Test" ------- the ------- of recent educational legislation, ridiculing the procedures used to formulate school policy.

   (A) reaffirms . . inflexibility
   (B) glorifies . . hypothesis
   (C) invalidates . . pitfalls
   (D) lampoons . . methodology
   (E) avoids . . dictates

6. Even though many doctors warn patients that high-cholesterol foods can increase risk of heart disease, some types of cholesterol are known to have ------- effects.

   (A) detrimental   (B) affable   (C) negligible
      (D) salutary   (E) peripheral

7. The physics professor designed his lectures to avoid ------- the material: his goal was to clarify difficult topics, not make them more confusing.

   (A) theorizing   (B) elucidating   (C) obfuscating
      (D) delineating   (E) accosting

8. Many voters believed that the new candidate ------- too often in his speeches: it seemed like he never chose one side of an issue and intentionally misled his audience

   (A) capitulated   (B) equivocated   (C) berated
      (D) vituperated   (E) debated

GO ON TO THE NEXT PAGE

Directions: Each passage below is followed by questions based on its content. Answer the questions on the basis of what is stated or implied in each passage and in any introductory material that may be provided.

Questions 9-12 are based on the following passages.

Passage 1

Educated by her father (the village rector), living out her days in secluded rural parishes, known as "Aunt Jane" to all her relations, Jane Austen seemed to embody the same
Line provincial and genteel way of life that she portrayed in her
5 novels. Generations of adoring fans have embraced her works, including *Emma* and *Pride and Prejudice*, as affectionate and witty portraits of the English gentry. For these readers, Austen's novels evoke an idyllic past, suffused with the classically English values of elegant charm and self-effacing
10 modesty, and refreshingly free of weighty political or philosophical concerns.

Passage 2

Often ignored in accounts of Austen's insular environment is the influence of her brother Henry, who introduced her to a sophisticated circle of London artists, writers, and other
15 intellectuals; these acquaintances gave Austen insight into social worlds not usually glimpsed from her small rural parish. She was acutely aware of the contradictions and hypocrisies of the British upper class, which she frequently subjected to withering criticism. Her irony is not humorous;
20 it is caustic and subversive, and seeks to undermine the assumptions of the society she lived in. In this sense, her work is profoundly political.

9. The author of Passage 1 would most likely argue that the interpretation of Jane Austen's work offered in Passage 2

   (A) is not representative of the way enthusiasts often view Austen's novels
   (B) exaggerates the impact of Austen's isolation from the outside world
   (C) is more reflective of how Austen was perceived in her own time than of how she is perceived today
   (D) is overly influenced by the popular interpretation of Austen's writing style
   (E) ignores the influence of the people she met through her brother Henry

10. The author of Passage 2 would probably argue that the "readers" (line 7, Passage 1) are likely to

   (A) support the notion that Austen expresses contempt for the British upper class
   (B) underestimate the degree to which Austen's works have a political purpose
   (C) dismiss the theory that Austen's works were influenced by her rural upbringing
   (D) identify with the difficulties that Austen faced as a female writer
   (E) exaggerate the relevance that Austen's novels have for the modern reader

11. Passage 1 suggests that Austen's depiction of the "British upper class" referred to in line 18, Passage 2, was

   (A) overly provincial
   (B) largely sympathetic
   (C) harshly critical
   (D) rigorously objective
   (E) highly unrealistic

12. The author of Passage 2 and the "adoring fans" mentioned in line 5, Passage 1, would most likely disagree about which of the following concerning Jane Austen?

   (A) Whether her family was a significant influence on her work
   (B) Whether her work accurately portrays the British upper class
   (C) Whether English society was a central topic of her novels
   (D) The extent to which her work is critical of certain segments of society
   (E) The extent to which she should be considered an important author

GO ON TO THE NEXT PAGE

Questions 13-24 are based on the following passage.

The following passage, adapted from a 2005 article, discusses the common garden slug.

As a professional ecologist, I find one image held by amateur gardeners to be particularly irksome: the idea that a "pest-free" garden, cleansed of any creatures that might
Line threaten the gardener's precious plants, is a healthy garden.
5   As an example, consider *Deroceras reticulatum*, otherwise known as the common garden slug. The average gardener believes that this creature is nothing more than an enemy to be exterminated. In attempting to beautify their yards, gardeners utilize an impressive arsenal of chemical
10 weapons designed to bombard the slugs from the air as well as attack them on the ground. Success is attained only when no trace of slugs can be found, although the wary gardener must watch and wait for their return, since permanently ridding a garden of slugs can prove nearly impossible.
15   There are important consequences that result from viewing the slug as mortal enemy. Repeated spraying of chemicals damages topsoil and saps it of essential nutrients. To compensate, gardeners frequently apply artificial fertilizers, which encourage plant growth in the short
20 term, but damage the soil in the long term. As a result, the weakened garden is left susceptible to invasion by all sorts of pests, requiring further application of chemical sprays. Thus, in attempting to attain the cherished ideal of a pristine, pest-free garden, amateur gardeners create a vicious circle:
25 contamination, followed by artificial regeneration and a slow depletion of natural resources, followed by more contamination.
   It seems to me that a solution to this dilemma starts with the recognition that a healthy garden is not one that has been
30 emptied of every organism that we find objectionable. Even creatures as repulsive as slugs have a role to play in a properly functioning ecosystem. Instead of trying to rid ourselves of slugs, wouldn't we be better off coming to some sort of accommodation with them?
35   The gardener who decides to coexist with the garden slug soon discovers that its nefarious reputation is at least partially unwarranted. Although it is true that the slug can devour garden plants from the roots up with frightening efficiency, it also produces nutrients for the soil, helping other plants to
40 grow. The diet of a slug consists not just of living plants, but also of plant waste and mold, making this diminutive creature into a sort of natural recycling center. The unique structure of a slug's digestive system enables it to take these discarded products, transform them into the nutrients that plants need to
45 thrive, and then release these nutrients into the soil by means of viscous, slime-like excretions.
   In order to reap the benefits that slugs provide while at the same time minimizing the slug's destructive effects, the gardener should focus on two tasks: reducing the slug
50 population to manageable proportions, and diverting the slug's efforts into activities that do the least harm. There are a number of ways to control the population of slugs without resorting to noxious chemicals, but one of the easiest

is to welcome a few of the slug's natural predators into
55 the garden. Ground beetles, toads, and hedgehogs are all naturally predisposed to hunt slugs. Providing a habitat for these creatures will ensure that the slug population is held to reasonable levels.
   To limit the slug's destructive effects, the gardener should
60 provide sacrificial plants for the slug to dine on. Lettuce, Zinnias, and Marigolds are all considered delicacies by slugs; the loss of a few of these plants will not distress the typical gardener. At the same time, natural barriers of white ash or diatomaceous earth should be placed around plants that are
65 held in higher esteem by the gardener. These barriers will naturally deter slugs, especially if tastier and more accessible treats are available nearby.
   It is true that these measures may seem cumbersome, but in the long run the benefits outweigh the temporary
70 inconvenience to the gardener. A garden should not be a place devoid of all creatures that the gardener finds troublesome; it should be a place in which competing forces balance each other out. By exchanging the ideal of a pest-free garden for one in which pests are tolerated and managed, the gardener
75 ensures a healthier garden and minimizes the hazards associated with chemical pesticides.

13. In line 1, "image" most nearly means

(A) resemblance
(B) apparition
(C) correspondent
(D) perception
(E) reputation

14. In the second paragraph, the author critiques "the average gardener" (lines 6-7) by describing the situation in terms of a

(A) political campaign
(B) sporting event
(C) military strategy
(D) scientific experiment
(E) criminal trial

15. The author would most likely describe the "important consequences" (line 15) as

(A) a decisive victory
(B) a complicated affair
(C) a superior result
(D) an unintended reaction
(E) an idealistic attitude

GO ON TO THE NEXT PAGE

16. The author would most probably characterize the "cherished ideal" (line 23) as

    (A) carefully planned
    (B) deeply insightful
    (C) inconclusive
    (D) unintelligible
    (E) misguided

17. The primary purpose of lines 28-34 (It seems . . . with them) is to

    (A) explain people's responses to certain animals
    (B) propose an alternative course of action
    (C) offer evidence of environmental destruction
    (D) praise the scope of a comprehensive effort
    (E) argue in favor of an unpopular position

18. The discussion in lines 35-46 ("The gardener . . . excretions") is best characterized as

    (A) a defense
    (B) a theory
    (C) an exception
    (D) an allusion
    (E) a comparison

19. The author uses the phrase "natural recycling center" (line 42) to suggest that slugs can

    (A) provide a model of environmentalism that people can emulate
    (B) help gardeners save money and increase productivity
    (C) heal a garden by absorbing and neutralizing harmful chemicals
    (D) eliminate all of the problems associated with artificial fertilizers
    (E) enable plants to make productive use of waste materials

20. The author's attitude toward the "viscous, slime-like excretions" (line 46) is best described as one of

    (A) ambivalence
    (B) revulsion
    (C) appreciation
    (D) uncertainty
    (E) irritation

21. In line 54, "welcome" most nearly means

    (A) acknowledge
    (B) thank
    (C) return
    (D) introduce
    (E) please

22. Lines 59-63 ("To limit . . . gardener") imply that

    (A) predators will inevitably destroy a garden unless the gardener takes drastic action
    (B) plants that appeal to slugs are not necessarily considered valuable by gardeners
    (C) slugs prefer Lettuce, Zinnias, and Marigolds to all other types of plants
    (D) gardeners should be sensitive to the needs of other species
    (E) people are often unwilling to compromise until forced to do so by circumstances

23. The implication of the phrase "It is true" (line 68) is that the author

    (A) recognizes that his suggestions may be viewed as burdensome
    (B) agrees with the conventional approach to an issue
    (C) is concerned that his ideas will not be taken seriously
    (D) is pleased by the willingness of gardeners to change their opinions
    (E) accepts that a solution to a problem may never be found

24. The last paragraph chiefly serves to

    (A) restate the author's evidence
    (B) suggest a direction for further study
    (C) intensify an emotional effect
    (D) downplay the impact of an approach
    (E) underscore the author's position

STOP

**If you finish before time is called, you may check your work on this section only.
Do not turn to any other section in the test.**

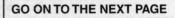

SECTION 6
Time — 25 minutes
35 Questions

Turn to Section 6 of your answer sheet to answer the questions in this section.

Directions: For each question in this section, select the best answer from among the choices given and fill in the corresponding circle on the answer sheet.

The following sentences test correctness and effectiveness of expression. Part of each sentence or the entire sentence is underlined; beneath each sentence are five ways of phrasing the underlined material. Choice A repeats the original phrasing; the other four choices are different. If you think the original phrasing produces a better sentence than any of the alternatives, select choice A; if not, select one of the other choices.

In making your selection, follow the requirements of standard written English; that is, pay attention to grammar, choice of words, sentence construction, and punctuation. Your selection should result in the most effective sentence—clear and precise, without awkwardness or ambiguity.

EXAMPLE:

Bobby Flay baked his first cake <u>and he was thirteen years old then</u>.

(A) and he was thirteen years old then
(B) when he was thirteen
(C) at age thirteen years old
(D) upon the reaching of thirteen years
(E) at the time when he was thirteen

Ⓐ●ⒸⒹⒺ

1. Although the senator <u>has been involved</u> in unethical behavior, her constituents continue to show strong support for her.

   (A) has been involved
   (B) involved
   (C) being involved
   (D) has yet to be involved
   (E) is involving

2. Like many freshmen, <u>a sense of homesickness was felt by</u> my roommates for the first few weeks of college.

   (A) a sense of homesickness was felt by
   (B) a sense of homesickness feeling by
   (C) my roommates felt homesick
   (D) my roommates, who felt a sense of homesickness
   (E) there was a sense of homesickness felt by my roommates

3. Because <u>Alberto set a state record in the 400-meter dash is the reason why</u> the university offered him a full athletic scholarship.

   (A) Alberto set a state record in the 400-meter dash is the reason why
   (B) Alberto set a state record in the 400-meter dash,
   (C) Alberto set a state record in the 400-meter dash and is why
   (D) Alberto setting a state record in the 400-meter dash,
   (E) Alberto set a state record in the 400-meter dash is why

4. Exceptional teachers not only convey information about subjects such as history, literature, and mathematics, <u>but instill in their students a love for learning</u> that leads them to investigate concepts beyond the classroom walls.

   (A) but instill in their students a love for learning
   (B) and instill in their students also a love of learning
   (C) but instill in their students a love to learn
   (D) but also instill in their students a love of learning
   (E) and instill in their students loving for learning

5. A comedic outlet well-suited to Meadowlark Lemon was the Harlem Globetrotter's brand of <u>basketball, it let him reinterpret</u> the sport without the limitations required by official regulations.

   (A) basketball, it let him reinterpret
   (B) basketball, which let him reinterpret
   (C) basketball that lets him reinterpret
   (D) basketball; letting him reinterpret
   (E) basketball by letting him do reinterpretation of

6. The success of many start up companies may depend on both the regulation of taxes on small businesses <u>and the education of the public</u> about the security of internet commerce.

   (A) and the education of the public
   (B) educating the public
   (C) and the public being educated
   (D) along with the education of the public
   (E) in combination with public education

GO ON TO THE NEXT PAGE ➡

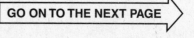
7. No one reason given for the fall of Rome, though many causes have been proposed over the centuries, <u>are adequate explanations for</u> why the mighty empire did not last.

- (A) are adequate explanations for
- (B) are an adequate explanation for
- (C) adequately explain
- (D) an adequate explanation of
- (E) is an adequate explanation for

8. The architect visited the remote village because <u>many were known there to construct</u> homes much like their predecessors had built.

- (A) many were known there to construct
- (B) many were known there for constructing
- (C) many of the people there were known to construct
- (D) of the many people, they were there constructing
- (E) of knowing that many people constructed there

9. During the Great Depression of 1929, Roosevelt's program to boost the failing economy by implementing the New Deal <u>were met with</u> overwhelming support.

- (A) were received with
- (B) having been met with
- (C) it met
- (D) met with
- (E) met their

10. When for the past week the weather service warned of a hurricane, island residents should have realized that a storm <u>was imminent and could strike very soon</u>.

- (A) was imminent and could strike very soon
- (B) could happen imminently very soon
- (C) will be imminent and happening soon
- (D) is an imminent thing
- (E) might be imminent

11. Speaking, writing, and body language are <u>all effective, if disparate, forms of communication</u>.

- (A) all effective, if disparate, forms of communication
- (B) effective forms of communication, being, however, disparate
- (C) disparate forms of communications, whereas they are effective
- (D) disparate forms of communication when effective
- (E) forms of communication that are different although being effective

GO ON TO THE NEXT PAGE

> The following sentences test your ability to recognize grammar and usage errors. Each sentence contains either a single error or no error at all. No sentence contains more than one error. The error, if there is one, is underlined and lettered. If the sentence contains an error, select the one underlined part that must be changed to make the sentence correct. If the sentence is correct, select choice E. In choosing answers, follow the requirements of standard written English.
>
> EXAMPLE:
>
> The other players and her significantly improved
>   A   B   C
>
> the game plan created by the coaches. No error
>   D   E
>
> Ⓐ ● Ⓒ Ⓓ Ⓔ

12. Harper Lee's first novel, which was published in 1960
                                              A
by J.B. Lippincott, and translated into editions in over
                     B   C   D
forty languages. No error
                    E

13. Over the last four months, Steven has fought to funding
        A   B   C
the reconstruction of the recreation center for the purpose
                                             D
of creating a venue for after-school programs. No error
                                                   E

14. Taking a small dose of aspirin causes thinning of the
                                             A
blood but delay the moment when a heart attack
          B   C
may occur. No error
   D   E

15. According to the results of the questionnaire, most
audience members were supportive of magicians'
                   A   B
unwillingness revealing secrets of the trade. No error
              C   D   E

16. Those body builders who competed in the Mr. Universe
                           A   B
Contest were either on steroids or incredible strong.
                 C   D
No error
E

17. The reviews for the restaurant are so good that even with
                                           A   B
the option of calling ahead, most patrons can rarely get
                             C   D
a table within two hours. No error
                             E .

18. When Gordon baked the pecan pie and served slices of it
        A
with various toppings—including vanilla ice cream and
     B
sprinkles—he had been the first to eat a slice. No error
            C   D   E

19. Ever since her promotion to manager last year,
                      A
Bretney is the hardest-working employee of this small
        B   C
and highly industrious company. No error
    D   E

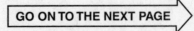

GO ON TO THE NEXT PAGE

20. One of the <u>dangers</u> facing the Kemp's ridley turtle, the
               A

smallest <u>of all sea turtles,</u> is that the female nests only
        B

<u>on a small stretch</u> <u>of beach</u> in Mexico that is now the
     C   D

target of developers. <u>No error</u>
              E

21. The salve made from the leaves of cactus plants <u>are</u>
                                A

highly efficient <u>in healing</u> minor sunburns, <u>thus</u>
          B   C

offering a solution <u>to small desert</u> camping fiascos.
             D

<u>No error</u>
 E

22. <u>Throughout</u> the 1990s, swing dancing enjoyed a
    A

resurgence <u>when both</u> musicians and dancers <u>listened to</u>
         B   C

the songs of the 1940s <u>for</u> inspiration. <u>No error</u>
              D   E

23. Most of the residents of Heard County <u>no longer</u> attend
                              A

church on Sunday, an activity that <u>formerly</u> <u>served</u> to
                      B   C

<u>tie the community's</u> families together. <u>No error</u>
    D   E

24. <u>In order</u> for the class to pay attention to and
    A

<u>be respectful of</u> the substitute teacher, <u>they have</u> to be
    B   C

convinced that the <u>instructor</u> is knowledgeable.
              D

<u>No error</u>
 E

25. The accounting department <u>is presenting</u> requests
                     A

<u>to both</u> vice presidents <u>in</u> the hope <u>to receive</u>
  B   C   D

permission to create a company spa. <u>No error</u>
                         E

26. <u>Rather than</u> view her <u>glass as</u> either half full <u>or</u> half
    A   B   C

empty, Reneé chose to see it as <u>overflowing from</u>
                      D

possibilities. <u>No error</u>
       E

27. At the concert, Lucy <u>enjoyed listening</u> to her friend
                  A

Noah's experimental music, <u>which she</u> thought was
                    B

<u>more original</u> than <u>the other bands.</u> <u>No error</u>
  C   D   E

28. The reason for <u>dramatically raising</u> fines for litering
            A

<u>is that</u> many pet owners would simply decide <u>to pay it</u>
  B   C

<u>rather than</u> pick up their pet's waste. <u>No error</u>
  D   E

29. No matter how many times a person <u>has driven</u> in
                           A

inclement weather, <u>they should</u> be <u>especially</u> careful
             B   C

when driving down a road <u>that</u> is covered with wet snow.
                  D

<u>No error</u>
 E

GO ON TO THE NEXT PAGE

Questions 30-35 are based on the following passage.

(1) Puccini's opera *La Bohème* is a timeless tale of love and art and tenderness in trying times and situations. (2) The epic is timeless for many reasons, one of the reasons is that people still relate to it, some even cry over the characters' fates. (3) Because it is timeless, recent artists have tried to bring the story to today's audiences.

(4) Director Baz Lurhmann brought the opera to the musical stage in 2002. (5) He did not change the words or the Italian language in which they were sung. (6) To reach his young audience, he jazzed up the costumes, set, and choreography. (7) The vibrant costumes, including black leather jackets, reflected the 1950s, the time period Lurhmann uses. (8) The set was stark and more reminiscent of the modern day than of a Bohemian ghetto. (9) The choreography transformed the singers into performers, so the show had the dynamic energy of a musical than the stilted movements of traditional opera; the show generally got rave reviews.

(10) Composer Jonathan Larson created the musical *Rent* in 1996, it takes much of the storyline and characters from *La Bohème*. (11) *Rent* was written in the 1990s; accordingly, it talks about issues relating to modern city youth. For example, tuberculosis in the original show became AIDS in the new one. (12) However, despite the rock music and modern slang, starving artists were still starving artists and greedy landlords were still greedy landlords; the musical was a huge success.

(13) Although all these updates of *La Bohème* have come to being, the original by Puccini is still incredibly popular. (14) Performances are given around the world and sell out frequently. (15) Interestingly, even though it is timeless, modern artists have still felt the need to update it.

30. Of the following, which would most improve the first paragraph (sentences 1-3) ?

   (A) a plot synopsis of *La Bohème*
   (B) a history of Puccini's life
   (C) a comparison of Puccini, Lurhmann, and Larson's backgrounds
   (D) an analysis of what audiences appreciate in theater
   (E) a description of tuberculosis and AIDS

31. Which of the following is the best version of sentence 7 (reproduced below) ?

The vibrant costumes, including black leather jackets, reflected the 1950s, the time period Lurhmann uses.

   (A) The vibrant costumes and black leather jackets, reflected the 1950s, the time period Lurhmann uses.
   (B) The black leather jackets and other vibrant costumes echo the 1950s, the time period Lurhmann used in his production.
   (C) Lurhmann uses black leather jackets and other vibrant costumes of the 1950s in his production to suggest the time period of the production.
   (D) The vibrant costumes, and jackets imitated those of the 1950s, the time period Lurhmann uses in his production.
   (E) The black leather jackets and other vibrant costumes reproduced the time period of the 1950s of which Lurhmann uses in his production.

32. The purpose of the second paragraph is to

   (A) illustrate the way an artist transformed *La Bohème*
   (B) show how artists have updated *La Bohème* for modern audiences
   (C) explain the differences between *Rent* and *La Bohème*
   (D) explore the plight of tuberculosis victims
   (E) update Puccini's opera for today's youth

33. Which of the following is the best version of sentence 10 (reproduced below) ?

Composer Jonathan Larson created the musical Rent *in 1996, it takes much of the storyline and characters from* La Bohème.

   (A) (As it is now)
   (B) Composer Jonathan Larson, who created the musical *Rent* in 1996, taking much of the storyline and characters from *La Bohème*.
   (C) Much of the storyline and characters from *La Bohème* were included in *Rent*, which is a musical created by composer Jonathan Larson in 1996.
   (D) *Rent*, a musical by composer Jonathan Larson in 1996, was created by using much of the storyline and characters from *La Bohème*.
   (E) Composer Jonathan Larson created the musical *Rent* in 1996 using much of the storyline and many of the characters from *La Bohème*.

GO ON TO THE NEXT PAGE ▷

34. What is the primary purpose of sentence 12 (reproduced below) ?

However, despite the rock music and modern slang, starving artists were still starving artists and greedy landlords were still greedy landlords; the musical was a huge success.

(A) To demonstrate that all cultures use modern slang
(B) To focus on the tribulations of starving artists who cannot pay their rent
(C) To convey that certain constants attract audiences, regardless of presentation
(D) To show that cultures frequently change and reinvent themselves
(E) To determine that artists, regardless of era, evolve into different forms and appearance

35. Which is the best sentence to put after sentence 15 ?

(A) *Rent* has grossed over $280 million, far more than Lurhmann's *La Bohème*.
(B) Unlike *Rent*, *La Bohème* was first put on by Lurhmann in Australia before traveling to New York.
(C) Lurhmann's *La Bohème* garnered 7 Tony Award nominations in addition to other honors.
(D) Seemingly, artists are as compelled to revisit the story of Puccini's opera as are audiences worldwide.
(E) Lastly, the new interpretations of Puccini's opera, *La Bohème*, show no signs of slowing.

STOP
If you finish before time is called, you may check your work on this section only. Do not turn to any other section in the test.

SECTION 7
Time — 25 minutes
18 Questions

Turn to Section 7 of your answer sheet to answer the questions in this section.

Directions: This section contains two types of questions. You have 25 minutes to complete both types. For questions 1-8, solve each problem and decide which is the best of the choices given. Fill in the corresponding circle on the answer sheet. You may use any available space for scratchwork.

Notes

1. The use of a calculator is permitted.

2. All numbers used are real numbers.

3. Figures that accompany problems in this test are intended to provide information useful in solving the problems. They are drawn as accurately as possible EXCEPT when it is stated in a specific problem that the figure is not drawn to scale. All figures lie in a plane unless otherwise indicated.

4. Unless otherwise specified, the domain of any function f is assumed to be the set of all real numbers x for which $f(x)$ is a real number.

Reference Information

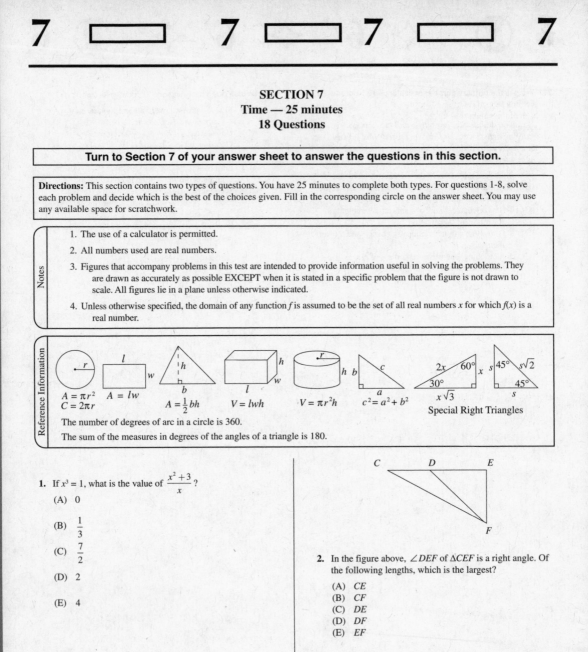

$A = \pi r^2$
$C = 2\pi r$

$A = lw$

$A = \frac{1}{2}bh$

$V = lwh$

$V = \pi r^2 h$

$c^2 = a^2 + b^2$

Special Right Triangles

The number of degrees of arc in a circle is 360.

The sum of the measures in degrees of the angles of a triangle is 180.

---

1. If $x^3 = 1$, what is the value of $\dfrac{x^2 + 3}{x}$?

(A) 0

(B) $\dfrac{1}{3}$

(C) $\dfrac{7}{2}$

(D) 2

(E) 4

2. In the figure above, $\angle DEF$ of $\triangle CEF$ is a right angle. Of the following lengths, which is the largest?

(A) CE
(B) CF
(C) DE
(D) DF
(E) EF

GO ON TO THE NEXT PAGE

3. The average (arithmetic mean) of the numbers in set A is 8. If a second set of numbers, B, if created by dividing each of the numbers in set A by two, then what is the average of the numbers in set B?

(A) $\frac{1}{2}$

(B) 4

(C) 8

(D) 12

(E) 16

4. If the positive four-digit integer JKLM contains the digits J, K, L, and M, what is the decimal equivalent of JKLM $\times$ 10^{-3}?

(A) 0.JKLM
(B) J.KLM
(C) JK.LM
(D) JK,LM0
(E) J,KLM,000

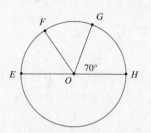

5. In the figure above, $\overline{EH}$ is a diameter of the circle with center O. If $\overline{FO}$ bisects $\angle EOG$, what is the measure of $\angle FOH$?

(A) 180
(B) 125
(C) 110
(D) 105
(E) 90

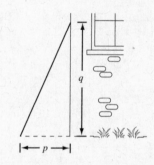

6. The figure above illustrates a ladder extended from a vertical wall to the ground. If the ladder has a slope of $\frac{5}{3}$ feet and p is 9 feet, what is q, in feet?

(A) 15
(B) 10
(C) 7.5
(D) 5
(E) 4.5

GO ON TO THE NEXT PAGE

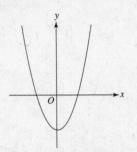

7. The parabola in the graph above is given by the equation $y = ax^2 - 3$. If a new parabola, given by the equation $y = 2ax^2 - 3$, is graphed on the same axes, which of the following best describes the resulting parabola as compared with the parabola above?

(A) It will move 2 units upward.
(B) It will be wider.
(C) It will be narrower.
(D) It will be moved to the left.
(E) It will be moved to the right.

8. Serena has three photographs from Brazil—a landscape, a street scene, and a portrait. She also has three photographs from Kenya—a landscape, a street scene, and a portrait—and three photographs from Istanbul—a landscape, a street scene, and a portrait. Serena wants to display three photographs: one landscape, one street scene, and one portrait, and also wants to use one each from Brazil, Kenya, and Istanbul. How many different possibilities does she have?

(A) 1
(B) 3
(C) 6
(D) 9
(E) 27

GO ON TO THE NEXT PAGE

Directions: For Student-Produced Response questions 9-18, use the grids at the bottom of the answer sheet page on which you have answered questions 1-8.

Each of the remaining 10 questions requires you to solve the problem and enter your answer by marking the circles in the special grid, as shown in the examples below. You may use any available space for scratch work.

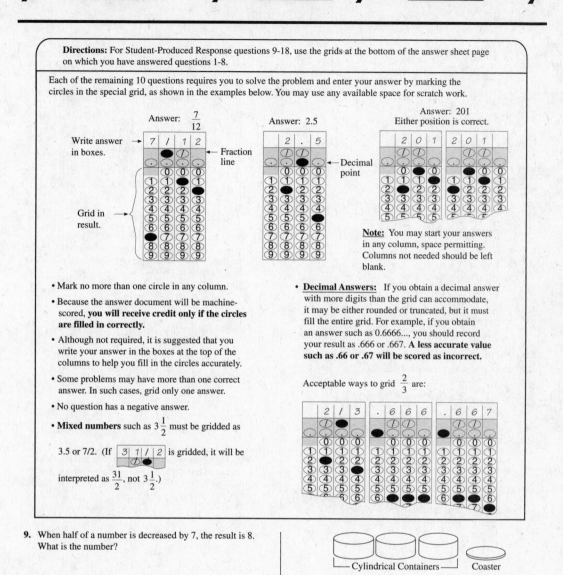

Answer: $\frac{7}{12}$

Write answer in boxes.

← Fraction line

Grid in result.

Answer: 2.5

← Decimal point

Answer: 201
Either position is correct.

Note: You may start your answers in any column, space permitting. Columns not needed should be left blank.

- Mark no more than one circle in any column.
- Because the answer document will be machine-scored, **you will receive credit only if the circles are filled in correctly.**
- Although not required, it is suggested that you write your answer in the boxes at the top of the columns to help you fill in the circles accurately.
- Some problems may have more than one correct answer. In such cases, grid only one answer.
- No question has a negative answer.
- **Mixed numbers** such as $3\frac{1}{2}$ must be gridded as 3.5 or 7/2. (If 3 1 / 2 is gridded, it will be interpreted as $\frac{31}{2}$, not $3\frac{1}{2}$.)

- **Decimal Answers:** If you obtain a decimal answer with more digits than the grid can accommodate, it may be either rounded or truncated, but it must fill the entire grid. For example, if you obtain an answer such as 0.6666..., you should record your result as .666 or .667. **A less accurate value such as .66 or .67 will be scored as incorrect.**

Acceptable ways to grid $\frac{2}{3}$ are:

9. When half of a number is decreased by 7, the result is 8. What is the number?

└─ Cylindrical Containers ─┘ Coaster

10. Each of the 3 right cylindrical containers shown has interior dimensions measuring 5 inches in height and 4 inches in diameter. At most, how many circular coasters, each with a 4-inch diameter and a height of $\frac{1}{3}$ inches, can fit inside the three containers altogether?

GO ON TO THE NEXT PAGE ⟹

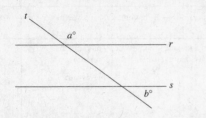

11. In the figure above, $r \parallel s$ and $a = 4b$. What is the value of a ?

_____

12. Let the function $f(x)$ be defined by $f(x) = |2x - 3|$. If p is a real number, what is one possible value of p for which $f(p) < p$?

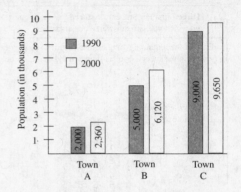

13. The bar graph shown above gives the populations for Town A, Town B, and Town C in 1990 and 2000. What is the average (arithmetic mean) population increase of the three towns from 1990 to 2000 ?

_____

14. A bowl contains 30 blue marbles and 30 green marbles. If 17 blue marbles are removed, what is the maximum number of green marbles that can be removed so that there are at least twice as many green marbles as there are blue marbles?

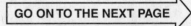

GO ON TO THE NEXT PAGE

15. If $\dfrac{4a + 3b}{2b} = \dfrac{5}{3}$, what is the value of $\dfrac{b}{a}$?

16. At shipping company A, sending a package costs a flat rate of \$10 for any package weighing up to and including 10 pounds, plus an additional \$0.60 per pound for every pound over 10 pounds. The cost of sending a package using shipping company B is \$0.80 per pound for any weight. If the cost of sending a package using Company 1 is the same as the cost of sending a package using Company 2, then how much does the package weigh?

17. A number is considered "odd-mult" if it is the multiple of exactly two consecutive odd numbers. How many positive numbers less than 400 are "odd-mult"?

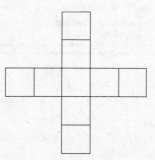

18. The figure above shows an arrangement of 9 squares, each with a side of length s inches. The perimeter of the figure is p inches and the area of the figure is a inches. If $p = a$, then what is the value of s ?

STOP
If you finish before time is called, you may check your work on this section only.
Do not turn to any other section in the test.

SECTION 8
Time — 20 minutes
16 Questions

Turn to Section 8 of your answer sheet to answer the questions in this section.

Directions: For this section, solve each problem and decide which is the best of the choices given. Fill in the corresponding circle on the answer sheet. You may use any available space for scratchwork.

Notes

1. The use of a calculator is permitted.

2. All numbers used are real numbers.

3. Figures that accompany problems in this test are intended to provide information useful in solving the problems. They are drawn as accurately as possible EXCEPT when it is stated in a specific problem that the figure is not drawn to scale. All figures lie in a plane unless otherwise indicated.

4. Unless otherwise specified, the domain of any function f is assumed to be the set of all real numbers x for which $f(x)$ is a real number.

Reference Information

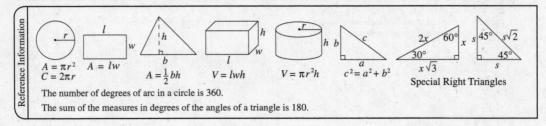

$A = \pi r^2$
$C = 2\pi r$

$A = lw$

$A = \frac{1}{2}bh$

$V = lwh$

$V = \pi r^2 h$

$c^2 = a^2 + b^2$

Special Right Triangles

The number of degrees of arc in a circle is 360.
The sum of the measures in degrees of the angles of a triangle is 180.

1. It takes 72 minutes to drive along a certain route at a constant speed. What fraction of the ride is completed after 12 minutes?

(A) $\frac{1}{4}$

(B) $\frac{1}{5}$

(C) $\frac{1}{6}$

(D) $\frac{1}{7}$

(E) $\frac{1}{12}$

x	1	2	3	4	5	6
$f(x)$	9	16	t	30	37	44

2. If the table above defines a linear function, what is the value of t ?

(A) 23
(B) 24
(C) 25
(D) 26
(E) 27

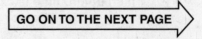

GO ON TO THE NEXT PAGE

3. The diameter of a basketball is 4 times the diameter of a racquetball. What is the ratio of the radius of the basketball to that of the racquetball?

(A) 1 : 2
(B) 3 : 2
(C) 4 : 1
(D) 4 : 3
(E) 8 : 1

SHORT STORY GENRES

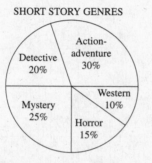

4. In a creative-writing course, 60 students chose from among 5 genres for each assignment. The graph above shows the distribution of the stories turned in for one assignment. If there were 6 assignments during the semester, and the same number of students turned in Detective stories for each assignment, what is the total number of Detective stories turned in during the semester?

(A) 72
(B) 100
(C) 120
(D) 240
(E) 300

5. Janet produced 4 more paintings than three times the number of paintings Sam produced. Last year, Sam produced p paintings. Of the expressions below, which represents the number of paintings Janet produced last year?

(A) $4 - 3p$
(B) $4p - 3$
(C) $4p + 3$
(D) $3p - 4$
(E) $3p + 4$

6. For the inequality $c - d > c$, which of the following must be true?

(A) $c < 0$
(B) $c > 0$
(C) $c < d$
(D) $d < 0$
(E) $d > 0$

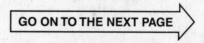

GO ON TO THE NEXT PAGE

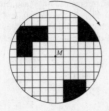

7. Which of the following is a representation of the result if the figure above were rotated 270° clockwise about point *M* ?

(A)

(B)

(C)

(D)

(E)

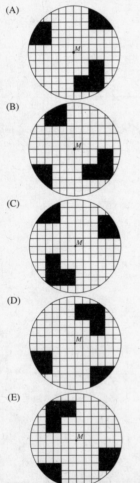

8. If $a > 0$ and $b < 0$, which of the following must be true?

(A) $a + b = 0$

(B) $\dfrac{a}{b} < 0$

(C) $a + b < 0$

(D) $a + b > 0$

(E) $ab > 0$

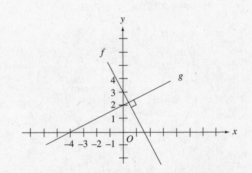

9. In the *xy*-coordinate plane above, line *f* and line *g* are perpendicular to one another. What is the slope of line *f* ?

(A) -2

(B) $-\dfrac{1}{2}$

(C) $\dfrac{1}{2}$

(D) 2

(E) 3

GO ON TO THE NEXT PAGE

10. A bag of candy contains chocolate hearts, vanilla hearts and gumballs. The number of pieces of heart shaped candy is 5 times the number of gumballs. If one piece of candy is to be chosen at random from the bag, the probability that a vanilla heart will be chosen is 4 times the probability that a chocolate heart will be chosen. If there are 16 vanilla hearts in the bag, what is the total number of pieces of candy in the bag?

(A) 48
(B) 44
(C) 36
(D) 24
(E) 20

11. If $ab = 8$, $bc = 4$ and $ac = 2$, and $c > 0$, then what is the value of abc ?

(A) 2
(B) 4
(C) 8
(D) 32
(E) 64

12. If six less than four times a number is greater than or equal to −2, which of the following represents all possible values of that number?

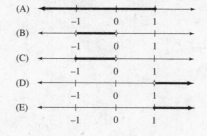

13. In a certain polygon, all of the angles are equal and all of the sides are of equal length. Point Q is a vertex of the polygon. If four diagonals can be drawn from point Q to the other vertices of the polygon, how many sides does the polygon have?

(A) Eight
(B) Seven
(C) Six
(D) Five
(E) Four

GO ON TO THE NEXT PAGE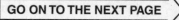

14. When n is a positive integer, $9 + 3^{n+2} = m$. What is the value of 3^n in terms of m ?

(A) $m + 3$

(B) $m^2 - 3$

(C) $\dfrac{m+1}{9}$

(D) $\dfrac{m-9}{9}$

(E) $\dfrac{1}{3}m$

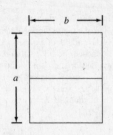

16. A gardener wants to enclose a patch of soil with length a and width b with fencing. He also wants to put a fence down the middle of the patch, to divide it into two smaller rectangular gardens, as seen in the figure above. If the area of the patch is 20 square feet, how many feet of fence, in terms of b, must the gardener use?

(A) $b + \dfrac{20}{b}$

(B) $b + \dfrac{40}{b}$

(C) $3b + \dfrac{40}{b}$

(D) $3b + \dfrac{20}{3b}$

(E) $3b + \dfrac{40}{3b}$

15. In $\triangle ABC$ two sides, AB and BC, are equal. Side AC has a length of 5, and the perimeter of $\triangle ABC$ is 13. If the measure of angle ABC is x , which of the following must be true about x ?

(A) $x < 60$
(B) $60 < x < 90$
(C) $x = 90$
(D) $x > 90$
(E) It cannot be determined from the information given.

STOP
**If you finish before time is called, you may check your work on this section only.
Do not turn to any other section in the test.**

NO TEST MATERIAL ON THIS PAGE.

SECTION 9
Time — 20 minutes
19 Questions

Turn to Section 9 of your answer sheet to answer the questions in this section.

Directions: For each question in this section, select the best answer from among the choices given and fill in the corresponding circle on the answer sheet.

Each sentence below has one or two blanks, each blank indicating that something has been omitted. Beneath the sentence are five words or sets of words labeled A through E. Choose the word or set of words that, when inserted in the sentence, best fits the meaning of the sentence as a whole.

Example:

Desiring to ------- his taunting friends, Mitch gave them taffy in hopes it would keep their mouths shut.

(A) eliminate   (B) satisfy   (C) overcome
    (D) ridicule   (E) silence

Ⓐ Ⓑ Ⓒ Ⓓ ●

1. The belief that bats are blind is a widespread -------: they are actually very sensitive to excessive light.

    (A) hypothesis   (B) conviction   (C) misconception
        (D) speculation   (E) observation

2. Because Donald frequently involved himself in the affairs of others, he gained the reputation of a -------, and even his own friends regarded him as an -------.

    (A) meddler . . interloper
    (B) traitor . . authority
    (C) mediator . . impostor
    (D) negotiator . . arbiter
    (E) conciliator . . intruder

3. Although Devon was viewed by his coworkers as a ------- and reliable employee, his boss viewed him as undependable and easily swayed.

    (A) staunch   (B) apprehensive   (C) incessant
        (D) diffident   (E) singular

4. The safety expert argued that even though the new helmet designs were ------ for their superior protective structures, the unreliable materials suggested for production made the helmets more -------.

    (A) banned . . prohibitive
    (B) lauded . . precarious
    (C) extolled . . advantageous
    (D) analyzed . . useless
    (E) tested . . functional

5. The prosecutor mocked the defendant's lack of -------, noting the lack of evidence or testimony to support the version of events offered by the defense.

    (A) respectability   (B) objection   (C) fidelity
        (D) eloquence   (E) corroboration

6. In spite of the ------- atmosphere at the gathering, John seemed unhappy and detached from the rest of the group.

    (A) reticent   (B) quixotic   (C) despondent
        (D) fortuitous   (E) convivial

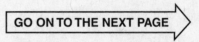

GO ON TO THE NEXT PAGE

Directions: Each passage below is followed by questions based on its content. Answer the questions on the basis of what is <u>stated</u> or <u>implied</u> in each passage and in any introductory material that may be provided.

Questions 7-19 are based on the following passage.

This passage, adapted from a novel written in the nineteenth century, portrays two characters—William Crimsworth and Mr. Hunsden, a business associate. At the beginning of the passage, William is out for a walk.

No man likes to acknowledge that he has made a mistake in the choice of his profession, and any human being, worthy of the name, will row long against wind and tide before he
Line allows himself to cry out, "I am baffled!" and submits to be
5 floated passively back to land. From the first week, I felt my occupation oppressive. The thing itself—the work of copying and translating business-letters—was a dry and tedious task enough, but had that been all, I should long have borne with the nuisance. But this was not all; the antipathy which had
10 sprung up between myself and Mr. Crimsworth struck deeper root and spread denser shade daily, excluding me from every glimpse of the sunshine of life.
   Antipathy is the only word which can express the feeling Edward Crimsworth had for me. My accent annoyed him; the
15 degree of education evinced in my language irritated him; my punctuality and industry fixed his dislike, and gave it the high flavour and poignant relish of envy. Had I been in anything inferior to him, he would not have hated me so thoroughly. I had long ceased to regard Mr. Crimsworth as my brother—he
20 was a hard, grinding master; he wished to be an inexorable tyrant: that was all. Thoughts, not varied but strong, occupied my mind; two voices spoke within me; again and again they uttered the same monotonous phrases. One said: "William, your life is intolerable." The other: "What can you do to alter
25 it?"
   I had received my weekly wages, and was returning to my lodgings, speculating on the general state of my affairs, when I encountered a familiar figure.
   "Mr. Hunsden! Good evening."
30 "Good evening, indeed!"
   For a moment, Mr. Hunsden fell silent. He seemed possessed of a great urge to speak, yet unsure of how to proceed. Presently, he recovered his composure, and starting from his silent fit, began:
35 "William! What a fool you are to live in those dismal lodgings of Mrs. King's, when you might take rooms in Grove Street, and have a garden like me!"
   "I should be too far from the mill."
   "What of that? It would do you good to walk there and
40 back two or three times a day; besides, are you such a fossil that you never wish to see a flower or a green leaf?"
   "I am no fossil."

   "What are you then? You sit at that desk in Crimsworth's counting-house day by day and week by week, scraping
45 with a pen on paper; you never get up; you never say you are tired; you never ask for a holiday; you never take change or relaxation; you give way to no excess of an evening; you neither keep wild company, nor indulge in strong drink."
   "Do you, Mr. Hunsden?"
50 "Don't think to pose me with short questions; your case and mine are diametrically different, and it is nonsense attempting to draw a parallel. I say, that when a man endures patiently what ought to be unendurable, he is a fossil."
   "Whence do you acquire the knowledge of my patience?"
55 "Why, man, do you suppose you are a mystery? What do you think I do with my eyes and ears? I've been in your counting-house more than once when Crimsworth has treated you like a dog; called for a book, for instance, and when you gave him the wrong one, or what he chose to consider the
60 wrong one, flung it back almost in your face!"
   "Well, Mr. Hunsden, what then?"
   "I can hardly tell you what then; the conclusion to be drawn as to your character depends upon the nature of the motives that guide your conduct; if you are patient because
65 you expect to make something eventually out of Crimsworth, notwithstanding his tyranny, you are what the world calls interested and mercenary, but if you are patient because you think it a duty to meet insult with submission, you are an essential sap, and in no shape the man for my money."
70 His brow darkened, his thin nostrils dilated a little.
   "You'll make nothing by trade," continued he; "nothing more than the crust of dry bread on which you now live; your only chance of getting a competency lies in marrying a rich widow, or running away with an heiress."
75 "I leave such shifts to be put in practice by those who devise them," said I.
   "And even that is hopeless," he went on coolly. "What widow would have you? Much less, what heiress? You're not bold and venturesome enough for the one, nor handsome and
80 fascinating enough for the other."
   Hunsden saw his advantage; he followed it up.
   "You should have been a nobleman, William Crimsworth! You are cut out for one; pity Fortune has cheated Nature! Now, if you'd only an estate, a mansion, and a title, how you
85 could play the part! As it is, you've no power; you're wrecked and stranded on the shores of commerce; forced into collision with practical men, with whom you cannot cope. You'll never succeed as a tradesman!"

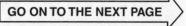
GO ON TO THE NEXT PAGE

7. The episode in the passage is best described as a

(A) dispute between two enemies
(B) collaboration between two coworkers
(C) disagreement between two friends
(D) conversation between two brothers
(E) confrontation between two acquaintances

8. Lines 1-5 ("No man . . . land") suggest that a person who is "worthy of the name" is one who

(A) enjoys the challenge of navigating in adverse conditions
(B) is determined to achieve wealth and respectability in business
(C) is reluctant to abandon a plan once it has been chosen
(D) is unwilling to work hard to attain his goals
(E) has difficulty expressing feelings and emotions

9. William's comments in lines 5-12 ("From . . . life") suggest that his primary objection to his job is his

(A) increasing resentment of his fellow employees
(B) growing disenchantment with his employer
(C) frequent conflicts with demanding customers
(D) annoyance with the tedious nature of the work
(E) frustration with working long hours for low pay

10. The list in lines 14-17 ("My accent . . . envy") indicates that Edward Crimsworth is

(A) angered by William's condescending and scornful manner
(B) exasperated by William's casual attitude toward his work
(C) jealous of William's cultivated and professional demeanor
(D) resentful of the fact that William was favored by their parents
(E) bewildered by William's tendency to speak in an affected accent

11. In line 42, Mr. Hunsden uses the word "fossil" to suggest that William is

(A) incapable of walking long distances
(B) suspicious of anything out of the ordinary
(C) inhibited by his strict sense of morality
(D) desensitized by his unvarying routine
(E) older than the other workers at the counting-house

12. Mr. Hunsden responds to the question posed by William in line 49 by

(A) denying that the same criteria apply to both of them
(B) complaining that William's responses are ill-considered
(C) demanding that William stop questioning his character
(D) deliberately misunderstanding the meaning of the question
(E) casually dismissing the importance of the topic

13. Lines 62-69 ("I can . . . money") indicate that Mr. Hunsden is

(A) uncertain about the reasons underlying William's actions
(B) confused about whether William really likes his brother
(C) suspicious about William's plan to take over the family business
(D) surprised that William refuses to accept his offer of financial assistance
(E) pleased that William has finally decided to make something of his life

14. Mr. Hunsden's statement in lines 71-74 ("You'll make . . . heiress") is best described as a

(A) criticism of unconventional relationships
(B) warning about romantic illusions
(C) confession of his own failures
(D) prediction of a bleak future
(E) confession of secret desires

15. William responds to the statement in lines 71-74 ("You'll make . . . heiress") by implying that

(A) a goal remains out of reach
(B) an outcome appears uncertain
(C) a plan is considered promising
(D) a strategy is unlikely to succeed
(E) an idea is unworthy of consideration

16. In line 75, "shifts" most nearly means

(A) substitutions
(B) occupations
(C) schemes
(D) directions
(E) adjustments

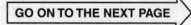

GO ON TO THE NEXT PAGE

17. In lines 77-80 ("And even . . . other"), Mr. Hunsden suggests that William is

(A) clever but unattractive
(B) drab but appealing
(C) timid and bland
(D) assertive and impoverished
(E) dashing and mysterious

18. In context, the phrase "Fortune has cheated Nature" (line 83) refers to the idea that William is

(A) cruel to members of the lower classes
(B) ill-suited to his chosen profession
(C) prone to making reckless decisions
(D) accustomed to insults from Mr. Hunsden
(E) envious of those who have power and wealth

19. William and Mr. Hunsden most likely agree on which point?

(A) William needs to think more carefully about his future.
(B) William will never succeed as a tradesman.
(C) William should feel fortunate to have a career.
(D) William is treated poorly by his employer.
(E) William should seek marriage with an aristocratic woman.

STOP

**If you finish before time is called, you may check your work on this section only.
Do not turn to any other section in the test.**

SECTION 10
Time — 10 minutes
14 Questions

Turn to Section 10 of your answer sheet to answer the questions in this section.

Directions: For each question in this section, select the best answer from among the choices given and fill in the corresponding circle on the answer sheet.

The following sentences test correctness and effectiveness of expression. Part of each sentence or the entire sentence is underlined; beneath each sentence are five ways of phrasing the underlined material. Choice A repeats the original phrasing; the other four choices are different. If you think the original phrasing produces a better sentence than any of the alternatives, select choice A; if not, select one of the other choices.

In making your selection, follow the requirements of standard written English; that is, pay attention to grammar, choice of words, sentence construction, and punctuation. Your selection should result in the most effective sentence—clear and precise, without awkwardness or ambiguity.

EXAMPLE:

Bobby Flay baked his first cake <u>and he was thirteen years old then</u>.

(A) and he was thirteen years old then
(B) when he was thirteen
(C) at age thirteen years old
(D) upon the reaching of thirteen years
(E) at the time when he was thirteen

Ⓐ●ⒸⒹⒺ

1. In everything from obedience training to home protection, pet owners have become so <u>knowledgeable, and</u> professional trainers often adopt their methods.

   (A) knowledgeable, and
   (B) knowledgeable, also
   (C) knowledgeable that
   (D) knowledgeable therefore
   (E) knowledgeable when

2. Since hiking trails need to be clearly marked, <u>parks departments requiring significant funds</u>.

   (A) parks departments requiring significant funds
   (B) parks departments being what requires significant funds
   (C) parks departments require significant funds
   (D) significant funds are required by parks departments
   (E) significant funds is what they require in parks departments

3. To commemorate its centennial, the town has installed an <u>exhibit, it consists of</u> five parts, each focusing on twenty years of the community's history.

   (A) exhibit, it consists of
   (B) exhibit, it consisting
   (C) exhibit, and it will consist of
   (D) exhibit that consists of.
   (E) exhibit, they consist of

4. With audiences following reality shows with unprecedented frequency, <u>producers are urging networks to increase their reality programming, which</u> may ultimately replace other, more substantive, programs.

   (A) producers are urging networks to increase their reality programming
   (B) producers have been urging that networks increase its programming of reality television; those
   (C) the networks ought to increase their programming of reality television, as urged by producers, because they
   (D) producers urge about increasing reality television programming, which
   (E) more reality television should be programmed by networks, urge producers, which

GO ON TO THE NEXT PAGE ➡

5. Contest judges argue about <u>what is the determination of the ultimate Halloween costume and how to critique it</u>.

(A) what is the determination of the ultimate Halloween costume and how to critique it
(B) how to determine the ultimate Halloween costume, and also its critique
(C) how to determine and critique the ultimate Halloween costume
(D) determining the ultimate Halloween costume as well as critique it
(E) the determination of the ultimate Halloween costume and critiquing it

6. In the sixteenth century Michelangelo was as celebrated for his sculpture <u>and also for his</u> painting, and he furthermore found success in architecture, poetry and engineering.

(A) and also for his
(B) as well as for his
(C) as he was for his
(D) but for his
(E) but also for his

7. Although she had previously been pleased to be photographed and written about, <u>it was after her brief and mysterious disappearance that Agatha Christie had an avoidance of publicity</u>.

(A) it was after her brief and mysterious disappearance that Agatha Christie had an avoidance of publicity
(B) it was after her brief and mysterious disappearance that Agatha Christie avoided publicity
(C) the brief and mysterious disappearance of Agatha Christie who then avoided publicity
(D) Agatha Christie's brief and mysterious disappearance an avoidance of publicity
(E) Agatha Christie avoided publicity after her brief and mysterious disappearance

8. One of the most unusual animals in the world, <u>eggs are laid by the platypus, which is a mammal</u>.

(A) eggs are laid by the platypus, which is a mammal
(B) the platypus, who is a mammal, lays eggs
(C) the platypus who is an egg-laying mammal
(D) the platypus is a mammal that lays eggs
(E) the mammal which lays eggs is the platypus

9. Many pre- and post-World War II military pilots <u>were believers in their commanding officers' authority, demonstrate national pride</u>, and the importance of discipline.

(A) were believers in their commanding officers' authority, demonstrate national pride
(B) are believers in the authority of their commanding officers, national pride being demonstrated
(C) who believed in the authority of their commanding officers, demonstrate national pride
(D) believed in the authority of their commanding officers, to demonstrate national pride
(E) believed in the authority of their commanding officers, the demonstration of national pride

10. A psychological novel, such as George Eliot's *Middlemarch*, is characterized by its focus on the ways the characters' internal states can trigger <u>events in the external</u>.

(A) events in the external
(B) external events
(C) events external
(D) events externally
(E) in external events

11. Many of William Blake's <u>etchings were inspired by his notions of good and evil, accompanied by</u> subject-appropriate writings.

(A) etchings were inspired by his notions of good and evil, accompanied by
(B) etchings had their inspiration from his notions of good and evil, accompanied by
(C) etchings, inspired by his notions of good and evil, were accompanied by
(D) etchings, which were inspired by his notions of good and evil and which are accompanied by
(E) etchings, being inspired by his notions of good and evil, accompanied by

12. Among the most inspirational and humanitarian films of all time, <u>Frank Capra has long been known for his</u> uplifting messages about the basic goodness within people.

(A) Frank Capra has long been known for his
(B) Frank Capra, having become well-known for long
(C) and the films of Frank Capra are known for
(D) films by Frank Capra have become known because they have
(E) the films of Frank Capra have long been known for their

GO ON TO THE NEXT PAGE

13. When the students take a trip on the intracoastal waterway system next month, they will learn <u>facts with which they have heretofore been unacquainted</u>.

   (A) facts with which they have heretofore been unacquainted
   (B) facts with which they haven't been acquainted with yet
   (C) facts, being, heretofore, unacquainted with them
   (D) facts with which they haven't never been acquainted
   (E) facts, being unacquainted with them heretofore beforehand

14. The painting style of Picasso, a mix of classical composition and innovative techniques, was regarded as more <u>progressive than his contemporaries</u>.

   (A) progressive than his contemporaries
   (B) progressive than his contemporaries were painting
   (C) progressive than were his contemporaries
   (D) progressive than that of his contemporaries
   (E) progressive than his contemporaries, when it came to painting

STOP
**If you finish before time is called, you may check your work on this section only.
Do not turn to any other section in the test.**

Chapter 6
Practice Test 2
Answers and
Explanations

PRACTICE TEST 2: ANSWER KEY

2 Reading	3 Math	5 Reading	6 Writing	7 Math	8 Math	9 Reading	10 Writing
1. D	1. D	1. A	1. A	1. E	1. C	1. C	1. C
2. D	2. B	2. B	2. C	2. B	2. A	2. A	2. C
3. E	3. E	3. E	3. B	3. B	3. C	3. A	3. D
4. C	4. B	4. B	4. D	4. B	4. A	4. B	4. A
5. B	5. D	5. D	5. B	5. B	5. E	5. E	5. C
6. D	6. A	6. D	6. A	6. A	6. D	6. E	6. C
7. A	7. A	7. C	7. E	7. C	7. C	7. E	7. E
8. A	8. E	8. B	8. C	8. C	8. B	8. C	8. D
9. D	9. D	9. A	9. D	9. 30	9. A	9. B	9. E
10. D	10. C	10. B	10. E	10. 45	10. D	10. C	10. B
11. B	11. C	11. B	11. A	11. 144	11. C	11. D	11. C
12. A	12. D	12. D	12. B	12. $1 < x < 3$	12. E	12. A	12. E
13. C	13. E	13. D	13. C	13. 710	13. B	13. A	13. A
14. E	14. D	14. C	14. B	14 4	14. D	14. D	14. D
15. A	15. E	15. D	15. C	15. 12	15. B	15. E	
16. A	16. E	16. E	16. D	16. 20	16. C	16. C	
17. C	17. A	17. B	17. E	17. 10		17. C	
18. D	18. B	18. A	18. C	18. $\dfrac{20}{9}$ or 2.22		18. B	
19. B	19. A	19. E	19. B			19. D	
20. C	20. D	20. C	20. E				
21. A		21. D	21. A				
22. E		22. B	22. E				
23. B		23. A	23. E				
24. B		24. E	24. C				
			25. D				
			26. D				
			27. D				
			28. C				
			29. B				
			30. A				
			31. B				
			32. A				
			33. E				
			34. C				
			35. D				

EXPLANATIONS

Section 2

1. **D** Who is Douglas? Someone who *misses deadlines and finishes projects late.* He puts things off. He is a *procrastinator.*

2. **D** What do we know about the referee's decision? Well, after fifteen minutes the rain cleared up, so the decision was probably made too early. (B) and (D) work, but keep any answer choices that you don't know. Considering the second blank, the game was canceled, so conditions must have been bad originally, which means that now they are good. Only (C) and (D) work, so (D) must be the right answer.

3. **E** *Most fish* are one way, and the *labyrinth fish* is another way. Since the *labyrinth fish* is different from *most fish*, a good word for the first blank would be "different" or "unusual." Since it is different from the majority of fish who breathe only water, it must be able to breathe air as well. So it is "able to" breathe air. We have a word for the second blank. The phrase "able to" is a little awkward alongside *breathing*, but as long as its meaning matches the sentence, it is fine. (E) most closely matches the meanings of "different" and "able to."

4. **C** We know we are looking for a word that means something negative because of *sapping strength* and *depriving one of energy.* Hopefully that helps you eliminate a few answers, but the words here are tough. If you don't know the meaning of at least three words, this probably a good one to skip. (C) is the only answer choice here that means *sapping strength.*

5. **B** What do we know about Bearden's talents? He produced paintings, wrote music, and was a baseball player. That is a really wide range of abilities; so our word must mean "wide ranging." Only (B) *eclectic* fits. The words here are really tough, if you don't know the vocab, or you can't eliminate anything, skip this question.

6. **D** The author states that for a *true craftsman…the slightest variation* (in the sound a tool makes) *will cause him to alter his stroke, or pause to sharpen the tool's blade.* In other words, *subtle changes* cause him to *respond* (D). The other answers are not supported by the passage.

7. **A** A metaphor is a comparison that is literally untrue, but conveys the author's point. Tools don't actually *sing, cough, wheeze,* or *hum.* Therefore (A) is the correct answer.

8. **A** Use Process of Elimination to cross off all answers that are true. *Big-stick approach* tells us (B) is true. *Curbed the abuse and exploitation of workers* shows that (C) is true. *Created the system of national parks long before environmentalism was fashionable* means that (D) is true. *Was awarded a Nobel Prize in 1906 for his diplomatic efforts* shows that (E) is true. Only (A) is false, because *used his executive authority to break up the monopolies of large companies* shows that he <u>did</u> have an *interest in regulating businesses.*

9. **D** Eliminate wrong answers. (A) is too broad; only one president is discussed in the passage. (B) is too narrow, because *foreign affairs* is only part of the passage (and *interest* is not really discussed). (C) is off base and too broad; the passage doesn't go beyond talking about Roosevelt. (E) is no good because there's no *character analysis.* (D) is the best answer.

10.   **D**   The narrator's *complex about music* involves *hopes* that *crashed too low* (lines 1–3), making her obsess negatively about the concert she performed in. Why is she so upset? The narrator relates that her poor performance at Town Hall made her doubt her ambition to be a singer, but she eventually resolved to do it anyway. This is best paraphrased in answer (D). The *complex* in this passage refers to an exaggerated concern or fear, and (A) is a trap answer that uses a different meaning of *complex*—complicated. In addition, the passage never mentions the narrator's musical tastes, so eliminate this answer choice. (B) is incorrect because the passage doesn't tell us if she changed careers, although it implies she did not. (C) may be true, but it does not explain the *complex*. (E) is incorrect because it contradicts the main idea.

11.   **B**   The author had wanted to be *one of the fortunate swimmers* in the *mainstream of American musical life*. She had wanted, in other words, to be famous. (B), *desire to be a popular singer*, is basically saying that she wanted to be famous.

12.   **A**   This sentence describes the narrator's memories of the performance at Town Hall: Some are vivid, while she pushes (thrusts) others aside. What emotions does this image reveal? She keeps *rehashing the concert in my mind*—not because she's thrilled (the performance *lost money* and *she might have done better*)—but because, we find, she's upset (*the fiasco had shaken me*) (lines 7–22). (A) most nearly means "upset."

13.   **C**   The question asks which two contradictory statements or facts constitute the *misrepresentation*. Reading the reference in context, we find that the narrator believes she might have performed better if she *had not been told the auditorium was full*, and that *a misrepresentation like that can throw you off balance*. Tying together these two statements, we can conclude that the misrepresentation refers to the number of people

actually in attendance versus those the narrator expected to see. (C) best expresses this relationship. (A) is incorrect because the author's actual skill as a singer is not mentioned here. (B) is incorrect because the narrator states that she does not know how much money she was promised. (D) is incorrect because the reaction of the audience is never mentioned. (E) is incorrect because the narrator's desire to please everyone is not mentioned in this paragraph.

14. **E** The third paragraph says that, after the Town Hall performance, the author *stopped going regularly to Mr. Boghetti's studio*, because *the fiasco had shaken* her. So the paragraph is giving us some details about what happened to the author as a result of her Town Hall performance. (E), *the consequences of a performance*, matches this. (A), *the importance of rehearsals*, is not mentioned in the passage.

15. **A** According to the sentence, the author realizes that *the criticism was right* and that she had *given the critics the opportunity* to write negative reviews of her performance. This suggests that the author knows that she had a role in earning the unfavorable criticism. This is best paraphrased in (A). Answers (C) and (E) contradict the author's point in this sentence; she does not blame the critics, as far as we know, and she does take responsibility for her mediocre performance. (B) and (D) are incorrect because her career isn't mentioned at all in this reference.

16. **A** *The figure's face* is the only feature mentioned in both passages. Passage 1 mentions *that odd, skull-like face*, and Passage 2 mentions that *something in that face holds us rapt*.

17. **C** Monica Bohm-Duchen argues that *as the painting became more accessible, it became more admired*. The lines in Passage 1 refer to ways in which the painting was copied; Monica Bohm-Duchen believes it was those copies that helped to make *The Scream* well-known. So she would probably view the copying of the painting as (C) *events that*

may themselves have added to the renown of The Scream. (E) is incorrect because we don't know that the copies have *hindered art critics ability to judge The Scream objectively,* the copies have simply made more people view *The Scream* favorably.

18.   **D**   Both authors believe that *The Scream* (D) *ought to be viewed and analyzed.* The author of Passage 1 spends most of the passage describing what it's like to view *The Scream,* and the author of Passage 2 states that *the reader* should *judge the painting itself.* (A) and (C) are not mentioned in either passage. (B) is referred to only in the second passage. (E) is contradicted by both passages: the main features of *The Scream* are actually immediately understandable.

19.   **B**   The quote from Edvard Munch serves to tell us a little about the scream that gave *The Scream* its name. In other words, it's trying to (B) *establish a context.*

20.   **C**   The passage states that Munch has captured a *raw, gut feeling.* So we want a word that means something along the lines of *gut feeling,* or "direct and obvious." Only (C), *stark* matches this.

21.   **A**   The quotation marks are there to hint that the *aimless "masterpieces" of a bored child* are not actually masterpieces at all, and that the critics did not think too much of *The Scream.* So they were (A) *skeptical of The Scream's aesthetic properties.* The passage does not indicate whether or not the author of Passage 2 thought they were (C) *incorrect.*

22.   **E**   Leonard Bartin points out that *The Scream* is *able to provoke a response, and therefore great,* and that *something in that face holds us rapt.* The author of Passage 1 seems to agree, because he says that *the eye invariably falls upon that odd, skull-like face,* and that *Munch has captured a raw, gut feeling.* So they both agree that people (E) *tends to elicit a strong involuntary response from viewers.* None of the other answers are mentioned by both the author of Passage 1 and Leonard Bartin.

23. **B** The author of Passage 2 mentions *Mozart's Requiem* to show that *Devoid of context, the central figure is no longer a piece functioning in a larger work of art*. So just taking one little part of a work of art isn't enough to really understand it; we need to look at the whole thing. Viewing just the main figure of *The Scream* isn't the same as viewing the full painting, because it's lacking all those other things that the author of Passage 1 mentioned: the sky, the river, the overall composition, et cetera. So the author is trying to (B) *illustrate that a simplified version* (like just seeing the main figure of *The Scream*) *can lack crucial elements* (the rest of the painting). (A) is wrong because the author isn't simply listing works of art that *are often best known in shorter forms*, he's mentioning another work of art that is missing something when shortened.

24. **B** Let's cross off some wrong answers. (A) is wrong because the second passage does not *argue for a purely intellectual interpretation*, it instead argues that the painting should be judged on its own merits. Similarly, (C) is wrong because the second passage does not *debate its artistic merits*. (D) is incorrect because the first passage does not *speculate about its intended meaning*. (E) is wrong because the first passage does not mention anything about *its unique place in art history*. (B) is the correct answer. The first passage *stresses its stylistic features*, because it talks for two paragraphs about what *The Scream* looks like. The second passage *emphasizes possible reasons for its cultural significance*, because it talks about why *The Scream* became so popular: it was copied a lot.

Section 3

1. **D** Begin by converting the 1 foot the snail traveled into 12 inches. Now set up a proportion: $\dfrac{12 \text{ inches}}{48 \text{ minutes}} = \dfrac{1 \text{ inch}}{x \text{ minutes}}$. Cross-multiply and solve for x: $12x = 48$, so $x = 4$.

2. **B** The question tells you that to get each term after the first, you multiply the previous by $\frac{1}{2}$ and add 1. For example, $\frac{1}{2} \times 66 + 1 = 33 + 1 = 34$, the second term. So $m = \frac{1}{2} \times 18 + 1 = 9 + 1 = 10$. You can double-check this by predicting that the next term will be $\frac{1}{2} \times 10 + 1 = 5 + 1 = 6$, which indeed it is.

3. **E** Translate the equation from English into math. It will read $3y + 4 = 11$. Although you can solve for y and then find $9y$, you can also solve for $3y$ and then triple the value to find $9y$. Because $3y = 7$, that means $9y = 21$. If you selected answer choice (A), you chose the value of y. If you selected answer choice (B), you chose the value of $3y$.

4. **B** Add the amounts given for 2001 and 2003: $12 + 15 = 27$. Subtract from that the amount given for 2002: $27 - 19 = 8$.

5. **D** A circle graph contains 360 degrees, so you need to determine the proportion of the circle that year 2005 will take up. So, add up all of the values from 2001 through 2006. The total is 90. The amount in 2005 (30) is one-third of the total, the central angle of the sector for 2005 must be one-third of the circle, or 120 degrees. If you selected (A), you chose the number from 2005, rather than its proportion of the whole. If you selected (C), you chose the total value of all years, rather than the proportion.

6. **A** A reflection means that the figure is simply flipped over the line of reflection, so a reflection about the x-axis means that the figure should end up like a mirror image below the x-axis. The figures in (C) and (E) are above the x-axis, so eliminate them. Of the three remaining, we need the flat edge of the figure facing the x-axis, so eliminate (C). Lastly, we need the figure that has the triangle on the right portion of

the figure, as it is in the original graph. (A) is the only graph that has all the qualities of a figure flipped over the *x*-axis.

7. **A** Draw a line to divide the figure into two rectangles. Then identify the lengths of all the sides. If you drew a horizontal line, the upper rectangle will measure 3 by 3, and the lower rectangle will measure 9 by 2. Find the area of both rectangles (9 and 18), and add the areas. If you drew a vertical line, the left rectangle will measure 3 by 5, and the right rectangle will measure 6 by 2. Find the area of both rectangles (15 and 12), and add them. Either way, the area is 27 (A).

8. **E** We need a value for *a* that results in either 6 or –6 in the parentheses so that the squared value is 36. Only (E), –2, gives us –6 in the parentheses. All the other answers give a much greater value than 36 when replacing *a* in the equation above.

9. **D** The easiest way to solve this problem is to fill in the variable with a number that fits the requirement $p < 0$. If $p = -2$, the four numbers from left to right are: 10, 6, –2, –6. Thus (D) has the least value. If you selected answer choice (A), you selected a positive *p* or missed that the two negative signs cancel out.

10. **C** Plug In the day value of any point from the graph into the equations in the answers to see which equation yields the corresponding calls value. Whatever point you select, the answer will be (C). For example, if you select day 4 ($D = 4$), you need an equation that yields 6 calls ($C = 6$). The four wrong equations, however, will yield *C* values of 2 or 8.

11. **C** The easiest way to tackle this is to come up with your own numbers for the variables. Of the two equations, $b = c^2$ is easier to work with. If $c = 2$, then $b = 4$. Use this value for *b* in the equation above the question. $a = (4)^2 + (4)^3 = 16 + 64 = 80$. Now use $c = 2$ in the answer choices and see which gives 80: (A) equals 32 and (B) will definitely be larger

than 80. (C) gives 16 + 64 = 80, a match, but check the rest: (D) gives 8 + 16 = 24; (E) gives 4 + 8 = 12. Only (C) matches. You could also use exponent rules to solve this. Replace b in the equation $a = b^2 + b^3$ with c^2 to get $a = (c^2)^2 + (c^2)^3 = c^4 + c^6$, answer (C).

12. **D** Note that triangle ABD and ECD share angle D. Also, angle C and angle B both have the measure m. Because two sets of the three pairs of angles are the same, the third set of angles must also be the same, meaning the triangles are similar. In similar triangles, the ratio of the lengths of any two common sides is the same as the ratio of the lengths of any other two common sides. Because the ratio of EC to AB is 6 to 9, the ratio of CD to BD will also be 6 to 9. However, the question asks for the ratio of BC to BD, so that ratio would be 3 to 9, which reduces to 1 to 3. If you selected answer choice (B), you found the ratio of CD to BD.

13. **E** Because the median is the middle number, write the numbers in order: 8, 8, 8, 10, 10, 10, 10, 12. Then, try out the answer choices. Although each of the five answer choices will result in a median of 10, answer choice (E) will create a second mode. The mode is number that appears most. There are four 10s; if $x = 8$, there would also be four 8s.

14. **D** To find the total number of items in A and C we need to add up all six numbers that are in any of the regions within A or C. 3 + 4 + 4 + 6 + 5 + 5 = 27, answer (D) is correct. (B) is the sum of the number of elements in A and C and the intersection of A and C. (C) is the total number of items in sets A, B, and C. (E) is the number of elements in the intersection of A and C.

15. E   Plug In numbers for x and y. If x is directly proportional to $\sqrt{y}$, then

it follows that $\dfrac{x_1}{\sqrt{y_1}} = \dfrac{x_2}{\sqrt{y_2}}$. Some good numbers to Plug In would be

$\dfrac{10}{\sqrt{25}} = \dfrac{8}{\sqrt{16}}$. Using these numbers, check the answers to see which

is inversely proportional to your value of y, which we found to be 25

when x is 10. The inverse proportion takes the form of $x_1 y_1 = x_2 y_2$.

With answer choice (E), the inverse proportion would be

$y_1 \times \dfrac{1}{x_1{}^2} = y_1 \times \dfrac{1}{x_2{}^2}$. If you Plug In your initial values for x and y, you get

$25 \times \dfrac{1}{100} = 16 \times \dfrac{1}{64} = \dfrac{1}{4}$. Because sides of the equation are equal,

(E) is the correct answer. If you chose (A), you used direct instead of

inverse variation.

16. E   Because function g is the absolute value of function f, no negative
points can appear on the graph of function g. Eliminate (A), (B), and
(C). Nothing else changed between $f(x)$ and $g(x)$, so the graph of g
should be the same as in f except any negative points will appear as a
mirror image reflected about the x axis, as in (E).

17. **A** Check each statement one at a time and eliminate answer choices. Because $f(x) = f(2y)$, you know $f(x) + f(x)$ is the same as $f(2y) + f(2y)$, which can be simplified as $2f(2y)$. Thus, statement I must be true—eliminate answer choices (B) and (D). Is $2f(2y)$ the same thing as $f(4y)$? Not necessarily—consider the function $f(x) = x^2$. In that case $2f(2y) = 2 \times 4y^2 = 8y^2$ while $f(4y) = 16y^2$. Thus, statement II is incorrect—eliminate (E). Now check statement III to see if $2f(2y)$ is the same thing as $2[f(y) + f(y)]$. The 2 in statement III must be distributed to both functions within the brackets, resulting in $2f(y) + 2f(y)$ is not equivalent to $2f(2y)$ if again, the function happens to be $f(x) = x^2$: $2y^2 + 2y^2 = 4y^2$ whereas previously we found $2f(2y) = 8y^2$. Only statement I is true, so (A) is correct.

18. **B** The formula for the volume of a cylinder is at the beginning of every SAT math section. $V = \pi r^2 h$. We need to know the increase in volume when the smaller cylinder is added to the water in the vase. One way to so this is to find the volume of the water without the smaller cylinder and the volume with the cylinder added and subtract to find the difference. A more straightforward way, since we know that the height of the water in the larger cylinder rises by 4 inches, is to use that height and the base measurement of the vase in the volume formula to find that $\pi 6^2 \times 4 = 36\pi \times 4 = 144\pi$—which equals the volume of the cylinder that was dropped into the larger cylinder. The question asks for the height of the smaller cylinder, which we can find since we know the base radius of the smaller cylinder and the volume: $144\pi = \pi 4^2 \times h = 16\pi h$. Divide both sides by 16π to get h alone and find that $\frac{144\pi}{16\pi} = h$, $s = 9$, choice (B).

19. **A** Let's figure out the coordinates of point C. Parabolas are symmetrical, so the left side looks like the right side. Since the point at $(2, 8)$ is 2 to the left of the middle point of the parabola, the point $(a, 8)$ will be 2 to the right of the middle point, so it's at $(6, 8)$. Now use the slope formula to find the slope of $\overline{BC}$, which is $\dfrac{2-8}{3-6} = \dfrac{-6}{-3} = 2$.

20. **D** Try each number for x. There is no mode, which means that no numbers can repeat themselves. Eliminate (B) and (E). Now try each number left. If $x = 2$, then $x^3 = 8$, which is not the median of $\dfrac{1}{4}$, $\dfrac{1}{2}$, 2, 4, and 8, respectively. Eliminate (A). If $x = \dfrac{1}{2}$, then $x^3 = \dfrac{1}{8}$, which is not the median of 4, 2, $\dfrac{1}{2}$, $\dfrac{1}{4}$, and $\dfrac{1}{8}$. Eliminate (C). (D) is the only answer left. If $x = -\dfrac{1}{2}$, then $x^3 = -\dfrac{1}{8}$, which is the median of 4, –2, $-\dfrac{1}{2}$, $\dfrac{1}{4}$, and $-\dfrac{1}{8}$.

Section 5

1. **A** The clue for the blank is *randomly occurring*. Since these reactions are *proof*, the blank should mean close to the clue. *Spontaneous* means *randomly occurring*, so (A) is the best choice.

2. **B** We don't know what is going on with the *patient* until the end of the sentence when we find out that the patient was able to go home, even sooner *than anticipated*. So originally the doctor must have been worried, *but after the surgery the patient* must have been better. The first

blank must mean "worry," so eliminate (A), (C), and (D). The second blank should mean "got better," so eliminate (E), leaving (B) as the only answer that fits.

3. E   The clue for the second blank is that *none of the petitioners were able to gather signatures*. The blank must mean something close to "not supporting." This eliminates choices (A), (C), and (D). The word that precedes the first blank, *obvious*, with the clue for the second blank tells us that the first blank must mean something close to "a showing." Between (B) and (E), choice (E) is closest.

4. B   The clue *code of conduct* tells us that the meaning of the first blank should be something related to the kind of conduct *school administrators* would approve of. (A), and (E) are completely unrelated to the clue and can be eliminated. The use of *in order to* tells us that the second blank should also be similar to the first blank. *Obedient* and *tractable* are close in meaning while the pairs of words in (C) and (D) are not synonymous. Thus (B) is the best answer.

5. D   The second half of the sentence serves as a clue that parallels the first half of the sentence. *Ridiculing* is the clue for the first blank. This alone points us to *lampoons*, which means "to mock" or "satirize." The word *procedures* is the clue for the second blank. The word *methodology* fits this clue best. All of the remaining answer choices "sound good." The words could all make sense in reference to an article and a piece of legislation, respectively. Remember not to go by how things "sound." Only one answer will agree with the clue.

6. D   The words *even though* tell us that the blank should mean something opposite of the clue *increase risk of heart disease*. A good word to use would be "beneficial." (A) is opposite of what we are looking for and (B), (C), and (E) do not mean "beneficial." *Salutary* in (D) means "beneficial to health" and is the best answer.

7. **C** The use of the colon tells us that the meaning of the first half of the sentence must mean something similar to the second half. The clue here is *clarify difficult topics*. Since the word before the blank is *avoid*, we need a word in combination with this one to produce the same thing as the clue. The word for the blank should mean something close to "making difficult." The closest in meaning is *obfuscating* in (C).

8. **B** The clue for the blank is *never chose one side* and *intentionally misled*. The blank must mean something similar because of the colon, which tells us that the first and second part of the sentence must have similar meanings. The best choice is *equivocated* which means "to use deliberately unclear language."

9. **A** Passage 2 says that Austen's work *is caustic and subversive, and seeks to undermine the assumptions of the society she lived in*. Passage 1, however, tells us that fans view Austen's works as *affectionate and witty portraits of the English gentry*. Therefore, the view offered in Passage 2 doesn't represent the view of most fans. (A) paraphrases this nicely. None of the other answers are supported by the passages.

10. **B** Passage 1 says that for the *readers, Austen's novels evoke an idyllic past… refreshingly free of weighty political or philosophical concerns*. However, the author of Passage 2 states that Austen's works are *profoundly political*. (B) clearly expresses this difference between the 2 passages. The other answers are not supported by the passages.

11. **B** The reference to Passage 2 in this question is mostly a distraction. We want to know what Passage 1 says about *Austen's depiction of the British upper class*. Passage 1 states that for fans, Austen's works are *affectionate and witty portraits of the English gentry*. Thus, they are *largely sympathetic* (B).

12. **D**   Passage 1 states that for the *adoring fans,* Austen's works are *affectionate and witty portraits of the English gentry.* Passage 2 states that Austen *frequently subjected* (the British upper class) *to withering criticism.* Therefore, the 2 passages disagree about *the extent to which her work is critical...of society* (D). We can also use process of elimination: Both passages suggest her family was important, so eliminate (A). Neither passage mentions the *accuracy* of her depictions, so eliminate (B). Both passages suggest that *English society was a central topic,* so eliminate (C). Both passages indicate Austen is an important author, so eliminate (E).

13. **D**   Come up with your own word to replace *image.* An important clue is the word *idea* right after the colon. So, something like "idea" or "belief" would work well. Only (D), *perception,* is a match.

14. **C**   In the second paragraph, the author uses words such as *enemy, arsenal, chemical weapons, bombard,* and *attack* to suggest that the gardener wages war on slugs. Thus (C), a *military strategy,* fits best. The other answers are not supported by the passage.

15. **D**   The author describes the *important consequences* as a vicious circle: *contamination, followed by...a slow depletion...,* *followed by more contamination.* (D), an unintended reaction, is a good match. The other answers are not supported by the passage.

16. **E**   Pursuing the *cherished ideal* leads to the vicious circle discussed in the explanation to question 15. Therefore, the author sees it as *misguided* (E).

17. **B**   In the previous paragraph, the author shows how trying to wipe out slugs doesn't work. In this paragraph, the author *proposes an alternative course of action*: learning to live with the slugs. Thus, the correct answer is (B). The author doesn't *explain people's responses* (A) or *offer evidence of destruction* (C); he doesn't *praise* anything (D), and there is no position that we know is *unpopular* (E).

18. **A** The lines provide evidence that the slug's *nefarious reputation is at least partially unwarranted.* (A), *a defense,* is the best answer. The other answer choices are not supported by the passage.

19. **E** The slug is like a recycling center in that it can take discarded products, transform them into the nutrients that plants need to thrive, and release these nutrients into the soil. (E) paraphrases this sentence. (A) and (B) are not supported at all. (C) looks good except for the part about harmful chemicals, which are not mentioned in this paragraph. (D) is extreme, and there's no direct discussion of artificial fertilizers in this paragraph.

20. **C** The author's attitude is positive because the *viscous, slime-like excretions* are beneficial; they provide the *nutrients that plants need to thrive.* (C) is the only answer choice that expresses a positive sentiment.

21. **D** Come up with your own word to replace *welcome.* Something like "bring" would work, because the author states that *providing a habitat for these creatures* would help to hold down the slug population. (D), *introduce,* is the best match. (C), return, is close, but we don't know that the natural predators had been in the garden before now, so there's no way of knowing if they are returning to the garden.

22. **B** The author tells us not only that slugs like certain plants (*Lettuce, Zinnias, and Marigolds are all considered delicacies*), but also that gardeners don't view these plants as terribly valuable (*the loss of a few of these plants will not distress the typical gardener*). Answer choice (B) paraphrases this nicely. (A) and (C) are too extreme, while (D) and (E) are not mentioned.

23. **A** The phrase *it is true* applies to the statement that *these measures may seem cumbersome* (if you don't know what cumbersome means, the word *inconvenience* can help you out). Thus, the author *recognizes that*

his suggestions may be viewed as burdensome (A). (B) is the opposite of what the author believes, while (C), (D), and (E) are not mentioned in the passage.

24.   E   The purpose of the last paragraph is to reiterate the author's main point, as stated in the first and fourth paragraphs. (E) is a good match. The last paragraph doesn't have *evidence* (A); it doesn't refer to *further study* (B); it doesn't *intensify* (C), and it doesn't *downplay the impact of an approach* (D).

Section 6

1.   A   The sentence is correct as written. (B) lacks a necessary helping verb to use with *involved*. (C) and (E) both use -ing forms, which are usually wrong, as they are here. (D) changes the direction and meaning of the sentence.

2.   C   The original sentence contains a misplaced modifier error and is passive. According to the original construction *a sense of homesickness* is *like many freshmen*. It should be *my roommates* who are *like many freshmen*. This eliminates (A) and (B). (D) is not a complete sentence, so we can eliminate it. (E) is redundant and passive and, therefore, not as good an answer as (C).

3.   B   The phrase *is the reason why* in the original sentence is redundant and therefore incorrect. (B) eliminates this construction and simplifies the sentence. (C) and (E) repeat the error found in (A). (D) awkwardly uses *resulting from*, which creates a modifying error.

4.   D   The correct idiom is *not only...but also*. (A), (B), (C), and (E) lack the correct idiom. (D) uses the idiom correctly and keeps *convey* and *instill* parallel.

5.   B   The easiest way to find the right answer in this one is to compare the verbs. You want the past tense *let*, so eliminate (C), (D), and (E). Answer (A) contains a comma splice which makes the sentence a run-on. You're then left with (B).

6.   A   The sentence is correct as written: it keeps the list parallel and has the proper idiom *both…and*. The first thing *success* depends on is *regulation of taxes for small businesses*, a noun followed by prepositional phrases. (C) and (E) don't fit the pattern. (D) doesn't join the parts of the list correctly; it sounds as if *education of the public* must be regulated. (B) is missing an "and" needed to join the parts of the list. (A) joins the parts correctly and has the same structure as the first part of the list.

7.   E   Watch out for subject-verb agreement errors when a lot of words separate the subject and the verb. In this case the phrase enclosed by the commas *though many causes…centuries* separate the singular subject *one reason* from the plural verb *are*. (A), (B), and (C) contain verb agreement errors. (D) creates an incomplete sentence. (E) correctly matches a singular verb to the singular noun *reason*.

8.   C   In the underlined portion of the sentence, it's unclear what *many* refers to, so you can eliminate (A), (B), and (E) because they don't include *people*. Between the two answers left, (C) is preferable because it's a clearer construction. The extra *they* and the *-ing* ending in answer (D) make the sentence awkward and confusing.

9.   D   This is a question where the right answer still sounds strange, but you can get there using POE. (A) can't be right because the subject *program* doesn't agree with the verb *were met*. (E) is wrong because the singular subject can't be paired with a plural pronoun. (B) uses the wrong verb tense, and you don't need the pronoun *it* in (C). You're left with (D), which may sound weird, but doesn't break any grammar rules.

10. E Eliminate (A), (B), and (C) because they're redundant. *Imminent* means something is about to happen, so you don't need to say it twice. (E) is a better choice than (D) because it's a clearer construction; there's no need for the word *thing* in (D).

11. A This sentence is correct as written. All the others use incorrect conjunctions.

12. B The sentence as written is a sentence fragment. The error is in (B) because it is missing a verb. You'd need to say it *was* translated in order for this to be a complete sentence.

13. C The wrong verb form is in (C). This sentence should use the infinitive form of "fund" in order to read *Steven has fought to fund*.

14. B Each verb should be in the same tense, so if aspirin *causes thinning* then it also "delays," instead of *delay*, as in (B).

15. C The underlined portion (C) is incorrect: *revealing* should be the infinitive form of "reveal" rather than the gerund. This sentence should read *magicians' unwillingness to reveal secrets of the trade*.

16. D *Incredible* modifies *strong*, so *incredible* needs to be in its adverb form: "incredibly" in (D).

17. E There are no errors in the sentence as it is written.

18. C *Had been* would mean that she had been the first to eat a slice, but now something changed, and she wasn't the first person any longer. Had been is called the "past perfect tense," and is used when something had gone on for a while, but then changed. Gordon ate a slice at one point in time, however, so we want "was" instead.

19. B Always check that verbs are in the correct tense. The verb *is* is in the simple present tense, yet the context tells us that Bretney was promoted *last year* and has been a hard worker *ever since*. To indicate that an action began in the past and continues to the present, use the present perfect tense, "has been."

20. E There are no errors in the sentence as it is written.

21. A The verb after *plants* refers to *the salve an*d, therefore, *are* must be singular *is* to read *The salve made from the leaves of cactus plants is highly efficient*.

22. E There are no errors in the sentence as it is written.

23. E There are no errors in the sentence as it is written.

24. C This sentence has a noun-pronoun agreement error. *The class* is a singular noun, but (C) contains the pronoun *they*. A collective noun like *group* agrees with the singular pronoun "it."

25. D This sentence has an idiom error in (D): the wrong preposition follows *hope*. The idiomatically correct phrase is *in the hope of receiving permission*.

26. D The correct idiom is phrased *overflowing with* rather than *overflowing from*.

27. D The words *more...than* tell us that the sentence compares two things, and the parts of the comparison need to be parallel. (D) is incorrect because it compares Noah's *music* to *other bands*, not to the music of other bands.

28. C This sentence has noun-pronoun agreement problem: Because the noun *fines* is plural, the singular pronoun *it* cannot be used to replace *fines*.

29. **B** The plural pronoun *they* refers to the singular noun person and is therefore incorrect. It should be replaced with "he or she."

30. **A** (B) would least help the paragraph. (D) and (E) might be interesting footnotes, but they would not add as much to the paragraph as (C) or (A). (C) would add another dimension to the passage but (B) is the most straightforward way to enhance the essay.

31. **B** (A) has the wrong verb tense compared to the past tense of the rest of the passage and has misplaced commas. (C) has redundant use of *production*. (D) changing the verb from something that means "were influenced by" for the more direct and active *imitated* changes the meaning of the sentence and the verb *uses* is in the wrong tense. (E) is wordy and uses the incorrect verb tense.

32. **A** (B) is tempting because it there is more than one artist mentioned in the passage, but this asks about a single paragraph. (C) is mentioned only in the third paragraph. (D) is the least supported answer. (E) is tempting, until one looks at the subject of the sentence—the essay's writer is not updating the opera; he's writing about Baz Lurhmann's updated version.

33. **E** The original sentence presented is actually a comma splice: It contains two complete ideas without any punctuation. (B) has an independent descriptive phrase between the commas, but the rest of the sentence cannot stand alone. The other problem with the original sentence is that it uses the phrase *much of* to refer to both something uncountable (the *storyline*) and something countable (the *characters*); *much of* can refer only to uncountable things. (C) and (D) don't fix this problem. (E) does without introducing any new problems that would disqualify it from being the credited response.

34. **C** (A) and (E) are not supported by the text. (D) is the opposite of the sentence. (B) looks appealing; however, the passage never discusses the actual tribulations of artists. (C) is the best answer in terms of finding the sentence's function.

35. **D** In deciding on what sentence fits best at the end of the passage we need to focus on flow. Sentence 15 introduces the idea that artists felt the need to change *La Bohème*. (D) correctly references this idea, while the rest of the answers do not. (E) starts well for the last sentence of a passage, but the content of the rest of the sentence do not fit with the paragraph.

Section 7

1. **E** Because 1 raised to the third power is still 1, we know that x is 1 (with x^2 we wouldn't be sure if 1 were negative or positive). Knowing this, we can replace x in the fraction in the question with 1: $\dfrac{1^2 + 3}{1} = \dfrac{4}{1} = 4$, answer (E).

2. **B** Indicate on the figure that $\angle DEF$ is a right angle. You will see that there are two right triangles contained in the figure—$\triangle CEF$ and $\triangle DEF$. The hypotenuse of a right triangle is the largest side of that triangle, meaning that CF is the largest side of $\triangle CEF$ and DF is the largest side of $\triangle DEF$. Note that the two triangles share side EF in common and that side DE is contained within side CE. Because $\triangle CEF$ has the larger second side, it will also have a larger hypotenuse.

3. **B** A good way to approach this problem is to make up simple numbers with an average of 8 for set A, such as 6, 8, and 10. When you cut these in half for set B, you have 3, 4, and 5. The average of those numbers is 4. If you picked (E), you doubled the numbers in set A.

4. **B** Because a negative exponent can be rewritten as a fraction with a positive exponent in the denominator, 10^{-3} is equivalent to $\frac{1}{10^3}$ or $\frac{1}{1,000}$. Thus, JKLM must be divided by 1,000. This requires moving the decimal point back three spaces, resulting in J.KLM. If you picked (E), you multiplied JKLM by 10^3.

5. **B** Because $\overline{EH}$ is a diameter, the measures of the three angles in the top half of the circle must add to 180°. The measure of $\angle EOG$ is $180 - 70 = 110°$. $\overline{FO}$ bisects it into two angles of 55° each. Now we can find the measure of $\angle FOH$: $70 + 55 = 125°$, answer (B).

6. **A** The wall and ground are at right angles, much like a coordinate plane. The slope formula can be simplified as "rise over run," or, in this case, the height where the ladder hits the wall over the length of ground between the ladder and the wall. A slope of $\frac{5}{3}$ indicates that for every 5 feet of height, there is a corresponding 3 feet distance from the wall. Because $p = 9$, or three times the of 3 units indicated by the slope, q must equal three times the 5 units indicated by the slope, so the correct answer is (A), 15.

7. **C** It is useful to know the transformative properties of parabolas, including that an increased coefficient a narrows the parabola. You can also pick an a and x value for each formula and compare the resulting

y values. Using *a* = 2 and *x* = 3, the original graph would have a *y* value of 15. Using the same *a* and *x* values in the new formula yields a *y* value of 33. If you roughly plot these points on the graph, you will see that the higher *y* value in the new formula generates a narrower parabola.

8. **C**   Take each photograph type one at a time in any order. For her landscape photograph, Serena has three choices—one each from Brazil, Kenya and Istanbul. For her street scene, however, she has only two choices, because one of the three countries is already represented by the landscape photograph. Thus, so far, there are six possible arrangements, because any of three landscape photographs could be paired with either of the two museum photographs. For the portrait, Serena has only one option, whichever country is not yet represented. Thus, the total number of possible arrangements is 3 × 2 × 1 = 6, (C). If you picked (E), you did not account for the fact that each country (as well as each photograph type) limits what can be included for each spot.

9. **30**   Translate the word problem into the equation $\frac{1}{2}x - 7 = 8$. Solve this equation to get *x* = 30.

10. **45**   Divide 5, the height of the container, by $\frac{1}{3}$, the height of a coaster, to get 15. Since there are 3 containers, multiply by three to find the total number of coasters that can fit into the containers.

11. **144**   When 2 parallel lines are intersected by a third line, 2 kinds of angles are created: Big angles and small angles. All the big angles are equal, all the small angles are equal, and any big angle plus any small angle equals 180. Therefore, *a* + *b* = 180. Substituting 4*b* for a yields the equation *b* + 4*b* = 180. 5*b* = 180 so *b* = 36 and from the equation in the question, *a* = 4*b* = 144.

12.   **$1 < x < 3$**

The easiest way to solve this problem is just to try small values for x. Substituting 2 for x yields $|2(2) - 3| < 2$, which is true. Another way to solve the problem is to write an equation: $|2x - 3| < x$. Remove the absolute value bars by turning this into two separate equations: $2x - 3 < x$, and $-(2x - 3) < x$. Solving both of these equations gives two solutions: $x > 1$, and $x < 3$.

13.   **710**   The increase in Town A is 360 (2,360 − 2,000); the increase in Town B is 1,120 (6,120 − 5,000); and the increase in Town C is 650 (9,650 − 9,000). The total population increase is 2,130. To get the average, divide the total by 3 to get 710.

14.   **4**   If 17 blue marbles are removed, there are 13 blue marbles left. Twice 13 is 26, so at most 4 green marbles can be removed to ensure that there are at least 26 green marbles, which is twice the number of blue marbles.

15.   **12**   One way to solve this problem is to Plug In values for b. If we say $b = 2$, then $\dfrac{4a + 6}{4} = \dfrac{5}{3}$. Cross multiply to get $12a + 18 = 20$. Now solve to get $a = \dfrac{1}{6}$. Thus, $\dfrac{a}{b} = \dfrac{2}{\frac{1}{6}} = 12$. Alternatively, you could cross-multiply to get $12a + 9b = 10b$. Now combine like terms to get $12a = b$.

Dividing by a yields $12 = \dfrac{b}{a}$.

16.   **20**   You can use some simple algebra to represent the information. If w represents the weight of the package, then the cost of using Company 1 is $10 + \$0.60(w - 10)$. The cost of using Company 2 is $\$0.80w$. You

can set the two expressions equal to each other and solve for *w*. Initially, $10 + 0.60(w - 10) = 0.80w$. Distribute on the left side and combine like terms to get $4 = 0.20w$. Solve for *w* and you get 20.

17.   **10**   The smallest *odd-mult* is 3 (1 × 3). You can continue to generate *odd-mults* by multiplying consecutive odd numbers: 15 (3 × 5), 35 (5 × 7), 63 (7 × 9), 99 (9 × 11), 143 (11 × 13), 195 (13 × 15), 255 (15 × 17), 323 (17 × 19), and 399 (19 × 21). There are a total of 10 less than 400: 21 × 23 is too big at 483.

18. $\dfrac{20}{9}$ or 2.22

The perimeter of the figure equals 20*s*, which you know because there are 20 sides of length *s*. Since there are 9 squares and the area of each square is s^2 (just *s* times *s*) the total area is $9s^2$. Set the perimeter equal to the area to get the following equation: $20s = 9s^2$. Divide both sides by *s* to get $20 = 9s$. Divide both sides by 9 to get $s = \dfrac{20}{9}$.

Section 8

1.   **C**   After 12 minutes, the fraction of the ride completed is $\dfrac{12}{72}$. This fraction reduces down to $\dfrac{1}{6}$, answer (C).

2.   **A**   In a linear function, the $f(x)$—or *y*-value—changes by the same amount for each unit change in *x*. Here, the $f(x)$ value increases by 7 each time the *x* value increases by 1. Because $f(x)$ is 16 when *x* is 2, $f(x)$ is $16 + 7$ when *x* is 3, and $t = 23$. (A) is correct.

3.   **C**   The basketball has 4 times the diameter of the racquetball. Make up diameters to work with: Let's start with the smaller ball: if the racquetball has a diameter of 2, the larger ball, the basketball, will have a

diameter 4 times larger, 2 × 2 = 8. The diameters of the basketball and the racquetball have a ratio of 8 : 2. The radius is half the diameter, so the radii have a ratio of 4 : 1, answer (C). The actual diameter of a basketball is 9 inches, while a racquetball's is 2.25 inches, but when you come up with your own numbers on the SAT, always pick numbers that are easy to work with.

4.   **A**   The first step is to find the number of students who turned in Detective stories for this assignment. 20% of 60 students is $\frac{20}{100}$ × 60 = 12 students. There are 6 assignments during the semester: 12 × 6 = 72.

5.   **E**   First translate the words into math: if Sam produced p paintings, then Janet produced $3p + 4$ paintings. This matches (E). You could also make up a number for p. If Sam produced 2 paintings ($p = 2$), then Janet produced 10 paintings, which is 4 more than three times the number Sam produced. Plugging $p = 2$ into all five answer choices shows that only (E) gives an answer of 10.

6.   **D**   Assign numbers to c and d that will satisfy the inequality. If $c = 5$, then d must be a negative number, such as –2, in order for $c – d$ to be greater than 5. This pair of numbers allows you to eliminate (A), (C) and (E). To choose between (B) and (D), try picking a negative number for c, such as –5. Now, d must be a negative number less than –5, such as –7, in order for $c – d$ to be greater than –5. So, eliminate (B).

7.   **C**   Rotate your test booklet clockwise 270 degrees (or counterclockwise 90 degrees) and take note of how the figure in the question looks. The L-shaped figure is at the bottom left corner, in the proper direction as a capital L would face. Only (C) has the L shape in that spot. If you selected (D), you rotated the original figure in the wrong direction.

8. **B** Test out some of your own numbers for *a* and *b*, and eliminate answer choices that are not always true. Try different sets of numbers until only one answer remains. If you try *a* = 2 and *b* = –2, you will be able to eliminate (C), (D), and (E). If you try *a* = 3 and *b* = –4, you will be able to eliminate (A). Basically the information given tells you that *a* is positive and *b* is negative. (B) is correct because dividing a positive number by a negative number always gives you a negative number.

9. **A** Line *f* has a negative slope, so eliminate (C), (D), and (E). Because the slope is steeper than a slope of –1, eliminate (B). You may also solve the slopes. Because the two lines are perpendicular, the slope of line *f* will be the negative reciprocal of the slope of line *g*. To find the slope of line *g*, identify the two points that are easily discernable—those at the intercepts. The *x*-intercept is (–4, 0) and the *y*-intercept is (0, 2). Thus, the slope of line *g* is $\dfrac{2-0}{0-(-4)}$, which reduces to $\dfrac{1}{2}$. The negative reciprocal is –2.

10. **D** There is a lot of information in the question. We know there are two flavors of heart-shaped candy and gumballs, and the ratio of hearts to gumballs is 5:1. We then learn that there are 4 times more vanilla hearts than chocolate hearts. Finally we are given the actual number of vanilla hearts: 16. Since there are 4 times more vanilla hearts than chocolate hearts, there must be 4 chocolate hearts. Now we know the total number of heart candies is 16 + 4 = 20. To find out the total number of pieces of candy we need to know the number of gumballs. There are 5 times more heart candies than gumballs: 20 ÷ 5 = 4. So there are 16 vanilla hearts, 4 chocolate hearts, and 4 gumballs, for a total of 24 pieces of candy.

11.   C   Try to come up with numbers that fit all three equations. If $a = 2$, $b = 4$, and $c = 1$, all three equations work. Now all you have to do is multiply. Another way to solve the problem is to multiply the three equations together to see what happens. On the left, you will have $(a^2 \, b^2 \, c^2)$, and on the right you will have 64. Take the square root of each side, which gives you $abc = 8$, answer (C). If you picked answer choice (E), you left out the final step of taking the square root of each side.

12.   E   Translate this into a math sentence: $4n - 6 \geq -2$. Solve for n to see that $n \geq 1$. Eliminate answers (A), (B), and (C) because they include numbers less than 1. Between (D) and (E), (E) is correct because a solid indicates that the number is included in the set of values (*greater than or equal to*), while a hollow dot shows that the number is not included in the set (*greater than*).

13.   B   Start drawing figures, and look for a pattern. If you draw a four-sided figure with equal sides and angles (a square), you can draw only one diagonal from any vertex. For the equivalent five-sided figure, you can draw two; for the six-sided figure, three. By now, you can see the pattern: from any given point in a equilateral polygon, it has three fewer diagonals than it has sides. Thus, if the polygon has four diagonals from a single vertex, it must have seven sides.

14.   D   An easy way to start this problem is to make up a number for n. Let's say $n = 2$. Then $m = 9 + 3^4 = 90$. $3^2 = 9$. So when we Plug In $m = 90$, we should get 9. (D) is the only answer that works.

15.   B   The first thing to do is draw this triangle. If $AC = 5$, and the perimeter is 13, then AB and BC add up to 8. Since the problem says that AB and BC are equal, then $AB = BC = 4$. We have a triangle with sides 4, 4, and 5. If it were an equilateral triangle, and $AC = 4$, then x would equal 60. But $AC > 4$, and as a side on a triangle gets larger, the opposite angle gets larger. So $x > 60$. Cross off (A). Now if this were a triangle

with sides 3, 4, and 5, then x would equal 90. But since $AC \neq 3$, then $x \neq 90$. Cross off (C). So we've got a triangle that's somewhere between an equilateral triangle and a right triangle. Which means that x is larger than 60, but smaller than 90, answer (B).

16.   C   Plug In numbers for a and b. Since we know ab must equal 20, since that's the area, $a = 5$ and $b = 4$ would work well. The length of fencing used is therefore $4 + 4 + 4 + 5 + 5 = 22$. Plug In 4 for b in the answer choices, and only (C) works out to be the target answer of 22. To solve the problem algebraically, first find a in terms of b. Because $ab = 20$, you know that $a = \dfrac{20}{b}$. The overall length of fence used on the window is $2a + 3b$. If you replace a with $\dfrac{20}{b}$, you get answer choice (C). If you chose answer choice (A), you found $a + b$. If you chose answer choice (B), you found $2a + b$.

Section 9

1.   C   Since we have a colon in the sentence, the first part of the sentence should have the same meaning as the second part. In the second part the clue *very sensitive to light* seems opposite of what is said in the first part—*bats are blind*. So the meaning of the blank must serve to make the first part more like the meaning of the second. A good word for the blank would be something close to "falsity." The closest choice is (C).

2.   **A**   Because *Donald* is *involved in the affairs of others*, his *reputation* should describe "someone who would become *involved*." For the first blank, only (A) and (B) have words close to this meaning. We also have the word *and*, which tells us that the second blank should mean something similar to the first blank. (A) has a closer meaning to the blank than (B).

3.   **A**   The clue for the blank is that Devon was *viewed as undependable and easily swayed*. The words *despite the fact* tell us that the blank should mean something opposite the clue. In addition, right before the blank we see another clue: *reliable*. The following word *and* tells us the blank should follow this is meaning. So, a good word to put into the blank would be something that means "reliable." The closest meaning is (A).

4.   **B**   The clue for the first blank, *superior protective structures*, must mean that the *helmet designs* were well-received. This allows only (B) and (C) to be possible answer choices. For the second blank, the words *even though*, tell us that the meaning will be opposite of the first blank. Since the clue for the second blank is *unreliable materials*, we can assume that the meaning of that blank should be close to "unreliable." Between *precarious and advantageous*, (B) is the better answer.

5.   **E**   The clue *lack of evidence or testimony to support* tells us that the blank must mean something close to "supporting evidence." None of the answer choices mean close to this except (E). (B) may be appealing because it is a word used in courtroom settings, but has no relationship to the sentence.

6.   **E**   The words *in spite of* tell us that blank will be opposite the clue *unhappy and detached*. The blank should then mean something like happy and social. None of the choices are close except for (E).

7. **E**   Use Process of Elimination. William and Mr. Hunsden are not *enemies* as far as we know, so eliminate (A). They're not *coworkers,* so eliminate (B). They don't seem to be *friends*, so eliminate (C). They're not *brothers*, so eliminate (D). The correct answer is (E).

8. **C**   The passage states that *any human being, worthy of the name, will row long against wind and tide before he allows himself to cry out, "I am baffled!"* In other words, he will keep going before admitting a mistake. (C) is a good paraphrase of this point. The other answers are not supported by the passage.

9. **B**   The *primary objection* William has is *the antipathy which had sprung up between myself and Mr. Crimsworth* (his brother). Answer choice (B) refers to this fact. (D) is true, but doesn't answer the question, because it's not his *primary* objection (he specifically states that the work *was a dry and tedious task enough, but had that been all, I should long have borne with the nuisance*). The other answers are not supported by the passage.

10. **C**   We know that William is characterized by his *punctuality and industry* (he's on time and works hard), and that he has a *degree of education* (he's educated). Furthermore, Edward finds this cause for *envy* (he's jealous). Answer choice (C) expresses this situation accurately. (A) is too strong, and while William might be condescending and scornful, we don't really know. (B) is false according to the passage. (D) and (E) are not indicated inn the passage.

11. **D**   Always read a few lines above and below the line reference. After William says *I am no fossil,* Mr. Hunsden supports his argument by noting how William does the same thing, day after day, never doing anything new or interesting. Thus, he's *desensitized by his unvarying routine.* None of the other answers are supported by the passage.

12. **A** Mr. Hunsden responds by stating that *your case and mine are diametrically different, and it is nonsense attempting to draw a parallel.* (A) summarizes this statement nicely. The other answers are not supported by the passage.

13. **A** Mr. Hunsden is unsure about *the conclusion to be drawn* (about William's character) because it *depends upon the nature of the motives that guide your conduct.* Therefore, he's *uncertain about the reasons underlying William's actions* (A). The other answers are not supported by the passage.

14. **D** Mr. Hunsden tells William he'll never make any money, and his only chance is to marry someone wealthy. But a few lines later, he notes that *even that is hopeless.* Thus, he's offering a *prediction of a bleak future* (D).

15. **E** William's response is that he'll leave such plans to those who come up with them, meaning he won't seriously consider such a plan. (E) paraphrases this nicely. He doesn't say anything about *a goal* (A); he's not *uncertain* as far as we know (B); there's no indication that he views Mr. Hunsden's idea as *promising* (C); he offers no opinion about whether the idea is *unlikely to succeed* (D).

16. **C** *Shifts* refers to Mr. Hunsden's idea of *marrying a rich widow, or…an heiress.* William regards this as a devious plan, or *scheme* (C). The other answers are not supported by the context of the passage.

17. **C** Mr. Hunsden states that William is *not bold and venturesome…nor handsome and fascinating.* In (C), *timid* is a good antonym for *bold*, and *bland* is a good antonym for *fascinating.*

18. **B** In context, *Fortune has cheated Nature* is used to suggest that William *should have been a nobleman,* because he's no good as a tradesmen. (B) paraphrases this point nicely. The other answers are not supported by the passage.

19. **D** At the beginning of the passage, William states that his brother is a hard and grinding master...an inexorable tyrant. Mr. Hunsden also notes that William's boss has treated (him) like a dog. Thus, they both agree that *William is treated poorly by his employer* (D). Choice (B) is tempting, but extreme, and we don't know if William thinks he'll never succeed as a tradesman; we just know he made a bad choice and hates his particular job (and employer).

Section 10

1. **C** This question is testing conjunctions; you need to choose the answer that most clearly connects the two parts of the sentence. (A) and (B) don't show a relationship between the two parts, (E) doesn't make sense, and (C) is better than (D) because the word *therefore* implies a stronger cause-effect relationship than the sentence gives us.

2. **C** The sentence as written is a fragment, so eliminate (A). (D) and (E) are passive constructions, so get rid of those. (B) uses the wrong form of the verb and also uses *being*, which is almost always wrong. You're left with (C).

3. **D** The sentence as written contains a comma splice—two clauses that stand on their own as complete sentences must be joined by a semicolon or other conjunction. (B) has a semicolon, but *it consisting* causes the phrase after the semicolon to be an incomplete sentence. (C) uses the future tense while the question is in the present. (E) still has the comma splice and a problem with pronoun agreement. Only (D) links the description of the exhibit in the second phrase with *exhibit* in the first phrase.

4. **A** The sentence is correct as written. (B) uses *its* instead of *they*, and (C), (D), and (E) are unclear compared to (A).

5. C   The sentence as written is awkward and ambiguous due to *it*. There are two things that must be done to the *Halloween costume*: it must be *determined* and *critiqued* and to be parallel, these verbs must be in the same form. (C) is the only answer with the verbs in parallel structure.

6. C   The sentence has an idiom error: the comparison begins, using the *as... as* construction, but does not finish correctly. Both (C) and (D) begin with *as*, but only (C) has a structure parallel to the beginning of the sentence.

7. E   The sentence as written is passive and wordy; also, since the phrase that starts the sentence describes *Agatha Christie*, her name should follow the comma. Only (E) does this. (D) might look close, but the subject is actually the *disappearance,* not *Agatha Christie*.

8. D   (A) has a misplaced modifier and is also in the passive voice. (B) and (C) both have pronoun errors—a *platypus* cannot be referred to as *who*. (C) also creates a fragment. (D) is in the active voice and lacks the pronoun error. Also, the introductory modifying clause correctly modifies *platypus*. (E) is awkward and incorrectly uses *which*.

9. E   Start by comparing the verbs in this one. You want *pilots believed*, because the sentence is in past tense; get rid of (A), (B), and (C). From there, you want to make the list of nouns parallel with *the importance of discipline*: we need *the authority of their commanding officers* and *demonstration of national pride,* which matches only (E).

10. B   The underlined portion is awkwardly phrased. Comparisons are correct when the terms are parallel to each other. An adjective-plural noun combo that matches *internal states* is the best solution, and (B) *external events* has this construction.

11.   **C**   (A) is a sentence fragment; the part after the comma is incomplete. (B) is wordy and awkward. (D) uses *which* too much and is a fragment. (E) is also a fragment and uses the -ing word *being*, which is unnecessary here.

12.   **E**   The sentence as written has a misplaced modifier or faulty comparison: this sentence is saying that *Frank Capra* is a *film*. (B) and (C) create incomplete sentences. (D) changes the meaning of the sentence. (E) fixes the modifier/comparison problem by making the subject *the films of Frank Capra* and the verb and pronoun agree with the plural subject *films*.

13.   **A**   The sentence is correct as written. (C) and (E) incorrectly use the word *being* (which is usually wrong). (B) has a redundant *with*. (D) has a double negative. (E) is redundant. (A) has none of these problems.

14.   **D**   As written, the sentence compares the *painting style of Picasso* to his contemporaries, but it should compare styles to styles. (A), (B), (C), and (E) don't fix the original problem. In (D), *that of* stands in for *styles* and creates a parallel comparison.

SAT SCORING WORKSHEET

For directions on how to score your SAT practice test, see pages 5–7.

SAT Writing Section

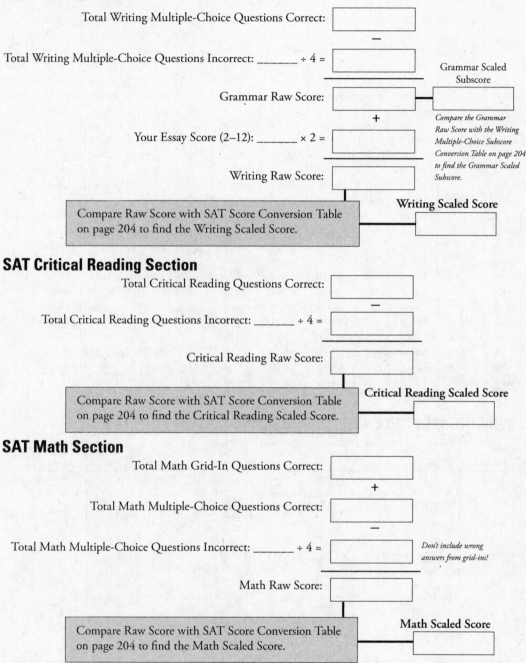

Total Writing Multiple-Choice Questions Correct: ☐

−

Total Writing Multiple-Choice Questions Incorrect: _____ ÷ 4 = ☐

Grammar Raw Score: ☐

Grammar Scaled Subscore ☐

+

Compare the Grammar Raw Score with the Writing Multiple-Choice Subscore Conversion Table on page 204 to find the Grammar Scaled Subscore.

Your Essay Score (2–12): _____ × 2 = ☐

Writing Raw Score: ☐

Compare Raw Score with SAT Score Conversion Table on page 204 to find the Writing Scaled Score.

Writing Scaled Score ☐

SAT Critical Reading Section

Total Critical Reading Questions Correct: ☐

−

Total Critical Reading Questions Incorrect: _____ ÷ 4 = ☐

Critical Reading Raw Score: ☐

Compare Raw Score with SAT Score Conversion Table on page 204 to find the Critical Reading Scaled Score.

Critical Reading Scaled Score ☐

SAT Math Section

Total Math Grid-In Questions Correct: ☐

+

Total Math Multiple-Choice Questions Correct: ☐

−

Total Math Multiple-Choice Questions Incorrect: _____ ÷ 4 = ☐

Don't include wrong answers from grid-ins!

Math Raw Score: ☐

Compare Raw Score with SAT Score Conversion Table on page 204 to find the Math Scaled Score.

Math Scaled Score ☐

SAT SCORE CONVERSION TABLE

Raw Score	Reading Scaled Score	Math Scaled Score	Writing Scaled Score	Raw Score	Reading Scaled Score	Math Scaled Score	Writing Scaled Score	Raw Score	Reading Scaled Score	Math Scaled Score	Writing Scaled Score
73			800	47	580–620	650–690	540–580	21	410–450	440–480	380–420
72			780–800	46	570–610	640–680	530–570	20	410–450	430–470	370–410
71			770–800	45	570–610	630–670	520–560	19	400–440	420–460	360–400
70			750–790	44	560–600	620–660	520–560	18	390–430	420–460	350–390
69			740–780	43	550–590	610–650	510–550	17	390–430	410–450	350–390
68			730–770	42	550–590	600–640	500–540	16	380–420	400–440	340–380
67	800		720–760	41	540–580	600–640	500–540	15	370–410	390–430	330–370
66	780–800		710–750	40	530–570	590–630	490–530	14	370–410	390–430	320–360
65	770–800		700–740	39	530–570	580–620	480–520	13	360–400	380–420	310–350
64	760–800		690–730	38	520–560	570–610	480–520	12	350–390	370–410	310–350
63	750–790		680–720	37	510–550	560–600	470–510	11	340–380	360–400	300–340
62	730–770		680–720	36	510–550	550–590	460–500	10	330–370	350–390	290–330
61	710–750		670–710	35	500–540	550–590	460–500	9	330–370	340–380	280–320
60	700–740		660–700	34	500–540	540–580	450–490	8	320–360	330–370	270–310
59	690–730		650–690	33	490–530	530–570	440–480	7	310–350	320–360	260–300
58	680–720		640–680	32	480–520	520–560	430–470	6	300–340	310–350	260–300
57	670–710		630–670	31	480–520	510–550	430–470	5	290–330	300–340	260–300
56	660–700		620–660	30	470–510	510–550	420–460	4	280–320	290–330	250–290
55	650–690		610–650	29	460–500	500–540	420–460	3	270–310	270–310	250–290
54	640–680	800	600–640	28	460–500	490–530	410–450	2	250–290	260–300	240–280
53	630–670	760–800	590–630	27	450–490	480–520	400–440	1	240–280	240–280	230–270
52	620–660	740–780	580–620	26	450–490	480–520	400–440	0	220–260	230–270	220–260
51	610–650	710–750	570–610	25	440–480	470–510	390–430	–1	200–220	210–250	200–220
50	600–640	690–730	560–600	24	430–470	460–500	390–430	–2	200–220	200–210	200–220
49	600–640	670–710	560–600	23	430–470	450–490	380–420	–3	200	200	200–220
48	590–630	660–700	550–590	22	420–460	450–490	380–420				

WRITING MULTIPLE-CHOICE SUBSCORE CONVERSION TABLE

Grammar Raw Score	Grammar Scaled Subscore	Grammar Raw Score	Grammar Scaled Subscore	Grammar Raw Score	Grammar Scaled Subscore	Grammar Raw Score	Grammar Scaled Subscore	Grammar Raw Score	Grammar Scaled Subscore
49	78–80	38	60–64	27	49–53	16	40–44	5	30–34
48	77–80	37	59–63	26	48–52	15	39–43	4	28–32
47	74–78	36	58–62	25	48–52	14	38–42	3	27–31
46	72–76	35	57–61	24	47–51	13	38–42	2	25–29
45	70–74	34	56–60	23	46–50	12	37–41	1	24–28
44	68–72	33	55–59	22	45–49	11	36–40	0	22–26
43	66–70	32	54–58	21	44–48	10	35–39	–1	20–22
42	65–69	31	53–57	20	43–47	9	34–38	–2	20–22
41	64–68	30	52–56	19	42–46	8	33–37	–3	20–22
40	62–66	29	51–55	18	42–46	7	32–36		
39	61–65	28	50–54	17	41–45	6	31–35		

Chapter 7
Practice Test 3

THIS PAGE INTENTIONALLY LEFT BLANK

○ I prefer NOT to grant the College Board the right to use, reproduce, or publish my essay for any purpose beyond the assessment of my writing skills, even though my name will not be used in any way in conjunction with my essay. I understand that I am free to mark this circle with no effect on my score.

SECTION 1

IMPORTANT: USE A NO. 2 PENCIL. DO NOT WRITE OUTSIDE THE BORDER!
Words written outside the essay box or written in ink **WILL NOT APPEAR** in the copy sent to be scored and your score will be affected.

Begin your essay on this page. If you need more space, continue on the next page.

Continue on the next page, if necessary.

PLEASE DO NOT WRITE IN THIS AREA

SERIAL #

COMPLETE MARK ●　EXAMPLES OF INCOMPLETE MARKS

You must use a No. 2 pencil and marks must be complete. Do not use a mechanical pencil. It is very important that you fill in the entire circle darkly and completely. If you change your responses, erase as completely as possible. Incomplete marks or erasures may affect your score.

SECTION 2

1 (A)(B)(C)(D)(E)　　11 (A)(B)(C)(D)(E)　　21 (A)(B)(C)(D)(E)　　31 (A)(B)(C)(D)(E)
2 (A)(B)(C)(D)(E)　　12 (A)(B)(C)(D)(E)　　22 (A)(B)(C)(D)(E)　　32 (A)(B)(C)(D)(E)
3 (A)(B)(C)(D)(E)　　13 (A)(B)(C)(D)(E)　　23 (A)(B)(C)(D)(E)　　33 (A)(B)(C)(D)(E)
4 (A)(B)(C)(D)(E)　　14 (A)(B)(C)(D)(E)　　24 (A)(B)(C)(D)(E)　　34 (A)(B)(C)(D)(E)
5 (A)(B)(C)(D)(E)　　15 (A)(B)(C)(D)(E)　　25 (A)(B)(C)(D)(E)　　35 (A)(B)(C)(D)(E)
6 (A)(B)(C)(D)(E)　　16 (A)(B)(C)(D)(E)　　26 (A)(B)(C)(D)(E)　　36 (A)(B)(C)(D)(E)
7 (A)(B)(C)(D)(E)　　17 (A)(B)(C)(D)(E)　　27 (A)(B)(C)(D)(E)　　37 (A)(B)(C)(D)(E)
8 (A)(B)(C)(D)(E)　　18 (A)(B)(C)(D)(E)　　28 (A)(B)(C)(D)(E)　　38 (A)(B)(C)(D)(E)
9 (A)(B)(C)(D)(E)　　19 (A)(B)(C)(D)(E)　　29 (A)(B)(C)(D)(E)　　39 (A)(B)(C)(D)(E)
10 (A)(B)(C)(D)(E)　　20 (A)(B)(C)(D)(E)　　30 (A)(B)(C)(D)(E)　　40 (A)(B)(C)(D)(E)

SECTION 3

1 (A)(B)(C)(D)(E)　　11 (A)(B)(C)(D)(E)　　21 (A)(B)(C)(D)(E)　　31 (A)(B)(C)(D)(E)
2 (A)(B)(C)(D)(E)　　12 (A)(B)(C)(D)(E)　　22 (A)(B)(C)(D)(E)　　32 (A)(B)(C)(D)(E)
3 (A)(B)(C)(D)(E)　　13 (A)(B)(C)(D)(E)　　23 (A)(B)(C)(D)(E)　　33 (A)(B)(C)(D)(E)
4 (A)(B)(C)(D)(E)　　14 (A)(B)(C)(D)(E)　　24 (A)(B)(C)(D)(E)　　34 (A)(B)(C)(D)(E)
5 (A)(B)(C)(D)(E)　　15 (A)(B)(C)(D)(E)　　25 (A)(B)(C)(D)(E)　　35 (A)(B)(C)(D)(E)
6 (A)(B)(C)(D)(E)　　16 (A)(B)(C)(D)(E)　　26 (A)(B)(C)(D)(E)　　36 (A)(B)(C)(D)(E)
7 (A)(B)(C)(D)(E)　　17 (A)(B)(C)(D)(E)　　27 (A)(B)(C)(D)(E)　　37 (A)(B)(C)(D)(E)
8 (A)(B)(C)(D)(E)　　18 (A)(B)(C)(D)(E)　　28 (A)(B)(C)(D)(E)　　38 (A)(B)(C)(D)(E)
9 (A)(B)(C)(D)(E)　　19 (A)(B)(C)(D)(E)　　29 (A)(B)(C)(D)(E)　　39 (A)(B)(C)(D)(E)
10 (A)(B)(C)(D)(E)　　20 (A)(B)(C)(D)(E)　　30 (A)(B)(C)(D)(E)　　40 (A)(B)(C)(D)(E)

CAUTION Grid answers in the section below for SECTION 2 or SECTION 3 only if directed to do so in your test book.

Student-Produced Responses

ONLY ANSWERS THAT ARE GRIDDED WILL BE SCORED. YOU WILL NOT RECEIVE CREDIT FOR ANYTHING WRITTEN IN THE BOXES.

Quality Assurance Mark ●

9　10　11　12　13

(grid-in bubbles: . / / . with 0–9)

14　15　16　17　18

(grid-in bubbles: . / / . with 0–9)

COMPLETE MARK ● EXAMPLES OF INCOMPLETE MARKS Ⓐ Ⓑ Ⓔ Ⓓ / Ⓐ Ⓧ Ⓔ Ⓓ

You must use a No. 2 pencil and marks must be complete. Do not use a mechanical pencil. It is very important that you fill in the entire circle darkly and completely. If you change your responses, erase as completely as possible. Incomplete marks or erasures may affect your score.

SECTION 4

1 Ⓐ Ⓑ Ⓒ Ⓓ Ⓔ	11 Ⓐ Ⓑ Ⓒ Ⓓ Ⓔ	21 Ⓐ Ⓑ Ⓒ Ⓓ Ⓔ	31 Ⓐ Ⓑ Ⓒ Ⓓ Ⓔ
2 Ⓐ Ⓑ Ⓒ Ⓓ Ⓔ	12 Ⓐ Ⓑ Ⓒ Ⓓ Ⓔ	22 Ⓐ Ⓑ Ⓒ Ⓓ Ⓔ	32 Ⓐ Ⓑ Ⓒ Ⓓ Ⓔ
3 Ⓐ Ⓑ Ⓒ Ⓓ Ⓔ	13 Ⓐ Ⓑ Ⓒ Ⓓ Ⓔ	23 Ⓐ Ⓑ Ⓒ Ⓓ Ⓔ	33 Ⓐ Ⓑ Ⓒ Ⓓ Ⓔ
4 Ⓐ Ⓑ Ⓒ Ⓓ Ⓔ	14 Ⓐ Ⓑ Ⓒ Ⓓ Ⓔ	24 Ⓐ Ⓑ Ⓒ Ⓓ Ⓔ	34 Ⓐ Ⓑ Ⓒ Ⓓ Ⓔ
5 Ⓐ Ⓑ Ⓒ Ⓓ Ⓔ	15 Ⓐ Ⓑ Ⓒ Ⓓ Ⓔ	25 Ⓐ Ⓑ Ⓒ Ⓓ Ⓔ	35 Ⓐ Ⓑ Ⓒ Ⓓ Ⓔ
6 Ⓐ Ⓑ Ⓒ Ⓓ Ⓔ	16 Ⓐ Ⓑ Ⓒ Ⓓ Ⓔ	26 Ⓐ Ⓑ Ⓒ Ⓓ Ⓔ	36 Ⓐ Ⓑ Ⓒ Ⓓ Ⓔ
7 Ⓐ Ⓑ Ⓒ Ⓓ Ⓔ	17 Ⓐ Ⓑ Ⓒ Ⓓ Ⓔ	27 Ⓐ Ⓑ Ⓒ Ⓓ Ⓔ	37 Ⓐ Ⓑ Ⓒ Ⓓ Ⓔ
8 Ⓐ Ⓑ Ⓒ Ⓓ Ⓔ	18 Ⓐ Ⓑ Ⓒ Ⓓ Ⓔ	28 Ⓐ Ⓑ Ⓒ Ⓓ Ⓔ	38 Ⓐ Ⓑ Ⓒ Ⓓ Ⓔ
9 Ⓐ Ⓑ Ⓒ Ⓓ Ⓔ	19 Ⓐ Ⓑ Ⓒ Ⓓ Ⓔ	29 Ⓐ Ⓑ Ⓒ Ⓓ Ⓔ	39 Ⓐ Ⓑ Ⓒ Ⓓ Ⓔ
10 Ⓐ Ⓑ Ⓒ Ⓓ Ⓔ	20 Ⓐ Ⓑ Ⓒ Ⓓ Ⓔ	30 Ⓐ Ⓑ Ⓒ Ⓓ Ⓔ	40 Ⓐ Ⓑ Ⓒ Ⓓ Ⓔ

SECTION 5

1 Ⓐ Ⓑ Ⓒ Ⓓ Ⓔ	11 Ⓐ Ⓑ Ⓒ Ⓓ Ⓔ	21 Ⓐ Ⓑ Ⓒ Ⓓ Ⓔ	31 Ⓐ Ⓑ Ⓒ Ⓓ Ⓔ
2 Ⓐ Ⓑ Ⓒ Ⓓ Ⓔ	12 Ⓐ Ⓑ Ⓒ Ⓓ Ⓔ	22 Ⓐ Ⓑ Ⓒ Ⓓ Ⓔ	32 Ⓐ Ⓑ Ⓒ Ⓓ Ⓔ
3 Ⓐ Ⓑ Ⓒ Ⓓ Ⓔ	13 Ⓐ Ⓑ Ⓒ Ⓓ Ⓔ	23 Ⓐ Ⓑ Ⓒ Ⓓ Ⓔ	33 Ⓐ Ⓑ Ⓒ Ⓓ Ⓔ
4 Ⓐ Ⓑ Ⓒ Ⓓ Ⓔ	14 Ⓐ Ⓑ Ⓒ Ⓓ Ⓔ	24 Ⓐ Ⓑ Ⓒ Ⓓ Ⓔ	34 Ⓐ Ⓑ Ⓒ Ⓓ Ⓔ
5 Ⓐ Ⓑ Ⓒ Ⓓ Ⓔ	15 Ⓐ Ⓑ Ⓒ Ⓓ Ⓔ	25 Ⓐ Ⓑ Ⓒ Ⓓ Ⓔ	35 Ⓐ Ⓑ Ⓒ Ⓓ Ⓔ
6 Ⓐ Ⓑ Ⓒ Ⓓ Ⓔ	16 Ⓐ Ⓑ Ⓒ Ⓓ Ⓔ	26 Ⓐ Ⓑ Ⓒ Ⓓ Ⓔ	36 Ⓐ Ⓑ Ⓒ Ⓓ Ⓔ
7 Ⓐ Ⓑ Ⓒ Ⓓ Ⓔ	17 Ⓐ Ⓑ Ⓒ Ⓓ Ⓔ	27 Ⓐ Ⓑ Ⓒ Ⓓ Ⓔ	37 Ⓐ Ⓑ Ⓒ Ⓓ Ⓔ
8 Ⓐ Ⓑ Ⓒ Ⓓ Ⓔ	18 Ⓐ Ⓑ Ⓒ Ⓓ Ⓔ	28 Ⓐ Ⓑ Ⓒ Ⓓ Ⓔ	38 Ⓐ Ⓑ Ⓒ Ⓓ Ⓔ
9 Ⓐ Ⓑ Ⓒ Ⓓ Ⓔ	19 Ⓐ Ⓑ Ⓒ Ⓓ Ⓔ	29 Ⓐ Ⓑ Ⓒ Ⓓ Ⓔ	39 Ⓐ Ⓑ Ⓒ Ⓓ Ⓔ
10 Ⓐ Ⓑ Ⓒ Ⓓ Ⓔ	20 Ⓐ Ⓑ Ⓒ Ⓓ Ⓔ	30 Ⓐ Ⓑ Ⓒ Ⓓ Ⓔ	40 Ⓐ Ⓑ Ⓒ Ⓓ Ⓔ

CAUTION Grid answers in the section below for SECTION 4 or SECTION 5 only if directed to do so in your test book.

Student-Produced Responses — ONLY ANSWERS THAT ARE GRIDDED WILL BE SCORED. YOU WILL NOT RECEIVE CREDIT FOR ANYTHING WRITTEN IN THE BOXES.

Quality Assurance Mark ●

9, 10, 11, 12, 13

14, 15, 16, 17, 18

COMPLETE MARK ● EXAMPLES OF INCOMPLETE MARKS Ⓐ Ⓑ ⊙ Ⓓ

You must use a No. 2 pencil and marks must be complete. Do not use a mechanical pencil. It is very important that you fill in the entire circle darkly and completely. If you change your responses, erase as completely as possible. Incomplete marks or erasures may affect your score.

SECTION 6

1 Ⓐ Ⓑ Ⓒ Ⓓ Ⓔ   11 Ⓐ Ⓑ Ⓒ Ⓓ Ⓔ   21 Ⓐ Ⓑ Ⓒ Ⓓ Ⓔ   31 Ⓐ Ⓑ Ⓒ Ⓓ Ⓔ
2 Ⓐ Ⓑ Ⓒ Ⓓ Ⓔ   12 Ⓐ Ⓑ Ⓒ Ⓓ Ⓔ   22 Ⓐ Ⓑ Ⓒ Ⓓ Ⓔ   32 Ⓐ Ⓑ Ⓒ Ⓓ Ⓔ
3 Ⓐ Ⓑ Ⓒ Ⓓ Ⓔ   13 Ⓐ Ⓑ Ⓒ Ⓓ Ⓔ   23 Ⓐ Ⓑ Ⓒ Ⓓ Ⓔ   33 Ⓐ Ⓑ Ⓒ Ⓓ Ⓔ
4 Ⓐ Ⓑ Ⓒ Ⓓ Ⓔ   14 Ⓐ Ⓑ Ⓒ Ⓓ Ⓔ   24 Ⓐ Ⓑ Ⓒ Ⓓ Ⓔ   34 Ⓐ Ⓑ Ⓒ Ⓓ Ⓔ
5 Ⓐ Ⓑ Ⓒ Ⓓ Ⓔ   15 Ⓐ Ⓑ Ⓒ Ⓓ Ⓔ   25 Ⓐ Ⓑ Ⓒ Ⓓ Ⓔ   35 Ⓐ Ⓑ Ⓒ Ⓓ Ⓔ
6 Ⓐ Ⓑ Ⓒ Ⓓ Ⓔ   16 Ⓐ Ⓑ Ⓒ Ⓓ Ⓔ   26 Ⓐ Ⓑ Ⓒ Ⓓ Ⓔ   36 Ⓐ Ⓑ Ⓒ Ⓓ Ⓔ
7 Ⓐ Ⓑ Ⓒ Ⓓ Ⓔ   17 Ⓐ Ⓑ Ⓒ Ⓓ Ⓔ   27 Ⓐ Ⓑ Ⓒ Ⓓ Ⓔ   37 Ⓐ Ⓑ Ⓒ Ⓓ Ⓔ
8 Ⓐ Ⓑ Ⓒ Ⓓ Ⓔ   18 Ⓐ Ⓑ Ⓒ Ⓓ Ⓔ   28 Ⓐ Ⓑ Ⓒ Ⓓ Ⓔ   38 Ⓐ Ⓑ Ⓒ Ⓓ Ⓔ
9 Ⓐ Ⓑ Ⓒ Ⓓ Ⓔ   19 Ⓐ Ⓑ Ⓒ Ⓓ Ⓔ   29 Ⓐ Ⓑ Ⓒ Ⓓ Ⓔ   39 Ⓐ Ⓑ Ⓒ Ⓓ Ⓔ
10 Ⓐ Ⓑ Ⓒ Ⓓ Ⓔ   20 Ⓐ Ⓑ Ⓒ Ⓓ Ⓔ   30 Ⓐ Ⓑ Ⓒ Ⓓ Ⓔ   40 Ⓐ Ⓑ Ⓒ Ⓓ Ⓔ

SECTION 7

1 Ⓐ Ⓑ Ⓒ Ⓓ Ⓔ   11 Ⓐ Ⓑ Ⓒ Ⓓ Ⓔ   21 Ⓐ Ⓑ Ⓒ Ⓓ Ⓔ   31 Ⓐ Ⓑ Ⓒ Ⓓ Ⓔ
2 Ⓐ Ⓑ Ⓒ Ⓓ Ⓔ   12 Ⓐ Ⓑ Ⓒ Ⓓ Ⓔ   22 Ⓐ Ⓑ Ⓒ Ⓓ Ⓔ   32 Ⓐ Ⓑ Ⓒ Ⓓ Ⓔ
3 Ⓐ Ⓑ Ⓒ Ⓓ Ⓔ   13 Ⓐ Ⓑ Ⓒ Ⓓ Ⓔ   23 Ⓐ Ⓑ Ⓒ Ⓓ Ⓔ   33 Ⓐ Ⓑ Ⓒ Ⓓ Ⓔ
4 Ⓐ Ⓑ Ⓒ Ⓓ Ⓔ   14 Ⓐ Ⓑ Ⓒ Ⓓ Ⓔ   24 Ⓐ Ⓑ Ⓒ Ⓓ Ⓔ   34 Ⓐ Ⓑ Ⓒ Ⓓ Ⓔ
5 Ⓐ Ⓑ Ⓒ Ⓓ Ⓔ   15 Ⓐ Ⓑ Ⓒ Ⓓ Ⓔ   25 Ⓐ Ⓑ Ⓒ Ⓓ Ⓔ   35 Ⓐ Ⓑ Ⓒ Ⓓ Ⓔ
6 Ⓐ Ⓑ Ⓒ Ⓓ Ⓔ   16 Ⓐ Ⓑ Ⓒ Ⓓ Ⓔ   26 Ⓐ Ⓑ Ⓒ Ⓓ Ⓔ   36 Ⓐ Ⓑ Ⓒ Ⓓ Ⓔ
7 Ⓐ Ⓑ Ⓒ Ⓓ Ⓔ   17 Ⓐ Ⓑ Ⓒ Ⓓ Ⓔ   27 Ⓐ Ⓑ Ⓒ Ⓓ Ⓔ   37 Ⓐ Ⓑ Ⓒ Ⓓ Ⓔ
8 Ⓐ Ⓑ Ⓒ Ⓓ Ⓔ   18 Ⓐ Ⓑ Ⓒ Ⓓ Ⓔ   28 Ⓐ Ⓑ Ⓒ Ⓓ Ⓔ   38 Ⓐ Ⓑ Ⓒ Ⓓ Ⓔ
9 Ⓐ Ⓑ Ⓒ Ⓓ Ⓔ   19 Ⓐ Ⓑ Ⓒ Ⓓ Ⓔ   29 Ⓐ Ⓑ Ⓒ Ⓓ Ⓔ   39 Ⓐ Ⓑ Ⓒ Ⓓ Ⓔ
10 Ⓐ Ⓑ Ⓒ Ⓓ Ⓔ   20 Ⓐ Ⓑ Ⓒ Ⓓ Ⓔ   30 Ⓐ Ⓑ Ⓒ Ⓓ Ⓔ   40 Ⓐ Ⓑ Ⓒ Ⓓ Ⓔ

CAUTION Grid answers in the section below for SECTION 6 or SECTION 7 only if directed to do so in your test book.

Student-Produced Responses ONLY ANSWERS THAT ARE GRIDDED WILL BE SCORED. YOU WILL NOT RECEIVE CREDIT FOR ANYTHING WRITTEN IN THE BOXES.

Quality Assurance Mark ●

9   10   11   12   13

14   15   16   17   18

COMPLETE MARK ● EXAMPLES OF INCOMPLETE MARKS Ⓐ Ⓑ ⦿ Ⓓ ⊘ ⊘ ⊘ ⊘

You must use a No. 2 pencil and marks must be complete. Do not use a mechanical pencil. It is very important that you fill in the entire circle darkly and completely. If you change your responses, erase as completely as possible. Incomplete marks or erasures may affect your score.

SECTION 8

1 Ⓐ Ⓑ Ⓒ Ⓓ Ⓔ
2 Ⓐ Ⓑ Ⓒ Ⓓ Ⓔ
3 Ⓐ Ⓑ Ⓒ Ⓓ Ⓔ
4 Ⓐ Ⓑ Ⓒ Ⓓ Ⓔ
5 Ⓐ Ⓑ Ⓒ Ⓓ Ⓔ
6 Ⓐ Ⓑ Ⓒ Ⓓ Ⓔ
7 Ⓐ Ⓑ Ⓒ Ⓓ Ⓔ
8 Ⓐ Ⓑ Ⓒ Ⓓ Ⓔ
9 Ⓐ Ⓑ Ⓒ Ⓓ Ⓔ
10 Ⓐ Ⓑ Ⓒ Ⓓ Ⓔ

11 Ⓐ Ⓑ Ⓒ Ⓓ Ⓔ
12 Ⓐ Ⓑ Ⓒ Ⓓ Ⓔ
13 Ⓐ Ⓑ Ⓒ Ⓓ Ⓔ
14 Ⓐ Ⓑ Ⓒ Ⓓ Ⓔ
15 Ⓐ Ⓑ Ⓒ Ⓓ Ⓔ
16 Ⓐ Ⓑ Ⓒ Ⓓ Ⓔ
17 Ⓐ Ⓑ Ⓒ Ⓓ Ⓔ
18 Ⓐ Ⓑ Ⓒ Ⓓ Ⓔ
19 Ⓐ Ⓑ Ⓒ Ⓓ Ⓔ
20 Ⓐ Ⓑ Ⓒ Ⓓ Ⓔ

21 Ⓐ Ⓑ Ⓒ Ⓓ Ⓔ
22 Ⓐ Ⓑ Ⓒ Ⓓ Ⓔ
23 Ⓐ Ⓑ Ⓒ Ⓓ Ⓔ
24 Ⓐ Ⓑ Ⓒ Ⓓ Ⓔ
25 Ⓐ Ⓑ Ⓒ Ⓓ Ⓔ
26 Ⓐ Ⓑ Ⓒ Ⓓ Ⓔ
27 Ⓐ Ⓑ Ⓒ Ⓓ Ⓔ
28 Ⓐ Ⓑ Ⓒ Ⓓ Ⓔ
29 Ⓐ Ⓑ Ⓒ Ⓓ Ⓔ
30 Ⓐ Ⓑ Ⓒ Ⓓ Ⓔ

31 Ⓐ Ⓑ Ⓒ Ⓓ Ⓔ
32 Ⓐ Ⓑ Ⓒ Ⓓ Ⓔ
33 Ⓐ Ⓑ Ⓒ Ⓓ Ⓔ
34 Ⓐ Ⓑ Ⓒ Ⓓ Ⓔ
35 Ⓐ Ⓑ Ⓒ Ⓓ Ⓔ
36 Ⓐ Ⓑ Ⓒ Ⓓ Ⓔ
37 Ⓐ Ⓑ Ⓒ Ⓓ Ⓔ
38 Ⓐ Ⓑ Ⓒ Ⓓ Ⓔ
39 Ⓐ Ⓑ Ⓒ Ⓓ Ⓔ
40 Ⓐ Ⓑ Ⓒ Ⓓ Ⓔ

SECTION 9

1 Ⓐ Ⓑ Ⓒ Ⓓ Ⓔ
2 Ⓐ Ⓑ Ⓒ Ⓓ Ⓔ
3 Ⓐ Ⓑ Ⓒ Ⓓ Ⓔ
4 Ⓐ Ⓑ Ⓒ Ⓓ Ⓔ
5 Ⓐ Ⓑ Ⓒ Ⓓ Ⓔ
6 Ⓐ Ⓑ Ⓒ Ⓓ Ⓔ
7 Ⓐ Ⓑ Ⓒ Ⓓ Ⓔ
8 Ⓐ Ⓑ Ⓒ Ⓓ Ⓔ
9 Ⓐ Ⓑ Ⓒ Ⓓ Ⓔ
10 Ⓐ Ⓑ Ⓒ Ⓓ Ⓔ

11 Ⓐ Ⓑ Ⓒ Ⓓ Ⓔ
12 Ⓐ Ⓑ Ⓒ Ⓓ Ⓔ
13 Ⓐ Ⓑ Ⓒ Ⓓ Ⓔ
14 Ⓐ Ⓑ Ⓒ Ⓓ Ⓔ
15 Ⓐ Ⓑ Ⓒ Ⓓ Ⓔ
16 Ⓐ Ⓑ Ⓒ Ⓓ Ⓔ
17 Ⓐ Ⓑ Ⓒ Ⓓ Ⓔ
18 Ⓐ Ⓑ Ⓒ Ⓓ Ⓔ
19 Ⓐ Ⓑ Ⓒ Ⓓ Ⓔ
20 Ⓐ Ⓑ Ⓒ Ⓓ Ⓔ

21 Ⓐ Ⓑ Ⓒ Ⓓ Ⓔ
22 Ⓐ Ⓑ Ⓒ Ⓓ Ⓔ
23 Ⓐ Ⓑ Ⓒ Ⓓ Ⓔ
24 Ⓐ Ⓑ Ⓒ Ⓓ Ⓔ
25 Ⓐ Ⓑ Ⓒ Ⓓ Ⓔ
26 Ⓐ Ⓑ Ⓒ Ⓓ Ⓔ
27 Ⓐ Ⓑ Ⓒ Ⓓ Ⓔ
28 Ⓐ Ⓑ Ⓒ Ⓓ Ⓔ
29 Ⓐ Ⓑ Ⓒ Ⓓ Ⓔ
30 Ⓐ Ⓑ Ⓒ Ⓓ Ⓔ

31 Ⓐ Ⓑ Ⓒ Ⓓ Ⓔ
32 Ⓐ Ⓑ Ⓒ Ⓓ Ⓔ
33 Ⓐ Ⓑ Ⓒ Ⓓ Ⓔ
34 Ⓐ Ⓑ Ⓒ Ⓓ Ⓔ
35 Ⓐ Ⓑ Ⓒ Ⓓ Ⓔ
36 Ⓐ Ⓑ Ⓒ Ⓓ Ⓔ
37 Ⓐ Ⓑ Ⓒ Ⓓ Ⓔ
38 Ⓐ Ⓑ Ⓒ Ⓓ Ⓔ
39 Ⓐ Ⓑ Ⓒ Ⓓ Ⓔ
40 Ⓐ Ⓑ Ⓒ Ⓓ Ⓔ

SECTION 10

1 Ⓐ Ⓑ Ⓒ Ⓓ Ⓔ
2 Ⓐ Ⓑ Ⓒ Ⓓ Ⓔ
3 Ⓐ Ⓑ Ⓒ Ⓓ Ⓔ
4 Ⓐ Ⓑ Ⓒ Ⓓ Ⓔ
5 Ⓐ Ⓑ Ⓒ Ⓓ Ⓔ
6 Ⓐ Ⓑ Ⓒ Ⓓ Ⓔ
7 Ⓐ Ⓑ Ⓒ Ⓓ Ⓔ
8 Ⓐ Ⓑ Ⓒ Ⓓ Ⓔ
9 Ⓐ Ⓑ Ⓒ Ⓓ Ⓔ
10 Ⓐ Ⓑ Ⓒ Ⓓ Ⓔ

11 Ⓐ Ⓑ Ⓒ Ⓓ Ⓔ
12 Ⓐ Ⓑ Ⓒ Ⓓ Ⓔ
13 Ⓐ Ⓑ Ⓒ Ⓓ Ⓔ
14 Ⓐ Ⓑ Ⓒ Ⓓ Ⓔ
15 Ⓐ Ⓑ Ⓒ Ⓓ Ⓔ
16 Ⓐ Ⓑ Ⓒ Ⓓ Ⓔ
17 Ⓐ Ⓑ Ⓒ Ⓓ Ⓔ
18 Ⓐ Ⓑ Ⓒ Ⓓ Ⓔ
19 Ⓐ Ⓑ Ⓒ Ⓓ Ⓔ
20 Ⓐ Ⓑ Ⓒ Ⓓ Ⓔ

21 Ⓐ Ⓑ Ⓒ Ⓓ Ⓔ
22 Ⓐ Ⓑ Ⓒ Ⓓ Ⓔ
23 Ⓐ Ⓑ Ⓒ Ⓓ Ⓔ
24 Ⓐ Ⓑ Ⓒ Ⓓ Ⓔ
25 Ⓐ Ⓑ Ⓒ Ⓓ Ⓔ
26 Ⓐ Ⓑ Ⓒ Ⓓ Ⓔ
27 Ⓐ Ⓑ Ⓒ Ⓓ Ⓔ
28 Ⓐ Ⓑ Ⓒ Ⓓ Ⓔ
29 Ⓐ Ⓑ Ⓒ Ⓓ Ⓔ
30 Ⓐ Ⓑ Ⓒ Ⓓ Ⓔ

31 Ⓐ Ⓑ Ⓒ Ⓓ Ⓔ
32 Ⓐ Ⓑ Ⓒ Ⓓ Ⓔ
33 Ⓐ Ⓑ Ⓒ Ⓓ Ⓔ
34 Ⓐ Ⓑ Ⓒ Ⓓ Ⓔ
35 Ⓐ Ⓑ Ⓒ Ⓓ Ⓔ
36 Ⓐ Ⓑ Ⓒ Ⓓ Ⓔ
37 Ⓐ Ⓑ Ⓒ Ⓓ Ⓔ
38 Ⓐ Ⓑ Ⓒ Ⓓ Ⓔ
39 Ⓐ Ⓑ Ⓒ Ⓓ Ⓔ
40 Ⓐ Ⓑ Ⓒ Ⓓ Ⓔ

SECTION 1
ESSAY
Time — 25 minutes

Turn to Section 1 of your answer sheet to write your essay.

The essay gives you an opportunity to show how effectively you can develop and express ideas. You should, therefore, take care to develop your point of view, present your ideas logically and clearly, and use language precisely.

Your essay must be written on the lines provided on your answer sheet—you will receive no other paper on which to write. You will have enough space if you write on every line, avoid wide margins, and keep your handwriting to a reasonable size. Remember that people who are not familiar with your handwriting will read what you write. Try to write or print so that what you are writing is legible to those readers.

You have twenty-five minutes to write an essay on the topic assigned below. DO NOT WRITE ON ANOTHER TOPIC. AN OFF-TOPIC ESSAY WILL RECEIVE A SCORE OF ZERO.

Think carefully about the issue presented in the following excerpt and the assignment below.

> There are times when it is easier to lie than it is to tell the truth. The truth may cause someone harm—financially, emotionally, or even physically—and so may do far greater damage than the damage of a lie, which harms only a person's trust.

Assignment: Are there instances when lying is the more appropriate action than telling the truth? Plan and write an essay in which you develop your point of view on this issue. Support your position with reasoning and examples taken from your reading, studies, experience, or observations.

DO NOT WRITE YOUR ESSAY IN YOUR TEST BOOK. You will receive credit only for what you write on your answer sheet.

BEGIN WRITING YOUR ESSAY IN SECTION 1 OF THE ANSWER SHEET.

STOP

**If you finish before time is called, you may check your work on this section only.
Do not turn to any other section in the test.**

SECTION 2
Time — 25 minutes
24 Questions

Turn to Section 2 of your answer sheet to answer the questions in this section.

Directions: For each question in this section, select the best answer from among the choices given and fill in the corresponding circle on the answer sheet.

Each sentence below has one or two blanks, each blank indicating that something has been omitted. Beneath the sentence are five words or sets of words labeled A through E. Choose the word or set of words that, when inserted in the sentence, best fits the meaning of the sentence as a whole.

Example:

Desiring to ------- his taunting friends, Mitch gave them taffy in hopes it would keep their mouths shut.

(A) eliminate   (B) satisfy   (C) overcome
(D) ridicule   (E) silence

Ⓐ Ⓑ Ⓒ Ⓓ ●

---

1. Ellie looked on ------- as Tom described his encounter with Bigfoot; she doubted such a creature even existed.

    (A) erroneously   (B) awkwardly   (C) miraculously
       (D) skeptically   (E) maliciously

2. Always looking for ------- theories, Hector was as eager to explore new possibilities as the more narrow minded scientists were to ------- them.

    (A) enlightening . . develop
    (B) relative . . disregard
    (C) innovative . . belittle
    (D) provocative . . study
    (E) exciting . . support

3. Despite painter Jean Michel Basquiat's ------- rise to prominence, he just as quickly ------- to the pressures of fame and died before turning thirty.

    (A) unprecedented . . appealed
    (B) swift . . yielded
    (C) graceful . . aspired
    (D) hasty . . ascended
    (E) lethal . . subsided

4. After he had been bitten by a jungle insect, Kei experienced a dull, pervasive discomfort rather than an -------, localized pain.

    (A) unstudied   (B) acute   (C) invasive
       (D) elevated   (E) obvious

5. Andy's best feature is his -------: he will always stick to his principles, no matter how daunting the opposition.

    (A) munificence   (B) efficacy   (C) intensity
       (D) tenacity   (E) eccentricity

6. Procrastination is often tempting, but circumstances sometimes demand ------- action.

    (A) prompt   (B) reckless   (C) caustic
       (D) protracted   (E) fallacious

7. In public, Chris is an amiable and generous donor, who gives freely of his time and money, yet his stinginess and ------- in private ------- this benevolent public image.

    (A) callousness . . belie
    (B) immorality . . display
    (C) perniciousness . . evaluate
    (D) austerity . . alleviate
    (E) contentment . . contradict

8. Nurses who work in emergency medicine departments are accustomed to handling urgent trauma situations in which every task must be performed with great -------.

    (A) passivity   (B) ineptitude   (C) alacrity
       (D) morbidity   (E) consternation

GO ON TO THE NEXT PAGE ⟩

Directions: Each passage below is followed by questions based on its content. Answer the questions on the basis of what is <u>stated</u> or <u>implied</u> in each passage and in any introductory material that may be provided.

Questions 9-12 are based on the following passages.

Passage 1

    The twentieth century will be remembered as one hundred years of great upheaval. All the major changes wrought in this century—from Picasso's paintings to James Joyce's novel
Line *Ulysses*—were profoundly influenced by Albert Einstein.
5 Einstein's theory of special relativity debunked the notions of Absolute Rest and Absolute Time, therefore implying that both time and space were subject to relative forces. Artists and writers applied this idea to their craft. Did all novels have to have plot, did all paintings have to be representational? The
10 answer of the twentieth century was an emphatic "no."

Passage 2

    Just as the Renaissance pulled Europe out of the Middle Ages, ideas of the twentieth century radically altered the ways that people think, interact, and live. While several aspects of the twentieth century are unique, there are still startling
15 parallels between the Renaissance and the last hundred years of the past millennium. Both time periods saw great advances in science; Copernicus caused as much furor as Einstein. Exploration—whether of the New World or of new world markets—led to trade expansion. Art moved in startlingly
20 different directions, away from the Gothicism of the fifteenth century and the dogmatic Realism of the nineteenth. It seems the twentieth century was not so different from the world of Shakespeare.

9. According to the author of Passage 1, which of the following is true of the twentieth century?

(A) There was a synthesis of ideas across various disciplines.
(B) Einstein proved the existence of Absolute Rest.
(C) Picasso was younger than Einstein.
(D) Literature was completely different from nineteenth century works.
(E) Einstein dabbled in art as well as science.

10. It can be inferred from Passage 2 that

(A) Realism was a precursor to both the Renaissance and the twentieth century
(B) the Renaissance and the twentieth century saw similar advances in science
(C) Shakespeare was a Renaissance figure
(D) the Renaissance saw the beginnings of capitalism
(E) advances during both the Renaissance and the twentieth century were mainly centered in Europe

11. The authors of both passages would probably agree with which of the following statements?

(A) Art and science are inextricably linked.
(B) Picasso was indirectly influenced by ideas of Copernicus.
(C) Einstein was one of the most important thinkers of the twentieth century.
(D) The twentieth century could not have existed without the model of the Renaissance.
(E) Classical music did not change much in the twentieth century.

12. How would each passage incorporate the ideas of the nineteenth century into its argument?

(A) Passage 1 would focus on parallels in ideas; Passage 2 would see the nineteenth century as an extension of the Renaissance.
(B) Passage 1 would establish contrasts; Passage 2 would explore links between the nineteenth century and a similar historical period.
(C) Passage 1 would discuss economic advances; Passage 2 would discuss art theory.
(D) Both passages would mention the importance of immigration.
(E) Both passages would discuss Shakespeare's influence on the nineteenth century.

GO ON TO THE NEXT PAGE ⟹

Questions 13-24 are based on the following passage.

In this excerpt from "Stride Toward Freedom," Martin Luther King, Jr. discusses the condition of the African American in American society. Written in 1958, it presents a number of problems facing African Americans and points the way to a solution.

Ever since the signing of the Declaration of Independence, America has manifested a schizophrenic personality on the question of race. She has been torn between selves—a self
Line in which she has proudly professed democracy and a self in
5 which she has sadly practiced the antithesis of democracy. The reality of segregation, like slavery, has always had to confront the ideals of democracy and Christianity. Indeed, segregation and discrimination are strange paradoxes in a nation founded on the principle that all men are created equal.
10 This contradiction has disturbed the consciences of whites both North and South, and has caused many of them to see that segregation is basically evil.

Climaxing this process was the Supreme Court's decision outlawing segregation in the public schools. For all men of
15 good will, May 17, 1954 marked a joyous end to the long night of enforced segregation. In unequivocal language the court affirmed that "separate but equal" facilities are inherently unequal, and that to segregate a child on the basis of his race is to deny that child equal protection of the law. This decision
20 brought hope to millions of disinherited Negroes who had formerly dared only to dream of freedom. It further enhanced the Negro's sense of dignity and gave him even greater determination to achieve justice.

This determination of Negro Americans to win freedom
25 from all forms of oppression springs from the same deep longing that motivates oppressed peoples all over the world. The rumblings of discontent in Asia and Africa are expressions of a quest for freedom and human dignity by people who have long been the victims of colonialism and
30 imperialism. So in a real sense the racial crisis in America is a part of the larger world crisis.

But the numerous changes which have culminated in a new sense of dignity on the part of the Negro are not of themselves responsible for the present crisis. If all men
35 accepted these historical changes in good faith there would be no crisis. The crisis developed when the collective pressures to achieve fair goals for the Negro met with tenacious and determined resistance. Then the emerging new order, based on the principle of democratic equalitarianism, came face
40 to face with the older order, based on the principles of paternalism and subordination. The crisis was not produced by outside agitators, NAACP'ers, Montgomery Protestors, or even the Supreme Court. The crisis developed, paradoxically, when the most sublime principles of American democracy—
45 imperfectly realized for almost two centuries—began fulfilling themselves and met with the brutal resistance of forces seeking to contract and repress freedom's growth.

The resistance has risen at times to ominous proportions. Many states have reacted in open defiance. The legislative
50 halls of the South still ring loud with such words as "interposition" and "nullification." Many public officials are using the power of their offices to defy the law of the land. Through their irresponsible actions, their inflammatory statements, and the dissemination of distortion and half-
55 truths, they have succeeded in rousing abnormal fears and morbid antipathies within the minds of underprivileged and uneducated whites, leaving them in such a state of excitement and confusion that they are led to acts of meanness and violence that no normal person would commit.
60 The present crisis in race relations has characteristics that come to the forefront in any period of social transition. The guardians of the status quo lash out with denunciation against the person or organization that they consider most responsible for the emergence of the new order. Often this denunciation
65 rises to major proportions. In the transition form slavery to restricted emancipation Abraham Lincoln was assassinated. In the present transition from segregation to desegregation the Supreme Court is castigated and the NAACP is maligned and subjected to extralegal reprisals.
70 This is a great hour for the Negro. The challenge is here. To become the instruments of a great idea is a privilege that history gives only occasionally. Arnold Toynbee says in *A Study of History* that it may be the Negro who will give the new spiritual dynamic to Western civilization that it so
75 desperately needs to survive. I hope this is possible. The spiritual power that the Negro can radiate to the world comes from love, understanding, good will, and nonviolence, so to challenge the nations of the world that they will seriously seek an alternative to war and destruction. In a day when
80 Sputniks and Explorers dash through outer space and guided ballistic missiles are carving highways of death through the stratosphere, nobody can win a war. Today the choice is no longer between violence and nonviolence. It is either nonviolence or nonexistence. The Negro may be God's appeal
85 to this age—an age drifting rapidly to its doom. The eternal appeal takes the form of a warning: "All who take the sword will perish by the sword."

13. The author's description of America's "schizophrenic personality" (line 2) refers to his belief that

(A) racial inequality can be viewed as an American disease

(B) this nation is dramatically split on the issue of racial segregation

(C) the practice of segregation is contradictory to the ideals of democracy that define America

(D) segregation is immoral, and therefore America must transform itself into an ethical society

(E) segregation is an illusion that has clouded the judgment of many otherwise well-meaning individuals

GO ON TO THE NEXT PAGE ➔

14. In the first paragraph, the contradiction that "disturbed the consciences of whites" (line 10) was

(A) the inconsistency of Dr. King's attitude as the leader of the Civil Rights movement
(B) the fact that the Supreme Court internally advocated desegregation, but passed laws that perpetuated segregation
(C) the fact that the principles of democracy and Christianity have little in common
(D) the fact that discrimination is rampant in a society that outwardly preaches equality
(E) differences in the attitudes of African Americans towards segregation in the North and the South

15. The passage suggests that as a result of the Supreme Court's decision (lines 13-14)

(A) the Civil Rights movement could be temporarily suspended
(B) schools were prevented from excluding students on the basis of skin color
(C) African Americans, inspired by the decision, became more involved in the educational system
(D) the political discontent in Asia and Africa intensified and spread to other regions
(E) the number of white supremacist groups in the South increased

16. In line 19 "deny" most nearly means

(A) dispute
(B) contradict
(C) disbelieve
(D) withhold from
(E) declare untrue

17. The third paragraph (lines 24-31) primarily emphasizes that

(A) society needs to concentrate on international issues before addressing domestic concerns
(B) the problems in Asia and Africa have received more international attention than the struggle for racial equality in America
(C) in order for freedom and human dignity to flourish, discontent needs to be suppressed
(D) the motivations for freedom are universal since the struggles in Africa and Asia are virtually identical
(E) the African Americans' struggle is not an isolated occurrence

18. The feature that distinguishes the "new order" (line 38) from the "older order" (line 40) is best described as which of the following?

(A) The older order has less democratic perceptions, believing that certain groups should be controlled by others.
(B) The new order is interested only in seizing social and political power by nonviolent means.
(C) The older order concerns itself only with issues that apply to the domestic situation and ignores matters of international importance.
(D) The new order consists of members whose affiliation with the NAACP and Montgomery Protesters has heightened their respectability.
(E) The older order cannot understand the arch-traditionalists who endorse a more resistant approach to minorities.

19. The author would consider which of the following responsible for the crisis mentioned in line 41 ?

(A) Supreme Court decisions that were unpopular with the majority of Americans
(B) conflict between the ideals of democracy and the realities of segregated society
(C) oppressed African Americans who stood up for the equal rights they deserved
(D) legislation that might have prevented the violence but was vetoed by the President
(E) intentional sabotage by alienated church leaders

20. In line 48, "resistance" most nearly means

(A) denial
(B) opposition
(C) underground
(D) distinction
(E) power

21. According to the author, "underprivileged and uneducated whites" (lines 56-57) act against integration by

(A) subtly ignoring the African American community in hopes that it might disintegrate
(B) engaging in haphazard acts of cruelty and destruction
(C) petitioning against any governmental agency that talks of "interposition"
(D) abusing officials who spread lies and half-truths that mislead the public
(E) issuing pleas to the government to block integration laws that would lead to mixed communities

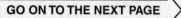

GO ON TO THE NEXT PAGE

22. It can be inferred that the author compares the assassination of Abraham Lincoln with the castigation of the Supreme Court (lines 65-69) in order to

(A) indicate that absence of morality during the Civil War

(B) denounce white supremacists as racists who are unwilling to change in spite of recent constitutional amendments

(C) prove that the Supreme Court justices installed during Lincoln's tenure were exemplary

(D) warn the Supreme Court justices about possible assassination attempts

(E) emphasize that the current response to the change in race relations is similar to that of the past

23. The author cites Toynbee's *A Study of History* in order to

(A) suggest that African Americans may contribute something of value to Western civilization

(B) predict the imminent destruction of American civilization

(C) extol the efforts of Abraham Lincoln to abolish slavery

(D) demonstrate that spirituality is a direct result of nonviolent resistance

(E) establish that the constant pressures of discrimination have suppressed the spirituality of African Americans

24. The author would be most likely to agree with which of the following?

(A) Abraham Lincoln was assassinated because he advocated restrictions on emancipation.

(B) The threat of "war and destruction" is due to the racist policies of the United States.

(C) The principles of American democracy will never be perfectly realized.

(D) The Supreme Court's decision to desegregate public schools had impacts outside of the field of education.

(E) Public officials are irresponsible and can no longer be trusted to be honest with citizens.

STOP

If you finish before time is called, you may check your work on this section only.
Do not turn to any other section in the test.

NO TEST MATERIAL ON THIS PAGE.

SECTION 3
Time — 25 minutes
20 Questions

Turn to Section 3 of your answer sheet to answer the questions in this section.

Directions: For this section, solve each problem and decide which is the best of the choices given. Fill in the corresponding circle on the answer sheet. You may use any available space for scratchwork.

Notes

1. The use of a calculator is permitted.

2. All numbers used are real numbers.

3. Figures that accompany problems in this test are intended to provide information useful in solving the problems. They are drawn as accurately as possible EXCEPT when it is stated in a specific problem that the figure is not drawn to scale. All figures lie in a plane unless otherwise indicated.

4. Unless otherwise specified, the domain of any function f is assumed to be the set of all real numbers x for which $f(x)$ is a real number.

Reference Information

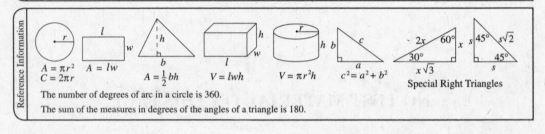

$A = \pi r^2$ $A = lw$ $A = \frac{1}{2}bh$ $V = lwh$ $V = \pi r^2 h$ $c^2 = a^2 + b^2$

$C = 2\pi r$ Special Right Triangles

The number of degrees of arc in a circle is 360.

The sum of the measures in degrees of the angles of a triangle is 180.

1. If $3x + 1 = 19$, then $6x - 2 =$

   (A)   6
   (B) 12
   (C) 34
   (D) 38
   (E) 40

2. The average (arithmetic mean) of a student's grades on four history tests is 86. If the student received two grades of 83 and one of 85, what grade did the student receive on the fourth test?

   (A) 95
   (B) 93
   (C) 90
   (D) 89
   (E) 88

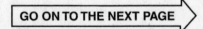

GO ON TO THE NEXT PAGE

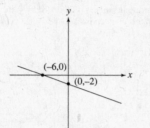

3. Which of the following equations defines the line in the *xy* coordinate system above?

(A) $y = -\dfrac{1}{3}x - 2$

(B) $y = -\dfrac{1}{2}x - 3$

(C) $y = -2x - 3$

(D) $y = -2x + 3$

(E) $y = -3x - 2$

4. Set *A* consists of all integers such that each element is equal to its square. How many elements are in set *A* ?

(A) Zero
(B) One
(C) Two
(D) Three
(E) Four

5. If $a^3 = 4$, what is the value of a^6 ?

(A) 8
(B) 10
(C) 12
(D) 16
(E) 64

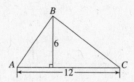

6. If the area of $\triangle ABC$ above is equal to the area of a square with side of length *x*, then $x =$

(A) 6
(B) $6\sqrt{2}$
(C) 9
(D) 12
(E) $12\sqrt{3}$

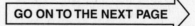

GO ON TO THE NEXT PAGE

7. If $x > 0 > y$, which of the following inequalities must be true?

   (A) $x^3 > y^3$

   (B) $x^2 < y^2$

   (C) $x - y < 0$

   (D) $\dfrac{1}{x^2} < \dfrac{1}{y^2}$

   (E) $\dfrac{1}{x} < \dfrac{1}{y}$

8. If $f(x) = |x - 4|$, which of the following has the LEAST value?

   (A) $f(8)$
   (B) $f(4)$
   (C) $f(0)$
   (D) $f(-4)$
   (E) $f(-8)$

9. When a certain number is increased by 4, the result is equal to that number divided by 7. What is the number?

   (A) $-\dfrac{14}{3}$

   (B) $\dfrac{4}{7}$

   (C) $\dfrac{2}{3}$

   (D) $\dfrac{14}{3}$

   (E) 28

10. In square $PQRS$, point T is the midpoint of side $\overline{QR}$. If the area of $PQRS$ is 3, what is the area of quadrilateral $PQTS$?

    (A) $\dfrac{3}{2}$

    (B) 2

    (C) $\dfrac{9}{4}$

    (D) $\dfrac{3\sqrt{3}}{2}$

    (E) $2\sqrt{3}$

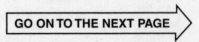

GO ON TO THE NEXT PAGE

11. Ron has a bucket of red, white, and blue marbles. The number of red marbles is two more than the number of blue marbles, and the number of white marbles is twice the number of red marbles. Which of the following could be the total number of marbles?

(A) 24
(B) 25
(C) 26
(D) 27
(E) 28

12. If $a = f - 2$ and $b = 4f + 5$, which of the following is an expression for b in terms of a ?

(A) $4a$
(B) $4a - 4$
(C) $4a + 2$
(D) $4a + 7$
(E) $4a + 13$

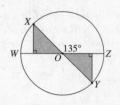

13. In the circle with center O, $\overline{WZ}$ and $\overline{XY}$ are diameters with lengths of 12. What is the area of the shaded region?

(A) 36
(B) 30
(C) 18
(D) 12
(E) 9

14. If x and y are positive integers, $(3^x)^y = 81$, and $3^x + 3^y = 84$, which of the following could be the value of x ?

(A) 2
(B) 3
(C) 4
(D) 5
(E) 6

GO ON TO THE NEXT PAGE

15. A triangle has vertices at points A, B, and C, which are located at $(1, 0)$, $(-3, 0)$, and $(0, 5)$ respectively. What is the distance from the midpoint of $\overline{AB}$ to point C ?

    (A) 3

    (B) 5

    (C) $\sqrt{26}$

    (D) $\sqrt{29}$

    (E) $\dfrac{\sqrt{26} + \sqrt{34}}{2}$

16. In the function $f(x) = \left(x^c\right)\left(x^{\frac{1}{c}}\right)$, c is a nonzero constant. If $f(2) = 4\sqrt{2}$, what is the value of c ?

    (A) 2

    (B) 3

    (C) 4

    (D) 16

    (E) 32

17. The cost for coal from a certain company is $15 for the first pound plus $6 for each additional pound of coal. Which of the following functions gives the total cost, in dollars, for p pounds of coal?

    (A) $C(p) = 6p - 15$
    (B) $C(p) = 6p - 9$
    (C) $C(p) = 6p$
    (D) $C(p) = 6p + 9$
    (E) $C(p) = 6p + 15$

18. If the members of set A are all the odd single-digit positive integers and the members of set B are all the prime integers, which of the following is the set of numbers common to both set A and set B ?

    (A) $\{1, 3, 5, 7\}$
    (B) $\{1, 3, 5, 7, 9\}$
    (C) $\{2, 3, 5, 7\}$
    (D) $\{3, 5, 7\}$
    (E) $\{3, 5, 7, 9\}$

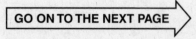
GO ON TO THE NEXT PAGE

19. The sum of 8 positive integers is 31. If no individual integer value can appear more than twice in the list of 8 integers, what is the greatest possible value one of these integers can have?

    (A) 16
    (B) 15
    (C) 10
    (D) 9
    (E) 7

20. Line q is given by the equation $y = -x + 8$, and line r is given by the equation $4y = 3x - 24$. If line r intersects the y-axis at point A, line q intersects the y-axis at point B, and both lines intersect the x-axis at point C, what is the area of $\triangle ABC$?

    (A) 14
    (B) 24
    (C) 48
    (D) 56
    (E) 112

STOP
**If you finish before time is called, you may check your work on this section only.
Do not turn to any other section in the test.**

SECTION 4
Time — 25 minutes
35 Questions

Turn to Section 4 of your answer sheet to answer the questions in this section.

Directions: For each question in this section, select the best answer from among the choices given and fill in the corresponding circle on the answer sheet.

The following sentences test correctness and effectiveness of expression. Part of each sentence or the entire sentence is underlined; beneath each sentence are five ways of phrasing the underlined material. Choice A repéats the original phrasing; the other four choices are different. If you think the original phrasing produces a better sentence than any of the alternatives, select choice A; if not, select one of the other choices.

In making your selection, follow the requirements of standard written English; that is, pay attention to grammar, choice of words, sentence construction, and punctuation. Your selection should result in the most effective sentence—clear and precise, without awkwardness or ambiguity.

EXAMPLE:

Bobby Flay baked his first cake and he was thirteen years old then.

(A) and he was thirteen years old then
(B) when he was thirteen
(C) at age thirteen years old
(D) upon the reaching of thirteen years
(E) at the time when he was thirteen

Ⓐ●ⒸⒹⒺ

1. The teacher's enthusiasm and obvious passion for the subject inspired students and before they had never been interested in Shakespeare.

(A) students and before they had never been interested in Shakespeare
(B) students, and they had never before been interested in Shakespeare
(C) students; before that they had never been interested in Shakespeare
(D) students who had never before been interested in Shakespeare
(E) students that Shakespeare had never before interested them

2. In the last twenty years, despite the chauvinism of European connoisseurs, California wines are respected throughout the world.

(A) are respected throughout the world
(B) are becoming better respected throughout the world
(C) which have gained respect throughout the world
(D) have gained respect throughout the world
(E) have since become respected throughout the world

3. In an effort to rouse her unconscious son, Mrs. Simpson shaked him and called out his name.

(A) Mrs. Simpson shaked him and called out his name
(B) shaking him, Mrs. Simpson called out his name
(C) Mrs. Simpson shook him and called out his name
(D) he was shaken and his name was called out by Mrs. Simpson
(E) he was shaken by Mrs. Simpson, who called out his name

4. As it is best known for its winter activities, which include skiing, skating, and sledding, the resort also has a complete summer program.

(A) As it is best known for its winter activities, which include skiing, skating, and sledding
(B) Best known for its winter activities, which include both skiing and skating, as well as sledding
(C) Best known for its winter activities, which include skiing, skating, and the riding of sleds
(D) By being best known for its winter activities, which include skiing, skating, and sledding
(E) Best known for its winter activities, which include skiing, skating, and sledding

5. Because the flight was non-stop, and so they were able to sleep for a number of hours.

(A) and so they were able to sleep for a number of hours
(B) therefore for a number of hours they slept
(C) they were able to sleep for a number of hours
(D) therefore they were sleeping for a number of hours
(E) sleeping for a number of hours was possible for them

GO ON TO THE NEXT PAGE

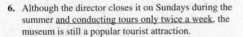

6. Although the director closes it on Sundays during the summer <u>and conducting tours only twice a week</u>, the museum is still a popular tourist attraction.

    (A) and conducting tours only twice a week
    (B) and is conducting tours only twice a week
    (C) and conducts tours twice a week
    (D) and twice a week conducts tours only
    (E) and conducts tours only twice a week

7. If mixed with a weak acid in a sealed container, <u>you can get an explosion from baking soda</u>.

    (A) you can get an explosion from baking soda
    (B) baking soda can explode
    (C) you could be getting an explosion from baking soda
    (D) baking soda, it can explode
    (E) then baking soda could be exploding

8. <u>Manet's work had a profound impact on his contemporaries</u>, including famous Impressionists such as Monet and Renoir.

    (A) Manet's work had a profound impact on his contemporaries
    (B) Manet's work had profoundly impacted his contemporaries
    (C) Manet profoundly influenced his contemporaries through his work
    (D) The work of Manet was profound on his contemporaries in its impact
    (E) Many of his contemporaries had felt the profound impact of the work of Manet

9. The testing procedures of the Food and Drug Administration <u>is an obstacle course which any new drug and its makers must run</u> before the drug is approved for sale to the public.

    (A) is an obstacle course which any new drug and its makers must run
    (B) are like an obstacle course through which any new drug and its maker must run
    (C) are an obstacle course run by its makers
    (D) which must be run as an obstacle course by any new drug
    (E) runs an obstacle course for any new drug

10. <u>Having lived there as a child, the street looked vaguely familiar to Judy.</u>

    (A) Having lived there as a child, the street looked vaguely familiar to Judy.
    (B) Having lived there as a child, Judy found the street to be vaguely familiar.
    (C) Living there as a child, the street was found by Judy to be vaguely familiar.
    (D) Living there as a child, Judy found the street vaguely familiar to her.
    (E) Judy lived there as a child, so to her the street was found to be vaguely familiar.

11. The major areas of medicine in which lasers are effective <u>is in the cutting and closing of blood vessels, and in the destruction of tumors</u>.

    (A) is in the cutting and closing of blood vessels, and in the destruction of tumors
    (B) are the cutting and closing of blood vessels, and also the case of destroying tumors
    (C) are the cutting, closing of blood vessels, and in the destroying of tumors
    (D) are the cutting and closing of blood vessels, and the destroying of tumors
    (E) is in the cutting and closing of blood vessels, and the destruction of tumors

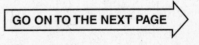

GO ON TO THE NEXT PAGE

The following sentences test your ability to recognize grammar and usage errors. Each sentence contains either a single error or no error at all. No sentence contains more than one error. The error, if there is one, is underlined and lettered. If the sentence contains an error, select the one underlined part that must be changed to make the sentence correct. If the sentence is correct, select choice E. In choosing answers, follow the requirements of standard written English.

EXAMPLE:

<u>The other</u> players and <u>her</u> <u>significantly</u> improved
　　A　　　　　　　　B　　　　C

the game plan <u>created by</u> the coaches. <u>No error</u>
　　　　　　　　　D　　　　　　　　　　E

Ⓐ ● Ⓒ Ⓓ Ⓔ

12. <u>Considering</u> how close the cafe was to his house, it is
　　A

surprising <u>that,</u> even though <u>he enjoyed</u> the ambiance,
　　　　B　　　　　　　　　　C

Chris hardly <u>never visited</u> it. <u>No error</u>
　　　　　　　D　　　　　　E

13. The trees <u>in</u> Bob's backyard <u>are</u> much
　　　　　　A　　　　　　　　B

<u>taller and greener</u> than <u>Henry.</u> <u>No error</u>
　　　C　　　　　　　　D　　　E

14. <u>To understand fully</u> William Shakespeare's body of work
　　A

we must analyze <u>not only</u> his most famous plays such
　　　　　　　　B

as *Hamlet,* <u>but also</u> his <u>lesser known</u> plays, poems, and
　　　　　　　C　　　　　　D

sonnets. <u>No error</u>
　　　　　E

15. <u>Last night</u> was not the first time Charles was exposed
　　A

<u>to her culinary</u> skills; Christine, a first-rate chef,
　　B

<u>has cooked</u> for him last week <u>as well.</u> <u>No error</u>
　　C　　　　　　　　　　　　　D　　　　E

16. Although the advertised price of a car may

<u>seem reasonable,</u> <u>the addition of</u> dealer preparation fees,
　　A　　　　　　　B

required options, <u>taxes, and delivery</u> charges may make
　　　　　　　　　C

the actual cost less attractive to a <u>prospective</u> buyer.
　　　　　　　　　　　　　　D

<u>No error</u>
E

17. <u>Also allowed</u> by the newer and more liberal investment
　　A

law <u>was</u> tax shelters, now <u>commonly used</u> by people
　　B　　　　　　　　C

<u>of all classes.</u> <u>No error</u>
　　D　　　　E

18. <u>While it may</u> appear that stewardesses are
　　A

<u>concerned solely to</u> passengers' comfort, they <u>are in fact</u>
　　B　　　　　　　　　　　　　　　C

extensively <u>schooled</u> in flight safety. <u>No error</u>
　　　　　D　　　　　　　　E

19. <u>After</u> dining on fish <u>from both</u> the Atlantic and Pacific
　　A　　　　　　　B

oceans, <u>I have decided</u> that Seattle's fish are superior to
　　　　　C

<u>Cape Cod.</u> <u>No error</u>
　　D　　　E

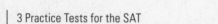

GO ON TO THE NEXT PAGE ⟩

20. <u>Whenever</u> Diana returns to the office after a long
    A

vacation, <u>she</u> finds <u>it</u> disorganized, dirty, and
      B   C

<u>an ugly place</u>. <u>No error</u>
   D   E

21. <u>While</u> the United States <u>may be lagging</u> behind Asia
    A   B

in the electronics market and Europe in the automobile

market, <u>we are</u> still a <u>leading</u> agricultural nation.
      C   D

<u>No error</u>
 E

22. The newspaper reporter enjoys reading the essays

<u>of</u> Orwell <u>during</u> his free time for <u>their</u> clarity,
A   B   C

conciseness, and <u>because they are persuasive</u>. <u>No error</u>
               D   E

23. After we had skipped <u>our</u> second class of the week,
              A

the <u>principal</u> called <u>Thomas and I</u> down to her office
     B   C

<u>for a conference</u>. <u>No error</u>
   D   E

24. Students who wish to become <u>a doctor</u> must begin
                A

planning <u>their</u> studies <u>long before</u> they <u>apply to</u>
      B   C   D

medical school. <u>No error</u>
         E

25. During the past several decades, <u>as</u> "super stores"
                    A

and national franchises have gained popularity, many

<u>locally owned</u> small businesses <u>are closing</u> <u>because of</u>
   B   C   D

the overwhelming competition. <u>No error</u>
                     E

26. Although <u>his term</u> <u>was much shorter</u> <u>than that of later</u>
         A   B   C

presidents, <u>President Lincoln instituted</u> the income tax,
            D

the draft, and the Thanksgiving holiday. <u>No error</u>
                         E

27. The <u>recently lowered</u> interest <u>rates allowed</u> my
      A   B

<u>wife and me</u> to buy a <u>larger home</u> for our family.
   C   D

<u>No error</u>
 E

28. Neither of America's major political parties <u>are interested</u>
                           A

<u>in making</u> the <u>trade balance</u> an important issue
   B   C

<u>in the recent</u> elections. <u>No error</u>
   D   E

29. Only after the Air Force <u>had ran</u> out of
              A

<u>other options</u> did it consider <u>launching</u> the new satellite
   B   C

<u>from the space shuttle</u>. <u>No error</u>
   D   E

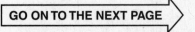

GO ON TO THE NEXT PAGE

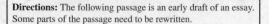
Directions: The following passage is an early draft of an essay. Some parts of the passage need to be rewritten.

Read the passage and select the best answers for the questions that follow. Some questions are about particular sentences or parts of sentences and ask you to improve sentence structure or word choice. Other questions ask you to consider organization and development. In choosing answers, follow the requirements of standard written English.

Questions 30-35 are based on the following passage.

(1) Starting on January 1, Bakersfield High School is planning to implement a dress code. (2) The administration has printed out a list of those items that students will be allowed to wear to school and those that will be considered unacceptable. (3) Even though I understand that the school had good intentions, I think that it is a bad idea overall.

(4) There are a number of problems with the dress code. (5) The rule against clothes that are "torn, ripped, or cut off" discriminates against many students. (6) Some students cannot afford to buy new clothes every year. (7) In the late spring and early summer, students forced to wear long pants will be so uncomfortable that they will not be able to concentrate on their studies. (8) Although girls can stay cool in skirts and dresses, boys have no such option.

(9) Even so, a dress code violates students' freedom of expression. (10) Students should be able to dress themselves in a way that expresses their tastes and creativity. (11) It is only through making decisions about ourselves and how we choose to present ourselves that we will grow into mature, independent adults.

30. In context, which version of the underlined section of sentence 2 (reproduced below) is the best?

    The administration has printed out a list of those items that students will be allowed to wear to school and those that will be considered unacceptable.

    (A) (as it is now)
    (B) school. Those that will be considered unacceptable
    (C) school; others that will be considered unacceptable
    (D) school as well as unacceptable clothing
    (E) school, and others that will not be considered acceptable

31. In sentence 3, the word "it" could best be replaced with which of the following?

    (A) the administration
    (B) the dress code
    (C) the list
    (D) the intention
    (E) the school

32. Which of the following is the best version of the underlined portion of sentence 9 (reproduced below)?

    Even so, a dress code violates students' freedom of expression.

    (A) (As it is now)
    (B) Most importantly,
    (C) To the extent that
    (D) It is true that
    (E) That notwithstanding,

33. Which of the following, if added immediately after sentence 11, would provide the best concluding sentence for the passage?

    (A) As near-adults, we should be allowed to decide how to dress ourselves.
    (B) In today's society, teenagers are required to make decisions about a number of extremely important issues.
    (C) Thus, the dress code will ultimately impede the educational process rather than aid it.
    (D) It is for a student and his or her parents to decide what clothing a student should wear, not a school administration.
    (E) If we must have a dress code, it should be one that does not discriminate against students on the basis of their gender or income level.

GO ON TO THE NEXT PAGE

34. The author's argument would be more balanced if it included a section on which of the following?

    (A) An outline of the steps that students will take to overturn the dress code, should it be implemented

    (B) A list of other bureaucratic policies that have angered students in the past

    (C) A discussion of the author's own clothing preferences

    (D) An acknowledgment of the positive aspects of the dress-code policy

    (E) The suggestion that the dress code be limited to ninth graders

35. In context, which of the following is the best way to revise the underlined wording in order to combine sentences 5 and 6 ?

The rule against clothes that are "torn, ripped or cut off" discriminates <u>against many students. Some students cannot afford to buy new clothes every year.</u>

    (A) against many students, some students cannot afford to buy new clothes every year.

    (B) against many of those students who cannot buy new clothes every year because they cannot afford it.

    (C) against students, many of which cannot afford to buy new clothes every year.

    (D) against those students who cannot afford to buy new clothes every year.

    (E) against many of the students being unable to afford to buy new clothes every year.

STOP

**If you finish before time is called, you may check your work on this section only.
Do not turn to any other section in the test.**

SECTION 5
Time — 25 minutes
18 Questions

Turn to Section 5 of your answer sheet to answer the questions in this section.

Directions: This section contains two types of questions. You have 25 minutes to complete both types. For questions 1-8, solve each problem and decide which is the best of the choices given. Fill in the corresponding circle on the answer sheet. You may use any available space for scratchwork.

Notes

1. The use of a calculator is permitted.

2. All numbers used are real numbers.

3. Figures that accompany problems in this test are intended to provide information useful in solving the problems. They are drawn as accurately as possible EXCEPT when it is stated in a specific problem that the figure is not drawn to scale. All figures lie in a plane unless otherwise indicated.

4. Unless otherwise specified, the domain of any function f is assumed to be the set of all real numbers x for which $f(x)$ is a real number.

Reference Information

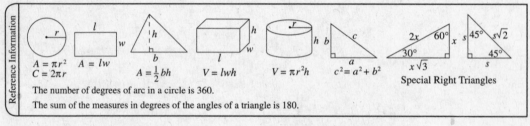

$A = \pi r^2$
$C = 2\pi r$

$A = lw$

$A = \frac{1}{2}bh$

$V = lwh$

$V = \pi r^2 h$

$c^2 = a^2 + b^2$

Special Right Triangles

The number of degrees of arc in a circle is 360.

The sum of the measures in degrees of the angles of a triangle is 180.

6, 12, 24, 48, . . .

1. Which of the following expressions represents the nth term in the sequence above?

(A) 2×6^n
(B) $2 \times 6^{n-1}$
(C) $6 \times 2^{n-1}$
(D) $6 \times n$
(E) $6 \times n^2$

2. If $3d - 2q = 17$ and $2d + 2q = -32$, what is the value of $10d$?

(A)   3
(B)   −3
(C)   −13
(D)   −15
(E)   −30

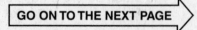

GO ON TO THE NEXT PAGE

3. Which of the following has the same area as a circle with an area of 16π ?

(A) A circle with a radius of 4π
(B) A circle with a circumference of 32π
(C) A circle with a radius of 8
(D) A circle with a diameter of 4
(E) A circle with a circumference of 8π

$$f(x) = x^2 - 5$$

4. If $y = f(x)$, which of the following represents all possible values of y ?

(A) $y < 5$
(B) $y \geq -5$
(C) $y < -5$
(D) $y > 5$
(E) All real numbers

5. Set A consists of all even integers from 1 to 100, inclusive. If a number is selected at random from set A, what is the probability that the number is less than 40 ?

(A) $\dfrac{19}{50}$

(B) $\dfrac{39}{100}$

(C) $\dfrac{2}{5}$

(D) $\dfrac{31}{50}$

(E) $\dfrac{9}{10}$

6. In a certain game, different colored tokens are worth different numbers of points. A blue token and a red token together are worth a total of 12 points, a blue token and a green token together are worth a total of 13 points, and a red token and a green token together are worth a total of 15 points. How many points is a blue token worth?

(A) 5 points
(B) 6 points
(C) 7 points
(D) 8 points
(E) 9 points

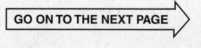

GO ON TO THE NEXT PAGE

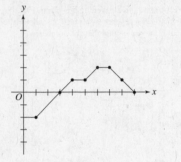

7. The figure above shows the graph of $y = f(x)$, where f is a function. If $f(c) = f\left(\dfrac{c}{3}\right)$, which of the following could be the value of c ?

(A) 3
(B) 5
(C) 6
(D) 8
(E) 9

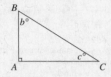

Note: Figure not drawn to scale.

8. In $\triangle ABC$ above, $AB < AC$. Which of the following must be true?

(A) $AC > BC$
(B) $AC = BC$
(C) $b > c$
(D) $b = 90$
(E) $c = 45$

GO ON TO THE NEXT PAGE

Directions: For Student-Produced Response questions 9-18, use the grids at the bottom of the answer sheet page on which you have answered questions 1-8.

Each of the remaining 10 questions requires you to solve the problem and enter your answer by marking the circles in the special grid, as shown in the examples below. You may use any available space for scratch work.

Answer: $\frac{7}{12}$

Write answer → in boxes.

← Fraction line

Grid in → result.

Answer: 2.5

← Decimal point

Answer: 201
Either position is correct.

Note: You may start your answers in any column, space permitting. Columns not needed should be left blank.

- Mark no more than one circle in any column.

- Because the answer document will be machine-scored, **you will receive credit only if the circles are filled in correctly.**

- Although not required, it is suggested that you write your answer in the boxes at the top of the columns to help you fill in the circles accurately.

- Some problems may have more than one correct answer. In such cases, grid only one answer.

- No question has a negative answer.

- **Mixed numbers** such as $3\frac{1}{2}$ must be gridded as

  3.5 or 7/2. (If $\boxed{3\ 1\ /\ 2}$ is gridded, it will be

  interpreted as $\frac{31}{2}$, not $3\frac{1}{2}$.)

- **Decimal Answers:** If you obtain a decimal answer with more digits than the grid can accommodate, it may be either rounded or truncated, but it must fill the entire grid. For example, if you obtain an answer such as 0.6666..., you should record your result as .666 or .667. **A less accurate value such as .66 or .67 will be scored as incorrect.**

Acceptable ways to grid $\frac{2}{3}$ are:

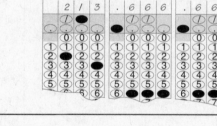

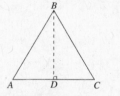

Note: Figure not drawn to scale.

9. If the area of $\triangle ABC$ is 40 and $AC = 10$, what is BD ?

10. If $f(x) = 2x - 10$, then $f(5) =$

GO ON TO THE NEXT PAGE

11. Sixty percent of Gateway High School's 300 students are female, and sixty percent of Riverdale High School's 400 students are male. How many more female students attend Gateway than attend Riverdale?

12. If $2(x + 2) + 4(x - 1) = 8$, then $x =$

13. If $3^{x+1} = 9^2$, what is the value of x^2 ?

14. What is the slope of the line in the xy-coordinate system above?

GO ON TO THE NEXT PAGE

15. If $n + \dfrac{n}{2} = \dfrac{n+1}{2}$, then $n =$

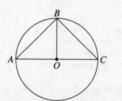

Note: Figure not drawn to scale.

16. In the figure above, $\overline{AC}$ is a diameter of the circle with center O. If the circumference of the circle is 32π, and the length of $\overline{AB}$ is 16, what is the degree measure of $\angle BAC$? (Disregard the degree symbol when gridding your answer.)

17. It took Garth $1\dfrac{1}{2}$ times as long to drive to the beach as it took him to drive home. If the trip was 60 miles in each direction and the total driving time for the round trip was $3\dfrac{1}{3}$ hours, what was Garth's average speed in miles per hour on the way to the beach?

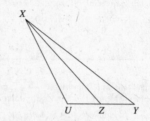

Note: Figure not drawn to scale.

18. If the length of $\overline{UZ}$ is 30 percent of the length of $\overline{UY}$ and the area of $\triangle XYZ$ is 210, what is the area of $\triangle UXZ$?

STOP

**If you finish before time is called, you may check your work on this section only.
Do not turn to any other section in the test.**

SECTION 6
Time — 25 minutes
24 Questions

Turn to Section 6 of your answer sheet to answer the questions in this section.

Directions: For each question in this section, select the best answer from among the choices given and fill in the corresponding circle on the answer sheet.

Each sentence below has one or two blanks, each blank indicating that something has been omitted. Beneath the sentence are five words or sets of words labeled A through E. Choose the word or set of words that, when inserted in the sentence, best fits the meaning of the sentence as a whole.

Example:

Desiring to ------- his taunting friends, Mitch gave them taffy in hopes it would keep their mouths shut.

(A) eliminate   (B) satisfy   (C) overcome
    (D) ridicule   (E) silence

Ⓐ Ⓑ Ⓒ Ⓓ ●

1. The new landlords were hampered by ------- resources and therefore unable to finance extensive improvements.

    (A) various   (B) sufficient   (C) inadequate
        (D) invalid   (E) fiscal

2. It was Mrs. Smedley's opinion that her daughter would ------- herself by marrying someone so obviously beneath her.

    (A) confuse   (B) indulge   (C) glorify
        (D) insinuate   (E) demean

3. The director did not consider her film ------- because her depiction of the sensitive topic was -------: it presented both sides of the issue fairly.

    (A) biased . . equitable
    (B) noteworthy . . balanced
    (C) challenging . . skewed
    (D) bombastic . . unconvincing
    (E) slanted . . apathetic

4. When Western contemporary art was first shown in Japan, Japanese artists were ------- it and sought to ------- its bold expressiveness.

    (A) oblivious to . . acquire
    (B) attracted to . . disclose
    (C) incensed by . . parallel
    (D) impressed by . . emulate
    (E) astonished by . . overrun

5. Nurses with ------- personalities were welcomed during the war because of their ability to uplift the dejected soldiers who were disabled.

    (A) winsome   (B) practical   (C) capricious
        (D) multifaceted   (E) cantankerous

GO ON TO THE NEXT PAGE ⟹

Directions: Each passage below is followed by questions based on its content. Answer the questions on the basis of what is <u>stated</u> or <u>implied</u> in each passage and in any introductory material that may be provided.

Questions 6-7 are based on the following passage.

Though most people know the definition of the word "boycott," few know its origin. Named for Captain Charles Boycott, the word as we know it owes less to him than to Irish
Line nationalist Charles Parnell. Parnell organized Irish farmers
5 and convinced them to fix their rent rates. When Boycott refused, Parnell unleashed the power of the people. A band of hostile peasants forced the Captain's servants to leave. There were no laborers to gather the harvest and no stablemen to care for the animals. Boycott was not allowed to enter stores
10 or make purchases. Eventually, Boycott and his wife fled Ireland, and Parnell was hailed as the workingman's hero.

6. The passage is best summarized by which of the following?

(A) The origin of a word is explored, and an explanation for its popularity is given.
(B) A word is introduced, and a history of its usage is related.
(C) The origin of a word is explored, and an unrelated story is told.
(D) A word is introduced, and the history of its coining is related.
(E) An event is described as the reason behind a shift in a word's meaning.

7. It can be most reasonably inferred from the passage that

(A) Boycott's land was not harvested that year
(B) the townspeople referred to were sympathetic to the farmers
(C) Parnell was popular among all Irishmen
(D) the farmers threatened Boycott with physical harm
(E) the farmers would never have organized without Parnell's help

Questions 8-9 are based on the following passage.

Hans Christian Andersen's story, "The Little Mermaid," contrary to popular perception, doesn't end happily. Instead of marrying her prince, the mermaid fails and is changed into
Line sea foam. The fate of this character mirrors that of many of
5 Andersen's fairy tales; throughout the years, his works have changed dramatically. As in the children's game of telephone, multiple translations altered both the words and meanings of the texts. In addition, the tales were bowdlerized to meet Victorian standards: risqué situations and inappropriate
10 language were cut. Finally, publishers edited them to fit in illustrations. While there is no one cause for the many changes to Andersen's stories, the original meanings departed as surely as sea foam on the shore.

8. What is the main idea of the passage?

(A) Unscrupulous publishers changed the story of "The Little Mermaid."
(B) There are many different reasons that Andersen's tales have changed through the years.
(C) Due to a number of factors, there can be no accurate version of a fairy tale.
(D) The Victorians insisted that Andersen's stories be changed to suit their standards.
(E) Happy endings in fairy tales are deceiving, as evidenced by "The Little Mermaid."

9. Sea foam is mentioned twice in the passage in order to

(A) mirror Andersen's obsession with sea imagery through allegory
(B) highlight a prevalent theme of loss and disappearance in the work of Hans Christian Andersen
(C) suggest that Hans Christian Andersen's fairy tales disappeared quickly after they were written in the Victorian age
(D) create a metaphor with the second citation which evokes the first time the word is used
(E) prove that the modern ending of "The Little Mermaid" is as arbitrary as the original ending

GO ON TO THE NEXT PAGE

Questions 10-15 are based on the following passage.

The following passage describes one battle in the bloody Anglo-Zulu War of 1879.

On a windswept hillside near a towering fortress of rock known to the Zulu as Isandlwana, a proletarian army from the world's foremost capitalist nation was defeated by a part-time
Line force of peasant farmers in a short, bloody, and eventually
5 inconclusive battle that rocked the British empire to its core. The Zulus attacked the red-coated British because they feared for their land and their independence. The British soldiers, drawn from the very poorest level of the working classes, fought back because they had been lured, like Private Moss
10 from Wales, to "take the Queen's shilling," thus placing a strain on royal finances.

Neither side had a clue as to why they were involved in desperate battle, not even the officers—on either side. In the words of an old soldier's song; "We're here because we're
15 here."

With the hindsight of history, it is perhaps simplest to say that the African peasants were fighting to stop themselves from becoming the same as their red-coated adversaries: the working class of a new capitalist South Africa modeled
20 on Britain. Most of the British dearly wished they were somewhere else, like the private who wrote to his family: "I repent the day I took the shilling. I have not had a bed since I left England. We have only one blanket, and are out every night in the rain—no shelter."

25 For the British officers, most of them from the landed classes and raised at dehumanizing boarding schools such as Tom Brown's Rugby, the war in the far-flung corners of the empire was more of a game than a serious instrument of imperial policy. For the Zulu, it was a war fought to defend
30 land, homes and families against unprovoked aggression by the most powerful military force in the world.

A British army sergeant who arrived at the battlefield later "could not help crying to see so many of our poor comrades lying dead on the ground, when only a few hours before that
35 we left them all well and hearty. Oh, father, such a sight I never witnessed in my life before. I could not help crying to see how the poor fellows were massacred."

His use of the word "massacre" gives another insight to the colonial view of the war—in which Zulu victories were
40 usually referred to as "massacres"; while the British won "victories" over their enemies—destroying homesteads, shooting down thousands with volley fire or blowing them to bloody rags with artillery.

Nevertheless, the British authorities were hard put to
45 explain how an army of "savages" had inflicted such a shattering defeat on their forces, and the myth was created that, because of a lack of screwdrivers, soldiers were unable to open reserve ammunition boxes—whose lids were secured by as many as nine screws, some "rusted into the wood." In
50 truth, the lids of the Mark V and VI ammunition boxes used in the campaign were each secured by only a single brass screw.

It is unlikely many of the working class soldiers who died at Isandlwana would have agreed with such myths. A
55 better tribute to them and the Zulu dead was paid by Bishop Colenso in a sermon after the battle: "We ourselves have lost very many precious lives, and widows and orphans, parents, brothers, sisters, friends are mourning bitterly their sad bereavements. But are there no griefs—no relatives that
60 mourn their dead—in Zululand? Have we not heard how the wail has gone up in all parts of the country for those who have bravely and nobly died in repelling the invader and fighting for the King and fatherland? And shall we kill ten thousand more to avenge that dreadful day?"

10. The primary purpose of the passage is to

(A) trace the specific reasons for British military action in South Africa
(B) describe the British-Zulu conflict and discuss the motivations of both parties
(C) disprove the myth that British-Zulu relations were amicable
(D) point to the factors that incited strong loyalty on both sides of the British-Zulu conflict
(E) present the history of British-Zulu relations

11. The author gives which of the following reasons for the lure felt by British soldiers such as Private Moss, in lines 7-11 ?

(A) The thrill of battling the primitive Zulu tribe
(B) The opportunity to show their loyalty to the Queen
(C) The fear that the Zulus might seize their land and independence
(D) The chance to make money from the country
(E) The fact that war could be both a game and a serious instrument of imperial policy

GO ON TO THE NEXT PAGE ⟩

12. The author cites which of the following reasons for the appropriateness of the lyric, "We're here because we're here," mentioned in lines 14-15 ?

   (A) The seemingly eternal nature of the war was paralleled in the repetition of the lyric.
   (B) Blind obedience to superior officers caused the soldiers to regard their position as unchanging.
   (C) The song served to rally the troops behind the Queen, enabling them to go forth to victory.
   (D) The British soldiers' uncertainty about the reasons for their participation in the war.
   (E) The song had once been the rallying cry of the Zulus.

13. The fourth paragraph primarily serves to illustrate the fact that

   (A) war was a dehumanizing reality for both the British and the Zulus
   (B) while the British officers saw the war as a diversion, the Zulus took the conflict quite seriously
   (C) the British military force consisted mainly of aristocrats while the Zulu army was comprised of homeowners and family men
   (D) Zulu tradition did not call for mourning of the dead
   (E) the Zulus were prepared to continue the war until 10,000 more British soldiers had been slain

14. The British device of calling Zulu victories "massacres," mentioned in lines 39-40, points to

   (A) the appalling brutality of the Zulus
   (B) the need on the part of the British to elevate their stature above that of the Zulus
   (C) the British tendency to avoid excessive violence when dealing with civilians
   (D) the British inability to win strategic battles
   (E) the Zulu's superior weaponry

15. In can be inferred that the "myth" mentioned in line 46 was created in order to

   (A) appease the defeated Zulus and advocate for more funds for the military
   (B) explain the uncivilized actions of the Zulu forces
   (C) mollify those in England who could not comprehend that a less powerful army could defeat the British
   (D) explain the British soldiers' inability to utilize all of their ammunition during the Anglo-Zulu war
   (E) cast doubt on the accuracy of the author's description of British atrocities

GO ON TO THE NEXT PAGE

Questions 16-24 are based on the following passage.

The following passage discusses critical reactions, both contemporary and modern, to Russian writer Karolina Pavlova's A Double Life, *an innovative literary work.*

Published in 1848, *A Double Life* was Karolina Pavlova's most successful original work among critics and readers alike. Although her translations were highly praised throughout
Line her literary career, her poetry was usually greeted by critical
5 reviews. Even admiration of her verse was often mixed with personal ridicule. A woman poet who took her work as seriously as any man was, to put it mildly, an oddity. Parodies of Pavlova were not uncommon and were usually satires of *her* rather than of her poetry. For example, the poet and publisher
10 Nikolay Nekrasov, one of Pavlova's more disdainful critics, bemoaned "the possibility that women might want to give up jelly-boiling and pickle-making for philosophy and literature."
Apart from the problems that Pavlova faced as a female poet in a male-dominated literary world, she was also forced
15 to contend with the general animosity that the utilitarian literary critics of the time had for many poets. The golden age of romanticism, these critics claimed, had come to an end in the 1830s, and the 1840s were heralded by Belinsky as the "era of action." Other critics such as Nekrasov, Panaev, and
20 Dobrolyubov felt that poetry should be useful and that people had lost their taste for dreamy, escapist poetry. Those poets who did not address contemporary issues in their verse or whose poetry was distinguished more by the beautiful sounds of the words rather than the poetic content were treated
25 harshly by critics. Thus Pavlova wrote *A Double Life* at a difficult time for poetry in general.
While it is true that many poets of the 1840s were still closely bound to the romantic tradition, their work was nevertheless developing, surmounting its romantic beginnings
30 and striving toward more objective narration and the new possibilities of revealing the lyric "I" in poetry. The direction in which poetry was moving revealed how intense an influence prose had on poetry. The appearance of so-called "stories in verse" helped to keep poetry alive in a prose-
35 oriented literary world.
A Double Life encompasses several themes and contains a wide variety of poetic styles. It is a reasonably successful marriage of prose and verse—not a "story in verse" exactly, but rather a work within which poetry is on equal footing
40 with prose, with neither truly subordinate to the other. In *A Double Life*, Pavlova has plenty of room to create "art for art's sake" as well as to address a contemporary social problem for her generation: the education of society women. The main criticism that *A Double Life* received from both nineteenth-
45 and twentieth-century critics was that it lacked "substance." Critics did not consider the problem of women's education to be a problem at all, and certainly not of the same import as the oppression of Russia's peasant class, a popular topic among writers of the time. These critics obviously overlooked the point
50 of Pavlova's work. The issues Pavlova raises are not relevant only to women, but speak more generally to the intellectual shortcomings and spiritual emptiness of members of her class.

16. According to the passage, Pavlova was most successful as

   (A) an innovator of poetic forms
   (B) an economic revolutionary
   (C) a cook and a baker
   (D) a translator of others' work
   (E) a teacher of philosophy and literature

17. It can be inferred that Panaev (line 19) would most likely prefer a literary work that

   (A) was not written by a woman
   (B) created an alternative reality superior to the actual one
   (C) contained lots of action and exciting plot twists
   (D) had harsh, discordant sounds and images
   (E) sought to offer solutions to current social problems

18. All of the following are true about the poets of the 1840s (line 27) EXCEPT

   (A) their work was judged differently than it would have been a decade earlier
   (B) they were unwilling to develop beyond the romantic tradition
   (C) they were interested in both lyrical and objective aspects of poetry
   (D) they had strong roots in the romantic past
   (E) their poetry was often influenced by contemporary trends in prose

19. What is the function of the third paragraph (lines 27-35) ?

   (A) It stresses the way in which Pavlova's work stood out from that of her contemporaries.
   (B) It establishes that the 1840s was an extremely difficult time in which to write poetry.
   (C) It lists what the utilitarians considered to be the attributes of poetry that lacks "substance."
   (D) It creates an artistic background within which to understand *A Double Life*.
   (E) It emphasizes the difficulties Pavlova faced as a female writer.

GO ON TO THE NEXT PAGE ⟩

20. According to the passage, a "story in verse" (line 38)

(A) was less objectionable to romantic critics than traditional poetry
(B) contains elements drawn from non-poetical works
(C) stresses class over issues such as gender and religion
(D) focuses on the narrative "I" to the exclusion of other characters
(E) was the most popular form of literature in the 1840s

21. It can be inferred that the critics mentioned in the final paragraph (lines 36-52) would have preferred Pavlova's work if she had

(A) written about the education of female peasants rather than society women
(B) focused more on artistic issues and ignored intellectual questions
(C) focused on issues such as class and politics
(D) been more concerned with goading the upper class into action
(E) explored the religious issues that were currently affecting Russia

22. In line 42, "address" most nearly means

(A) attend to
(B) situate in
(C) send to
(D) speak with
(E) leave space

23. Which of the following is a reason that the author disagrees with the criticism of Pavlova's work?

(A) The fact that the critics did not recognize the utilitarian thrust of Pavlova's work
(B) The critics' escapist attitude toward the realities of life for Russian peasants
(C) The critics' insistence that women are unable to write poetry as well as men
(D) The fact that the critics did not recognize Pavlova's skills as a translator
(E) The critics' inability to recognize Pavlova's wide ranging artistic and social interests

24. Which of the following, if true, would weaken the criticism leveled on *A Double Life*?

(A) The discovery that well-educated Russian society women were more concerned about the plight of the peasant class
(B) The fact that it was the most disdained blending of poetry and prose of any work of the 1840s
(C) A survey of readers of novels about society women that discovered the readers did not complain of spiritual emptiness
(D) A complaint by a peasant woman that *A Double Life* did not pertain to her life
(E) Proof that readers of the work were inspired to institute educational reform

STOP
**If you finish before time is called, you may check your work on this section only.
Do not turn to any other section in the test.**

SECTION 8
Time — 20 minutes
16 Questions

Turn to Section 8 of your answer sheet to answer the questions in this section.

Directions: For this section, solve each problem and decide which is the best of the choices given. Fill in the corresponding circle on the answer sheet. You may use any available space for scratchwork.

Notes

1. The use of a calculator is permitted.

2. All numbers used are real numbers.

3. Figures that accompany problems in this test are intended to provide information useful in solving the problems. They are drawn as accurately as possible EXCEPT when it is stated in a specific problem that the figure is not drawn to scale. All figures lie in a plane unless otherwise indicated.

4. Unless otherwise specified, the domain of any function f is assumed to be the set of all real numbers x for which $f(x)$ is a real number.

Reference Information

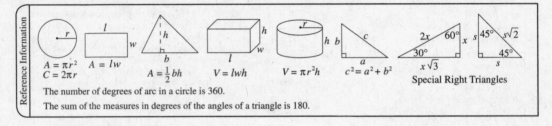

$A = \pi r^2$ $A = lw$
$C = 2\pi r$

$A = \frac{1}{2}bh$ $V = lwh$ $V = \pi r^2 h$ $c^2 = a^2 + b^2$

Special Right Triangles

The number of degrees of arc in a circle is 360.
The sum of the measures in degrees of the angles of a triangle is 180.

1. Which of the following numbers disproves the statement "A number that is divisible by 4 and 8 is also divisible by 12" ?

   (A) 24
   (B) 36
   (C) 40
   (D) 48
   (E) 60

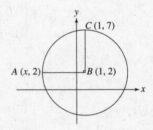

2. In the figure above, $\overline{AB}$ and $\overline{BC}$ are radii of the circle with center B. What is the value of x ?

   (A) −5
   (B) −4
   (C) −3
   (D) 3
   (E) 7

GO ON TO THE NEXT PAGE ⟩

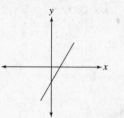

3. Which of the following equations could be represented by the line above?

(A) $y = 2x + 1$
(B) $y = 2x - 1$
(C) $y = -2x + 1$
(D) $y = -2x - 1$
(E) $y = -2x$

4. If, at a certain clothing store, three pairs of dress socks and four pairs of athletic socks cost a total of $27 and four pairs of dress socks and three pairs of athletic socks cost a total of $29, what is the combined cost of one pair of dress socks and one pair of athletic socks?

(A) $56
(B) $28
(C) $16
(D) $8
(E) $2

5. When the organizers of a bake sale sell brownies for $1.50 each, they sell 7 brownies every hour. When the brownies are sold for $2.00 each, 5 brownies are sold each hour. If x is the price per brownie in dollars, and f is the number of brownies sold per hour, then which of the following could represent f as a function of x?

(A) $f(x) = 4x + 1$
(B) $f(x) = 6x - 7$
(C) $f(x) = -3x + 11$
(D) $f(x) = -4x + 13$
(E) $f(x) = -6x + 16$

6. If $a < -1$ and $-1 < b < 0$, what are all of the possible values of ab?

(A) All negative numbers
(B) All negative numbers between −1 and 0
(C) All positive numbers less than 1
(D) All positive numbers greater than 1
(E) All positive numbers

GO ON TO THE NEXT PAGE

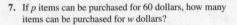

7. If p items can be purchased for 60 dollars, how many items can be purchased for w dollars?

(A) $\dfrac{wp}{60}$

(B) $\dfrac{w}{60p}$

(C) $\dfrac{60p}{w}$

(D) $\dfrac{60}{wp}$

(E) $\dfrac{60w}{p}$

SALES OF CDS

(bar graph: Number of CDs sold at the show vs. Price of CD in dollars)

Legend: ▦ Friday, ☐ Saturday

y-axis: Number of CDs sold at the show (0, 10, 20, 30, 40, 50, 60, 70, 80, 90)

x-axis: Price of CD in dollars (5, 10, 15, 20)

---

8. A musician goes on tour and sells CDs of his music. He varied the price of the CD on a nightly basis, kept track of how many were sold, and put this information in the graph above. Which of the following conclusions is best supported by the graph?

(A) Reducing the price of a CD will always increase the number of CDs sold.

(B) Above a certain price level, reducing the price of a CD will increase the number of CDs sold. Below that level reducing the price has no effect.

(C) The price of a CD has no effect on the number of CDs sold.

(D) Reducing the price of a CD will decrease the number of CDs sold.

(E) The price of the CD should be raised.

9. If $f(-3) = 1$, which of the following CANNOT be $f(x)$?

(A) $f(x) = x^2 - 8$

(B) $f(x) = x^2 + 2x - 4$

(C) $f(x) = \dfrac{x^2 - 3}{-2x}$

(D) $f(x) = x^2 + 3x + 1$

(E) $f(x) = |x - 3| - 5$

10. On her biology test, Cathy answered $\dfrac{5}{6}$ of the questions correctly. If Cathy answered 18 of the first 27 questions correctly, then the total number of questions on the test must be at <u>least</u>

(A) 32
(B) 36
(C) 45
(D) 48
(E) 54

GO ON TO THE NEXT PAGE ▷

11. A rectangular box is constructed from ten square tiles, each of which has a perimeter of 24 centimeters. If the box is formed so that the tiles do not overlap, what is the volume of the box in cubic centimeters?

A) 432
(B) 288
(C) 240
(D) 216
(E) 36

12. If $\dfrac{2x+10\sqrt{x}+12}{\sqrt{x}+3}=3\sqrt{x}$, what is the value of x ?

(A) 0
(B) 2
(C) 4
(D) 9
(E) 16

13. In a list of four positive even numbers, the mean, median, and mode are all equal. Which of the following CANNOT be done to the list if the mean, median, and mode are to remain equal?

(A) Add one number to the list.
(B) Add one number to the list that is greater than the mean.
(C) Add two distinct numbers to the list.
(D) Add 2 to each number in the list.
(E) Remove the first and last numbers from the list.

14. Points L, M, and N lie in a plane. If the distance between L and M is 4, and the distance between M and N is 9, which of the following could be the distance between L and N ?

   I. 5
  II. 8
 III. 13

(A) I only
(B) II only
(C) III only
(D) I and III
(E) I, II, and III

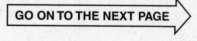

GO ON TO THE NEXT PAGE

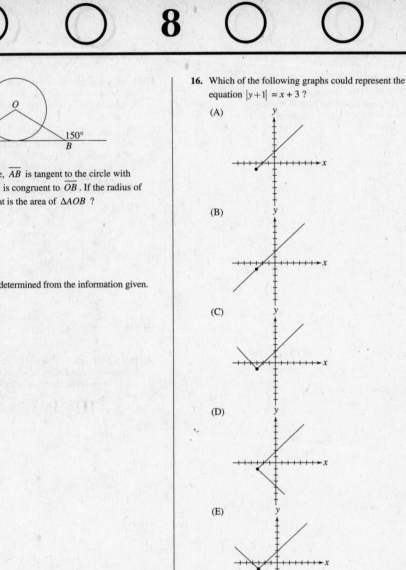

15. In the figure above, $\overline{AB}$ is tangent to the circle with center O, and $\overline{AO}$ is congruent to $\overline{OB}$. If the radius of the circle is 6, what is the area of $\triangle AOB$?

(A) $18\sqrt{2}$

(B) $18\sqrt{3}$

(C) $36\sqrt{2}$

(D) $36\sqrt{3}$

(E) It cannot be determined from the information given.

16. Which of the following graphs could represent the equation $|y+1| = x+3$?

(A)

(B)

(C)

(D)

(E)

STOP

If you finish before time is called, you may check your work on this section only.
Do not turn to any other section in the test.

8 ◯ ◯ **8** ◯ ◯ **8**

NO TEST MATERIAL ON THIS PAGE.

SECTION 9
Time — 20 minutes
19 Questions

Turn to Section 9 of your answer sheet to answer the questions in this section.

Directions: For each question in this section, select the best answer from among the choices given and fill in the corresponding circle on the answer sheet.

Each sentence below has one or two blanks, each blank indicating that something has been omitted. Beneath the sentence are five words or sets of words labeled A through E. Choose the word or set of words that, when inserted in the sentence, <u>best</u> fits the meaning of the sentence as a whole.

Example:

Desiring to ------- his taunting friends, Mitch gave them taffy in hopes it would keep their mouths shut.

(A) eliminate   (B) satisfy   (C) overcome
    (D) ridicule   (E) silence

Ⓐ Ⓑ Ⓒ Ⓓ ●

1. Many people find coyotes to be ------- creatures because their high-pitched and piercing howl tends to trigger humans' primordial fears.

   (A) unnerving   (B) anthropological   (C) sacrosanct
       (D) haughty   (E) suspicious

2. Lemony Snicket is only -------; the real name of the author of the popular children's book is Daniel Handler.

   (A) a hyperbole   (B) a prevarication   (C) a pseudonym
       (D) an epigram   (E) a non sequitur

3. Valued in traditional Chinese culture for its purifying qualities, the Quan Yin symbol is believed to ------- an environment after an argument or disagreement has occurred.

   (A) unsettle   (B) harmonize   (C) preserve
       (D) amplify   (E) pollute

4. Heather felt ------- regarding her work for the class, but Ms. Shockey was -------; she did not find Heather's essay particularly exceptional.

   (A) satisfied . . unconcerned
   (B) malcontent . . pleased
   (C) confident . . indifferent
   (D) glum . . impressed
   (E) energized . . soured

5. The seemingly ------- policy changes eventually resulted in a severe economic downturn, prompting critics to wonder if the intent of the changes was more ------- than once thought.

   (A) informed . . unintended
   (B) sinister . . malicious
   (C) obsolete . . fortuitous
   (D) harmless . . beneficial
   (E) benign . . pernicious

6. The editor refused to approve the story because the reporter had included some ------- statements that could not be verify by experts in the field.

   (A) substantiated   (B) serious   (C) ingenuous
       (D) indubitable   (E) specious

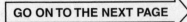
GO ON TO THE NEXT PAGE

Directions: Each passage below is followed by questions based on its content. Answer the questions on the basis of what is <u>stated</u> or <u>implied</u> in each passage and in any introductory material that may be provided.

Questions 7-19 are based on the following passages.

The following passages review the Shakespearean actors David Garrick and Charles Macklin. Passage 1, written by Thomas Davies in 1741, describes Garrick's abilities on the stage; Passage 2, written by James Boaden in 1849, compares Macklin's performing abilities with Garrick's.

Passage 1

On the 19th of October 1741, David Garrick acted Richard the Third, for the first time, at the playhouse in Goodman's Fields. So many idle persons, under the title of gentlemen
Line acting for their diversion, had exposed their incapacity at that
5 theatre, and had so often disappointed the audiences, that no very large company was brought together to see the new performer. However, several of his own acquaintance, many of them persons of good judgment, were assembled at the usual hour; though we may well believe that the greater part
10 of the audience was stimulated rather by curiosity to see the event, than invited by any hopes of rational entertainment.

An actor, who, in the first display of his talents, undertakes a principal character, has generally, amongst other difficulties, the prejudices of the audience to struggle with,
15 in favor of an established performer. Here, indeed, they were not insurmountable: Cibber, who had been much admired in Richard, had left the stage. Quin was the popular player; but his manner of heaving up his words, and his labored action, prevented his being a favorite Richard.
20 Mr. Garrick's easy and familiar, yet forcible style in speaking and acting, at first threw the critics into some hesitation concerning the novelty as well as propriety of his manner. They had been long accustomed to an elevation of the voice, with a sudden mechanical depression of its tones,
25 calculated to excite admiration, and to entrap applause. To the just modulation of the words, and concurring expression of the feature from the genuine workings of nature, they had been strangers, at least for some time. But after he had gone through a variety of scenes, in which he gave evident proofs
30 of consummate art, and perfect knowledge of character, their doubts were turned into surprise and astonishment, from which they relieved themselves by loud and reiterated applause. They were more especially charmed when the actor, after having thrown aside the hypocrite and politician,
35 assumed the warrior and the hero. When news was brought to Richard, that the Duke of Buckingham was taken, Garrick's look and action, when he pronounced the words,

—Off with his head!
So much for Buckingham!

40 were so significant and important, from his visible enjoyment of the incident, that several loud shouts of approbation proclaimed the triumph of the actor and satisfaction of the audience. The death of Richard was accompanied with the loudest gratulations of applause.

Passage 2

45 As I paid much attention to Macklin's performances, and personally knew him, I shall endeavor to characterize his acting, and discriminate it from that of others. If Macklin really was of the old school, that school taught what was truth and nature. His acting was essentially manly—there was
50 nothing of trick about it. His delivery was more level than modern speaking, but certainly more weighty, direct, and emphatic. His features were rigid, his eye cold and colorless; yet the earnestness of his manner, and the sterling sense of his address, produced an effect in Shylock, that has remained
55 to the present hour unrivalled. Macklin, for instance, in the trial scene, "stood like a TOWER," as Milton has it. He was "not bound to please" anybody by his pleading; he claimed a right, "grounded upon LAW," and thought himself as firm as the Rialto. To this remark it may be said, "You are here
60 describing SHYLOCK." True; I am describing Macklin. If this perfection be true of him, when speaking the language of Shakespeare, it is equally so, when he gave utterance to his own. Macklin was the author of *Love à la Mode* and the *Man of the World*. His performance of the two true born Scotsmen
65 was so perfect, as though he had been created expressly to keep up the prejudice against Scotland. The late George Cooke was a noisy Sir Pertinax compared with Macklin. He talked of *booing*, but it was evident he took a credit for suppleness that was not in him. He was rather Sir Giles than
70 Sir Pertinax. Macklin could inveigle as well as subdue; and modulated his voice, almost to his last year, with amazing skill.

It has been commonly considered that Garrick introduced a mighty change in stage delivery: actors had never, until his
75 time, been natural. If Macklin at all resembled his masters, as it is probable he did, he can certainly not be obnoxious to a censure of this kind. He abhorred all trick, all start and ingenious attitude; and his attacks upon Mr. Garrick were always directed to the restless abundance of his action and his
80 gestures, by which, he said, rather than by the fair business of the character, he caught and detained all attention to himself.

With respect to the alleged unfairness of Garrick in engrossing all attention to himself, a charge often repeated, it may, perhaps, be true, that this great master converged the
85 interest of the whole too much about his particular character; and willingly dispensed with any rival attraction, not because he shunned competition with it as *skill*, but because it might encroach upon, delay or divide that palm for which he labored—public applause.

GO ON TO THE NEXT PAGE

7. In line 6, the reference to "no very large company" is intended to convey that

(A) the cast of actors was very small
(B) the theatre received little support from businesses
(C) the audience was not very big
(D) the new performer's audition was seen by few of the theatre's producers
(E) the theatre was extremely understaffed

8. From lines 8-11, we may assume that the author of Passage 1 believes that the audience

(A) was assembled with high hopes of viewing a superior performance
(B) expected a mediocre performance
(C) had little enthusiasm for a careful, competent performance
(D) had never attended a theatrical event and was curious to see what it entailed
(E) was a rival of Garrick's who intended to distract the performers

9. The reference in line 22 to "novelty as well as propriety" is used to

(A) explain the critics' reluctance to embrace Garrick's unfamiliar acting style
(B) explain the enthusiasm the audience felt toward Garrick's exciting portrayal
(C) show that Garrick was not a serious actor, but a dilettante who rejected a studied performance in favor of haphazard indifference
(D) indicate that Garrick's naturalistic approach was inappropriate to the portrayal of King Richard III
(E) reinforce the notion that Garrick had no intention of giving a serious performance, since the critical community was determined to see him fail

10. The applause mentioned in the last sentence of Passage 1 signifies that

(A) the audience was thoroughly pleased with Garrick's portrayal of Richard
(B) the audience so disliked Garrick's portrayal that it cheered his death
(C) Richard's death scene was spectacularly gruesome
(D) the lengthy play had finally reached its conclusion
(E) the death of a principal character was customarily applauded in the eighteenth century

11. In line 49, "manly" most nearly means

(A) virile
(B) deceptive
(C) honest
(D) powerful
(E) emphatic

12. In line 52, Macklin's facial expressions while playing Shylock can best be described as

(A) colorfully animated
(B) difficult to understand
(C) easy to misinterpret
(D) stoic and unfeeling
(E) free and relaxed

13. Which of the following , if true, would most weaken the contention in lines 73-75 that "Garrick introduced . . . natural"?

(A) In Shakespeare's time, productions of his work were characterized in many cases by unexaggerated, lifelike performances.
(B) In the original productions of Shakespeare's plays, female parts were always played by boys.
(C) Shakespearean actors working before Garrick were taught to speak Shakespeare's words in a stilted and forced manner.
(D) Many modern productions of Shakespeare's plays emphasize a naturalistic, non-stylized approach to the language.
(E) Garrick was unwilling to teach his acting method to other Shakespearean actors of his time.

GO ON TO THE NEXT PAGE

14. In Passage 2, Macklin's main problem with Garrick concerns

(A) Garrick's tendency to be overly reserved in movement, and to focus too intently on his lines
(B) Garrick's dynamic physicality, which unjustly drew focus away from the other characters
(C) Garrick's emphasis on a more natural stage delivery
(D) Garrick's inability to make his body rigid and his demeanor stern in his portrayal of Shylock
(E) Garrick's lack of concern for the audience's approval

15. The author of Passage 2 views Macklin's criticism of Garrick as

(A) irrelevant, despite Garrick's outspoken scorn for the public
(B) justly forgotten, because of Macklin's strong prejudice against Scotland
(C) justifiable, even in light of Garrick's talents
(D) based primarily upon Macklin's groundbreaking portrayal of Shylock
(E) profoundly influential on the younger Garrick

16. In line 88, "palm" most nearly means

(A) promotion
(B) part of the hand
(C) leaf
(D) money
(E) symbol of triumph

17. The author of Passage 2 may have had a more favorable regard for the actor described in Passage 1 had the author

(A) viewed the actor's flexibility on stage
(B) seen first-hand a performance in which the audience's applause was the not the overriding impetus for Garrick's actions
(C) viewed a critically acclaimed production of Richard III
(D) seen the version of Richard IIII performed by Garrick's company before Garrick joined it
(E) taken into consideration "the old school's" influence on the actor

18. The author of Passage 1 describes Garrick's acting style as "familiar" (line 20) and the author of Passage 2 describes it as "natural" (line 75). What is the significance of these references?

(A) The adjectives refer to a style of acting that was not commonly used by actors prior to Garrick.
(B) Actors were becoming personally acquainted with their audiences.
(C) Acting was becoming an easier craft as playwrights improved their manuscripts.
(D) Performers were becoming better known to their audiences.
(E) No new plays were being written, so the actors knew their parts thoroughly.

19. Which of the following references from Passage 1 could that author present to support the statement in lines 73-75 ("It has been . . . natural") ?

(A) "Mr. Garrick's easy and familiar . . . manner." (lines 20-23)
(B) "An actor, who in the first . . . performer." (lines 12-15)
(C) "On the nineteenth . . . Fields" (lines 1-3)
(D) "The death of Richard . . . applause." (lines 43-44)
(E) "However several of his . . . entertainment." (lines 7-11)

STOP

If you finish before time is called, you may check your work on this section only.
Do not turn to any other section in the test.

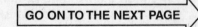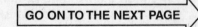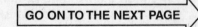
SECTION 10
Time — 10 minutes
14 Questions

Turn to Section 10 of your answer sheet to answer the questions in this section.

Directions: For each question in this section, select the best answer from among the choices given and fill in the corresponding circle on the answer sheet.

The following sentences test correctness and effectiveness of expression. Part of each sentence or the entire sentence is underlined; beneath each sentence are five ways of phrasing the underlined material. Choice A repeats the original phrasing; the other four choices are different. If you think the original phrasing produces a better sentence than any of the alternatives, select choice A; if not, select one of the other choices.

In making your selection, follow the requirements of standard written English; that is, pay attention to grammar, choice of words, sentence construction, and punctuation. Your selection should result in the most effective sentence—clear and precise, without awkwardness or ambiguity.

EXAMPLE:

Bobby Flay baked his first cake <u>and he was thirteen years old then.</u>

(A) and he was thirteen years old then
(B) when he was thirteen
(C) at age thirteen years old
(D) upon the reaching of thirteen years
(E) at the time when he was thirteen

Ⓐ●ⒸⒹⒺ

1. <u>Since one should not count</u> out the Yankees early in the season, as they always get stronger by the middle of August.

(A) Since one should not count
(B) One ought not to count
(C) Since one ought not count
(D) One had ought not to count
(E) One should not be counting

2. Historian Mike Wallace founded the Gotham Center for New York History in 200 <u>with the goal being to generate</u> greater interest in the city's wealth of historic spaces.

(A) with the goal being to generate
(B) and the goal was generating
(C) to generate
(D) therefore to generate
(E) he generated

3. The new bill is a move <u>to take the responsibility for welfare allocation from the federal government and that give</u> it to the state administration.

(A) to take the responsibility for welfare allocation from the federal government and that give
(B) to take the responsibility for welfare allocation from the federal government and give
(C) to take the responsibility for welfare allocation from the federal government for giving
(D) which takes the responsibility for welfare allocation from the federal government to give
(E) taking the responsibility for welfare allocation from the federal government and that give

4. In 1982, the Go-Go's <u>became the first all-woman band</u> to have a number-one album, garnering an enduring victory for women in popular music.

(A) became the first all-woman band to have
(B) are the first all-woman band that have had
(C) were the first all-woman band that had
(D) was the first all-woman band that had
(E) came to be the first all-woman band to receive

5. After moving farther away from downtown, <u>Ryan's commute being less time consuming than it had been was surprising to him.</u>

(A) Ryan's commute being less time consuming than it had been was surprising to him
(B) it was surprising to Ryan that his commute was less time consuming than it had been
(C) surprisingly, Ryan's commute was less time consuming than it had been
(D) Ryan was surprised that his commute was less time consuming than it had been
(E) taking less time than it had, Ryan's commute surprised him

GO ON TO THE NEXT PAGE

6. During one of the worst mudslides in California history, what began as flash flood soon raged out of control <u>and it roared downhill at 35 miles per hour, consuming everything in its path</u>.

(A) and it roared downhill at 35 miles per hour, consuming everything in its path

(B) and it roared downhill at 35 miles per hour, everything in its path having been consumed

(C) and the roaring downhill was at 35 miles per hour, consuming everything in its path

(D) and roared downhill at 35 miles per hour, consuming everything in its path

(E) and roaring at 35 miles per hour downhill; consuming everything in its path

7. Carrying an assortment of bats, balls, and helmets in several cumbersome bags, <u>the equipment manager's search for assistance was desperate</u>.

(A) the equipment manager's search for assistance was desperate

(B) the equipment manger's desperate search was for assistance

(C) assistance was what the equipment manager desperately searched for

(D) assistance for which the equipment manager desperately searched

(E) the equipment manager searched desperately for assistance

8. Members of the squash family include not only the pumpkin, <u>but the butternut, the Hubbard, and the acorn squash as well</u>.

(A) but the butternut, the Hubbard, and the acorn squash as well

(B) but also the butternut, Hubbard squash, and the acorn squash

(C) but also the butternut, Hubbard, and acorn squash

(D) and the butternut, Hubbard, and acorn as well

(E) and the butternut, Hubbard, and acorn squashes as well

9. College admission officers suggest that before submitting <u>your application, prospective students should proofread one's essay</u> carefully.

(A) your application, prospective students should proofread one's essay

(B) their application, a prospective applicant should proofread their essay

(C) their applications, proofread the essays

(D) their applications, prospective students should proofread their essays

(E) one's application, you should proofread your essay

10. The clear blue water off the coast of Fiji is home to aquatic life of such beauty and <u>variedness and the water has appealed</u> to both fisherman and underwater photographers alike.

(A) variedness and the water has appealed

(B) variety and the water has appeals

(C) variety and the water having appeal

(D) variety that have appealed

(E) variety that it appeals

11. The male weaverbird builds a nest of green grass and then clings, shrieking and fluttering, to his new home, attracting <u>what females, if any, that are</u> in his vicinity.

(A) what females, if any, that are

(B) any females

(C) females, if there might be any

(D) the females, so that if any are

(E) whatever females that are or may be

12. The problem of food and aid <u>distribution, frequently compounded in certain countries because</u> corrupt officials and poor infrastructure making accessing the neediest people all the more challenging.

(A) distribution, frequently compounded in certain countries because

(B) distribution, frequently compounded in certain countries and

(C) distribution, frequently compounded in certain countries when

(D) distribution is frequently compounded in certain countries where

(E) distribution is frequently compounded in certain countries and

GO ON TO THE NEXT PAGE

13. Since the early 1980s, many musicians have chosen to make themselves known mainly through <u>music videos, and playing small clubs affords</u> musicians a better opportunity to build a loyal fan base.

    (A) music videos, and playing small clubs affords

    (B) music videos, but playing small clubs is good in that in affords

    (C) music videos; however, playing small clubs affords

    (D) music videos, playing small clubs affording

    (E) music videos, when playing small clubs afford

14. The delicious and vast menu choices <u>contribute to the popularity of the Ethiopian restaurant, as does</u> the authentic and quaint decor.

    (A) contribute to the popularity of the Ethiopian restaurant, as does

    (B) contributes to the popularity of the Ethiopian restaurant as greatly as

    (C) contributes as greatly to the popularity of the Ethiopian restaurant as do

    (D) contribute to the popularity of the Ethiopian restaurant, so do

    (E) contribute greatly to the popularity of the Ethiopian restaurant, as it also comes from

S T O P

**If you finish before time is called, you may check your work on this section only.
Do not turn to any other section in the test.**

Chapter 8
Practice Test 3
Answers and
Explanations

PRACTICE TEST 3: ANSWER KEY

2 Reading	3 Math	4 Writing	5 Math	6 Reading	8 Math	9 Reading	10 Writing
1. D	1. C	1. D	1. C	1. C	1. C	1. A	1. B
2. C	2. B	2. D	2. E	2. E	2. B	2. C	2. C
3. B	3. A	3. C	3. E	3. A	3. B	3. B	3. B
4. B	4. C	4. E	4. B	4. D	4. D	4. C	4. A
5. D	5. D	5. C	5. A	5. A	5. D	5. E	5. D
6. A	6. A	6. E	6. A	6. D	6. E	6. E	6. D
7. A	7. A	7. B	7. E	7. B	7. A	7. C	7. E
8. C	8. B	8. A	8. C	8. B	8. B	8. B	8. C
9. A	9. A	9. B	9. 8	9. D	9. B	9. A	9. D
10. C	10. C	10. B	10. 0	10. B	10. E	10. A	10. E
11. C	11. C	11. D	11. 20	11. D	11. A	11. C	11. B
12. B	12. E	12. D	12. $\frac{4}{3}$ or 1.33	12. D	12. E	12. D	12. D
13. C	13. C	13. D	13. 9	13. B	13. B	13. A	13. C
14. D	14. C	14. E	14. $\frac{1}{3}$ or .333	14. B	14. E	14. B	14. A
15. B	15. C	15. C	15. $\frac{1}{2}$ or .5	15. C	15. D	15. C	15. C
16. D	16. A	16. E	16. 60	16. D	16. D	16. E	16. E
17. E	17. D	17. B	17. 30	17. E		17. B	
18. A	18. D	18. B	18. 90	18. B		18. A	
19. B	19. B	19. D		19. D		19. A	
20. B	20. D	20. D		20. B			
21. B		21. C		21. C			
22. E		22. D		22. A			
23. A		23. C		23. E			
24. D		24. A		24. A			
		25. C					
		26. C					
		27. E					
		28. A					
		29. A					
		30. A					
		31. B					
		32. B					
		33. C					
		34. D					
		35. D					

EXPLANATIONS

Section 2

1. **D** Because Ellie *doubted* Tom's story, the blank means something like "with doubt" (D) *skeptically* comes closest to this meaning.

2. **C** Start with the second blank. Hector is willing to *explore new possibilities,* which is different from how the *more narrow-minded scientists* feel about it. A good word for the second blank is "reject." Only (B) and (C) are appropriately negative Eliminate (A), (D), and (E) Because Hector is *eager to explore new possibilities,* "new" is a good word for the first blank, and only (C) matches both blanks.

3. **B** The phrase near the second blank, *he just as quickly* indicates that we need a word for the first blank that means "quick." Only (B) *swift* and (D) *hasty* have a meaning close to "quick." *Despite* indicates that the second blank will mean the opposite of *rise,* so "fell" is be a good word for the blank. Between (B) *yielded* and (D) *ascended* only (B) fits the meaning of both blanks.

4. **B** We know that Kai's pain was *dull* rather than whatever goes in the blank, so we need a word that means something like "sharp." Only (B) *acute* means "sharp."

5. **D** The colon indicates that the description following the punctuation is the meaning of the blank. We need a word that means "firmly sticking to one's principles," and (D) *tenacity* means "the quality of keeping a firm hold on something." These answers have some tough vocab, so look up any unfamiliar words.

6.   A   The word *but* indicates that the second part of the sentence will mean the opposite of *Procrastination*. The opposite of putting things off is "immediate" *action*. Eliminate any words that don't mean "immediate," leaving only (A) *prompt*.

7.   A   The word *and* indicates that the first blank will mean something close to *stinginess*. Eliminate (E)—all the other words describe someone mean or stingy. The second blank must be a word that describes his contrasting *public image* and his *private* behavior, so "go against" is a good meaning for the blank. Both (A) *belie* and (E) *contradict* fit this meaning, but only (A) matches the meaning of both blanks.

8.   C   Because the department handles *urgent situations* these are tasks which must be *performed with great* "urgency," or great speed. Only (C) *alacrity* fits this meaning.

9.   A   The main idea of Passage 1 is that Einstein's theories affected the works of artists and writers. This is paraphrased in (A). The opposite of (B) is true: Einstein *debunked*, or disproved *Absolute Rest*. (C), (D), and (E) are not mentioned in the passage.

10.   C   The passage is about the *startling parallels between the Renaissance* and the twentieth century and sums up by stating that *the twentieth century was not so different from the world of Shakespeare*, thus making (C) the only answer supported by the passage. *Realism* (A) is not mentioned in the passage. While both eras *saw great advances in science* the advances themselves were not necessarily similar, as in (B). There was *trade expansion* in the Renaissance, but not necessarily *capitalism* as in (D). There is no evidence that the advances were centered mainly in Europe as in (E). Remember, even an inference question must be supported by text in the passage.

11.   C   Both passages mention Einstein's influence on the twentieth century. While both passages are generally about science and art, (A) is too strong: art and science are somewhat linked in Passage 1, but not at all in Passage 2. There is no evidence in either passage for (B).

12.   B   Neither passage mentions the nineteenth century, but finding the main ideas of each passage will show how each would make a relevant use of the nineteenth century. Passage 1 is about how the twentieth century is one of *upheaval* and *major changes*, though it doesn't give any examples of life before the change. Passage 2 is about *startling parallels* between the twentieth century and another era. (B) is the best answer: *contrasts* would show the differences between the nineteenth and twentieth centuries, while *links between the nineteenth century and another period* does for the nineteenth century what Passage 2 did for the twentieth.

13.   C   The first paragraph discusses how America *proudly professed democracy* but acted against that belief. (C) is correct, because it addresses this *contradictory* practice that goes against the *ideals of democracy*. (A) has a trap answer in its mention of *disease*. The *nation's* feelings about *segregation* (B) are not mentioned in the passage. (D) may be true, but it doesn't address the issue of believing one thing and doing the opposite. (E) segregation was not *an illusion* and the answer does not address the split of belief and action needed to explain the *schizophrenic personality*.

14.   D   As with question 13, this *contradiction* is the difference between what is professed and actual actions of the nation: the passage states *segregation and discrimination are strange paradoxes in a nation founded on the principle that all men are created equal*, and this is paraphrased well in (D). (A) is not true—Dr. King is the author of the passage. The *Supreme Court* mentioned in (B) is in the passage, but doesn't relate to the *disturbed consciences* asked about in the question. (C) is not mentioned in the passage, and many people may be offended if the SAT considered this a true or correct answer. (E) is also not mentioned in the passage.

15. **B** The *Supreme Court's decision* outlawed segregation in schools. (A) is the opposite, while (C), (D), and (E) are not mentioned in the passage. (B) is a good paraphrase of the desegregation schools.

16. **D** Go back to the passage and use the context to come up with a word to replace *deny*. In the passage, segregation is described as *inherently unequal* and "does not allow" a child to have *equal protection of the law*. The correct answer should be something like "does not allow." While many of the answers do address certain meanings of *deny* only (D) *withhold from* matches the context of the passage.

17. **E** The main idea of the third paragraph is that the issues involved in segregation as the same as those *all over the world* and that the *racial crisis…is a part of the larger world crisis*. This is best reflected in (E), that this struggle *is not an isolated occurrence* since it is something addressed around the world. There is no evidence in the passage for any of the other answers.

18. **A** From the passage, the *new order* is based on democratic equality, while the *older order* is based on *subordination,* or keeping people down. (A) best reflects this, stating that the *older order* is *less democratic* and believes *certain groups should be controlled by others.* (B) and (C) are extreme, due to their use of *only.* (D) is much too specific, and not supported by the passage. (E) contradicts the passage: those of the *older order* are the traditionalists.

19. **B** The *crisis* mentioned in line 41 is explained in the rest of the paragraph: it is the *paradox* of the *principles of American democracy* clashing with the actions of people who would *repress freedom's growth.* This is paraphrased in (B) the *conflict between the ideals…and realities.* This also fits in with the main idea of the passage as a whole. (A) and (C) are contradicted by lines 41–43. (D) and (E) are not mentioned at all in the passage.

20. **B** Go back to the passage and use the context to come up with a word to replace *resistance*. In the passage the *principles of American democracy* came up against people who wanted the opposite, to *repress freedom*. (A) and (B) are both close, but in context, (A) *denial of forces* either means that those forces themselves were denied, or perhaps they just ignored what was going on, which does not fit with *brutal*. (B) *opposition* fits better, because it shows direct action of the part of the forces.

21. **B** The passage states in lines 57–59 that the *uneducated whites* were in a state of *confusion* that led them to commit *acts of meanness and violence*. This is paraphrased in (B). None of the other answers are mentioned in the passage.

22. **E** The author brings up *Lincoln* and the *castigation of the Supreme Court* to support the idea at the beginning of the paragraph: that there are *characteristics that come to the forefront in any period of social transition*. Therefore, these are two instances that have similarities, paraphrased best in (E). The rest of the answers are unsupported by evidence in the passage.

23. **A** The point of Toynbee's *A Study of History* is that African Americans have something to give that *Western civilization…desperately needs to survive*. This is best paraphrased in (A). (B) is the opposite of what's stated in the passage. (C), (D), and (E) are unsupported in the passage.

24. **D** There is no line reference, so go through the answers one by one to see if it is supported by the passage as a whole. (A) actually is the opposite of Lincoln's stance on emancipation. In (B) the connection is unsupported by the passage. (C) is too strong due to the use of *never* and (E) is also extreme in its implication that all *public officials* share the qualities listed. Only (D) is supported: the passage discusses how the Supreme Court's decision caused *resistance* by *older orders* of people who believed in segregation, not just of schools but as a general principle.

Section 3

1. **C** Manipulate the first equation to find that $3x = 18$. We don't have to solve for x itself, because we can multiply both sides by 2 to see that $6x = 36$. $36 - 2 = 34$, choice (C). There are trap answers in (A), which is the value of x, and in (D) which is the result if 2 is added to rather than subtracted from 36.

2. **B** The average on four tests is 86, so the total of all four tests added together is 344. Now we can subtract the actual values of the three tests we know the scores of: $344 - 83 - 83 - 85 = 93$. So the fourth test had a score of 93, answer (B).

3. **A** In the line formula, $y = mx + b$, b is the y-intercept. In the graph, the line crosses the y-axis at -2, so eliminate (B), (C), and (D) because they have a different y-intercept. The m value is the slope, so using the slope formula $\frac{y_2 - y_1}{x_2 - x_1}$ we get $\frac{(-2) - 0}{0 - (-6)} = -\frac{1}{3}$, which matches (A). (E) has the x and y values reversed.

4. **C** There are very few numbers that are equal to their square. Only 0 and 1 have this property: $0 \times 0 = 0$ and $1 \times 1 = 1$. -1 does not work, because a negative times a negative is a positive: $-1 \times -1 = 1$. Only two integers work; (C) is correct.

5. **D** When a number with an exponent is raised to another power, multiply the two exponents. Since we are given $a^3 = 4$, and we can get the value of a^6 by raising both sides of the equation to the second power. $(a^3)^2 = 4^2$ so $a^6 = 16$.

6.   A   The first step is to find the area of the triangle: Area of a triangle = $\frac{1}{2}bh$. $\frac{1}{2} \times 12 \times 6 = 36$. This is also the area of the square we need to find the side of. A square with sides of length 6 would have an area of 36, so (A) 6 is the correct answer.

7.   A   From the statement $x > 0 > y$, we know that x is positive and y is negative. The easiest way to solve this is to Plug In numbers for x and y and test out each answer. If $x = 3$ and $y = -2$, (A) and (D) are both true, while (B), (C), and (E) can be eliminated. If we change the numbers so that $x = 2$ and $y = -2$, (A) is still true, but (D) is no longer true, since $\frac{1}{4} = \frac{1}{4}$. The correct answer is (A).

8.   B   To solve this, try out all the answer choices: for (A) $8 - 4 = 4$, since the answer is positive, the absolute value is also 4. For (B) $4 - 4 = 0$, and the absolute value is also 0. For (C), $0 - 4 = -4$, which has an absolute value of 4. (D) gives 8 and (E) gives 12, leaving (B) as the lowest value. Because absolute value is always positive 0 is the lowest value that can be obtained.

9. **A** This can be solved algebraically by translating the question to

$x + 4 = \dfrac{x}{7}$. Multiply both sides by 7: $7x + 28 = x$. Get the variables

on one side and the numbers on the other: $6x = -28$, then solve for x:

$x = -\dfrac{28}{6}$ which simplifies to $-\dfrac{14}{3}$ answer (A). This can also be solved

by trying out each answer choice. In (A) $-\dfrac{14}{3} + 4 = -\dfrac{14}{3} + \dfrac{12}{3} = -\dfrac{2}{3}$.

Now we need to see if we get the same result when we divide $-\dfrac{14}{3}$ by

7: $-\dfrac{14}{3} \times \dfrac{1}{7} = -\dfrac{14}{21}$ which reduces to $-\dfrac{2}{3}$, making (A) correct.

10. **C** When a question describes a figure but doesn't show it, draw it yourself.

Square *PQRS* has an area of 3. Now add *T*, the midpoint of *QR*. Draw-

ing the line from point *T* to point *S* forms the fourth side of quadrilateral

PQTS. It also creates a triangle that is $\dfrac{1}{4}$ of the area of the square.

This means that quadrilateral *PQTS* is $\dfrac{3}{4}$ of the area of the square:

$\dfrac{3}{4} \times 3 = \dfrac{9}{4}$, answer (C).

11. **C** To solve this try out some numbers for the marbles: it's easiest to
start with red. If red is 6, blue must be two less than red, so that's
4. White is twice red, so that's 12. $6 + 4 + 12 = 22$, which is too low
for any of the answers. Trying red = 8, then blue = 6, and white = 16.

8 + 6 + 16 = 30, too big for anything on our list. That leaves only 7 as a possible value for red (we can't have half of a marble). 7 + 5 + 14 = 26, answer (C).

12.   E   Because there is an *f* in each of the equations, we can make up our own number for *f* and find values for *a* and *b* that agree with each other. If *f* = 5, then *a* must equal 3. Now use the second equation to find *b*: *b* + 4(5) + 5, so *b* + 25. The question asks us to find the value of *b*, so replace each *a* in the answers with 3, and the correct answer will be the one that gives our value for *b*, 25. (A) gives 12, so eliminate it. (B) gives 8, so that's out. (C) is 14, (D) is 19, and only (E) gives the number we were looking for, 25.

13.   C   The triangles within the circle are special right triangles. Because we are given a measure of 135° in the top half of the circle, the angle within the triangle must measure 45°, making the triangle a 45-45-90 triangle. The legs of these triangles have a ratio of $x : x : x\sqrt{2}$. We know that the hypotenuse is 6, because *XY* is a diameter, and each triangle takes up half the diameter of 12. If $6 = x\sqrt{2}$, then *x*, the legs of the triangles, each equal $\dfrac{6}{\sqrt{2}}$. The triangles together form a square, and the sides are $\dfrac{6}{\sqrt{2}}$, so to find the area of the shaded region, we just need to square $\dfrac{6}{\sqrt{2}}$:

$$\frac{6}{\sqrt{2}} \times \frac{6}{\sqrt{2}} = \frac{36}{2} = 18, \text{ answer (C).}$$

14.   C   We can use exponent rules here or simply try out some of the answer choices by substituting them in for x. If $x = 4$, the first equation becomes $3^{4y} = 81$, or $3^{4y} = 3^4$. Because the bases are equal, the exponents are equivalent, so $4y = 4$, which yields $y = 1$. $3^4 + 3^1 = 81 + 3 = 84$, so the answer is (C).

15.   C   When a question describes a figure but doesn't show it, draw it yourself. We know that A is at $(1, 0)$ and B is at $(-3, 0)$, and we need the midpoint of that. Since the distance between A and B is 4, the midpoint is at $(-1, 0)$. The question asks for the distance between $(-1, 0)$ and point C, which is at $(0, 5)$ If you have drawn the figure, you can see that the line we need to find the distance of is the hypotenuse of a triangle with legs of 1 and 5, so we can use the Pythagorean theorem to find the distance: $a^2 + b^2 + c^2$, so $1^2 + 5^2 = 26$, and the distance of the hypotenuse is $\sqrt{26}$, answer (C).

16.   A   For this question we need to use each of the answers and see which, when used as a replacement for c gives $4\sqrt{2}$ when $x = 2$. Using $c = 2$, as in (A) we get $\left(2^2\right)\left(2^{\frac{1}{2}}\right)$. A fractional exponent means that the base number is raised by the numerator of the fraction, and the root taken is determined by the denominator. Therefore, an exponent of $\frac{1}{2}$ means to take the square root of the base number. $\left(2^2\right)\left(\sqrt{2}\right) = 4\sqrt{2}$, the number given in the question for $f(2)$, so c must equal 2, answer (A). None of the other answer choices used as c give a result of $4\sqrt{2}$ when $x = 2$.

17. **D** It costs $15 to buy one pound of coal and $6 for each additional pound, represented by p. So each pound after the first would cost $6(p - 1)$. The total cost for al the coal would be $15 + $6(p - 1)$, which simplifies to $15 + 6p - 6$, or $6p + 9$. The answer is (D).

18. **D** The members of set A are $\{1, 3, 5, 7, 9\}$. The members of set B are $\{2, 3, 5, 7, 11,...\}$ There are more prime numbers, but since we need to find the elements the two sets have in common, and set A has only single-digit numbers, we've gone far enough. The numbers that these sets have in common are $\{3, 5, 7\}$, answer (D).

19. **B** The question asks for the greatest possible value of one of the integers in the group of 8 integers, so come up with the smallest numbers possible for the first 7 integers that fit the description given in the question. We can use numbers up to 2 times each, so $1 + 1 + 2 + 2 + 3 + 3 + 4 = 16$. We can find the value of the eighth (and largest possible) number by subtracting this from the sum of all 8 numbers: $31 - 16 = 15$, answer (B).

20. **D** When an equation is in the $y = mx + b$ format, b is the y-intercept. To find point A, put the equation for line r in $y = mx + b$:

$$4y = 3x - 24$$
$$y = \frac{3}{4}x - 6$$

This means that point A is located at $(0, -6)$. As line q is already in the right format, point B is located at $(0, 8)$, and the distance between points A and B is 14. To find point C, which is the x-intercept of both lines, using line q, substitute 0 for y in the equation of line q:

$$y = -x + 8$$
$$0 = -x + 8$$
$$x = 8$$

This means that point C is located at (8, 0). Therefore, we have a triangle with a base of 14 and a height of 8, so solve for area: Area $= \frac{1}{2}$ (14)(8) = 56, answer (D).

Section 4

1. D   The sentence as written uses a conjunction that awkwardly links the two parts of the sentence; eliminate (A). The addition of a comma in (B) does not fix the error. In (C) it is unclear what the pronoun *that* refers to. The pronoun *that* in (E) seemingly refers to *the students*, and thus should be *who*. (D) simplifies and clarifies the sentence by using the pronoun *who* to refer to *the students*. The correct answer is (D).

2. D   The sentence as written has a verb tense error: *the last twenty years* does not agree with *are*. Eliminate (A) and (B). (C) is an incomplete sentence, and *since* in (E) is redundant, as the time frame is already established in the sentence. This leaves only (D), which properly uses the present perfect tense as the correct answer.

3. C   The sentence as written uses the incorrect past tense of "shake:" *shaked* should be *shook*. Eliminate (A). (B) has an awkward construction. Both (D) and (E) have a misplaced modifier. Only (C) uses the correct verb construction without adding any further errors.

4. E   The word *As* should be used when describing a cause-and-effect relationship or two events happening at the same time. Neither is the case in the sentence as written, so eliminate (A). (B) fixes this, but should simply list the activities rather than using the *both…as well as* construction. The list of activities in (C) is not parallel. In (D), the phrase *By being* indicates a cause-and-effect relationship that does not exist in the sentence. Only (E) creates a sentence that has the correct relationship

between the *winter* and *summer* at *the resort* and has all the activities in a parallel list.

5. **C** The word *Because* sets up a cause-and-effect relationship, but this is disrupted by *and so* in the sentence as written, so eliminate (A). In (B) and (D), *therefore* is redundant since *Because* already establishes the relationship between the two parts of the sentence. (E) is awkward and passive, leaving only (C), which eliminates the unnecessary *and so.*

6. **E** In the sentence as written, the verbs *closes* and *conducting* should be in parallel form. Eliminate (A) and (B). (C) eliminates the necessary *only* that is part of the contrast set up by the sentence, while (D) puts *only* in the wrong place, which changes the meaning. Only (E) correctly puts the verbs in parallel form and introduces no other errors.

7. **B** The sentence as written has a misplaced modifier; the first word after the comma needs to be something that could be *mixed with a weak acid.* Eliminate (A) and (C). Both (D) and (E) are awkwardly phrased. Only (B) correctly puts *baking soda* immediately after the comma without introducing any other errors.

8. **A** The sentence is correct as written. The word *impacted* in (B) is not the correct form of the verb and since the end of the sentence describes the *contemporaries,* that is the word that should come before the comma, so (C), (D), and (E) are incorrect.

9. **B** The sentence as written has a subject-verb agreement error: *procedures* is plural while *is* is singular. The pronoun *its* in (C) is ambiguous, and seems to refer to *the course,* which changes the meaning of the sentence. (D) creates an incomplete sentence. The verb *runs* (E) confuses the sentence: *The testing procedures* could not run an obstacle course. Only (B) corrects the misplaced modifier and clearly shows the comparison of *the testing procedures* and *an obstacle course.*

10. B The sentence as written has a misplaced modifier, as does (C). (D) indicates that *Judy* is still a child, which changes the meaning of the sentence. (E) is awkwardly constructed and confuses the meaning of the sentence. Only (B) corrects the misplaced modifies and clearly describes the relationship between *Judy* and the street.

11. D The sentence as written has a subject-verb agreement error. Eliminate (A) and (E) for using the singular *is* with the plural *areas*. The areas listed in (B) and (C) are not in parallel form. (D) is correct because it uses the proper verb and has the list in parallel form.

12. D There is a double negative in (D). The correct construction is *hardly ever*.

13. D (D) creates a comparison error, the *trees* should not be compared to *Henry*. The correct construction is *than those in Henry's*.

14. E The sentence is correct as written. Don't just go by how things sound: check each underlined part for errors.

15. C The verb construction *has cooked* in (C) is not appropriate for the past tense established by *last week*.

16. E The sentence is correct as written. The list is in parallel form, and the verbs have correct constructions and tenses.

17. B (B) creates a subject-verb agreement error: *was* is singular while *tax shelters* is plural.

18. B (B) uses the wrong preposition with *concerned*. While prepositions *for* or *about* could be used with *concerned*, depending on context, *to* is never correct.

19. D *Cape Cod* in (D) creates a comparison error: it should be parallel to *Seattle's*.

20. D   The list is not in parallel form: (D) should simply be *ugly* to fit in with the adjectives in the rest of the list.

21. C   The pronoun *we* in (C) is incorrect: *The United States* is a singular, collective noun. *It* would be the appropriate pronoun to use in this case.

22. D   The list is not in parallel form: (D) should be *persuasiveness* to fit in with the nouns in the rest of the list.

23. C   The pronoun *I* in (C) is in the incorrect case. If *Thomas and* were not part of the sentence, it would read *the principal called I.* This makes it more evident that the pronoun should be "me."

24. A   The sentence has a noun agreement error: *Students* is plural, so *a doctor* should also be plural. All the students cannot become a single doctor, they must wish to become doctors.

25. C   The sentence has a verb tense error in (C). The time is given as *the past several decades* so the present perfect *have closed* is the appropriate verb construction in the sentence since the time frame is an unspecified point before now.

26. C   Because the *later presidents* had more than one term among them, the singular pronoun *that* in (C) is incorrect; it should be the plural *those.*

27. E   There is no error in this sentence. (C) might be tempting, but if *my wife and* is removed from the sentence, it is clear that the correct pronoun case is being used.

28. A   *Neither* is a singular, and needs to be followed with "is" rather than *are* as seen in (A).

29. A   (A) uses the incorrect verb construction, the past perfect "had run" is appropriate in the sentence since this is an action completed before something else that happened in the past.

30. **A**   The sentence is fine as it is. (B) and (C) are incomplete sentences. (D) is unclear, and makes it sound as if the students are allowed to wear unacceptable clothing. (E) is wordier than the original, and it also creates a run on, since a complete idea does not follow the comma.

31. **B**   While each of the nouns in the answer choices are mentioned in the passage, the context makes it clear that what is being discussed in the first paragraph is *the dress code.*

32. **B**   This is part of the list of problems begun in sentence 4. *Even so* indicates something opposite, when what we need is something that indicates a continuation, as *Most importantly* in (B) does.

33. **C**   A conclusion should tie in to the previous sentence, and effectively end the passage. *Thus* in (C) is a conjunction that connects two thoughts together in a cause and effect relationship, and the content of (C) and sentence 11 work together well in that sentence 11 is about how *making decisions about…*what to wear helps students *grow into mature adults* and (C) continues the theme in suggesting that this choice is part of *an educational process* that the lack of choice would *impede.* The other choices do not connect as well to 11 or introduce new ideas.

34. **D**   The argument as presented is pretty one-sided. It is overwhelmingly negative in its presentation of dress codes. Addressing some positive aspects of dress codes would be a more balanced argument, and would be more persuasive as it shows the author has weighed both pros and cons in coming to a thoughtful decision about whether dress codes are good or bad overall. Only (D) adds information that would create a more balanced argument.

35. **D**   (A) creates a comma splice. (B) is wordy. (C) uses the incorrect pronoun to refer to *students*: *which* should be *whom.* (E) is awkward: beware of sentences that use the word "being;" it's usually bad news on the SAT.

Only (D) clearly identifies the students with the correct pronoun and includes no other errors.

Section 5

1. **C** We want to know which expression gives the value of the nth term. There are four examples above the question. The 1st term (n = 1) has a value of 6; the 2nd term (n = 2) has a value of 12; the 3rd term (n = 3) has a value of 24 . Plug In each value of n into the answers and eliminate expressions that do not give the value of that term. Eliminate (A) and (B) because they don't give 6 when n = 1. Eliminate (E) because it doesn't give 12 when n = 2. Eliminate (D) because it doesn't give 24 when n = 1. Only (C) works with all the numbers.

2. **E** You can find the value of $10d$ by using simultaneous equations. By placing one equation on top of the other and adding the two equations, you are left with $5d$ = –15.

$$\begin{array}{r} 3d - 2q = 17 \\ + 2d + 2q = -32 \\ \hline 5d \qquad = -15 \end{array}$$

Now multiply the resulting equation by 2 on both sides to obtain $10d$ = –30. You don't even have to solve for d!

3. **E** A circle with an area of 16π has a radius of 4. (A) and (C) are too big. The circle in (B) has a radius of 16. The one in (D) has a radius of 2. (E) is correct because the formula for circumference is $2\pi r$, so a circle with a circumference of 8π has a radius of 4.

4. **B**   Test out numbers for x. If $x = 0$, x^2 is also 0, and $y = -5$. Eliminate (C) and (D). Because the square of any integer other than zero is positive, y can never be negative, so eliminate (E) since negative numbers are real numbers. If $x = 10$, then $y = 95$, which rules out (A). (B) is correct.

5. **A**   There are 50 even integers in set A since the question states that 100 is included in the list. The word *inclusive* is not applied *to less than 40* so we need to know how many numbers are 38 or below. From 2 through 38 there are 19 even integers out of the total of 50, so the probability is (A) $\dfrac{19}{50}$.

6. **A**   The answer choices represent the point value of the blue token. Since we are given the point values for blue and red together (12) and blue and green together (13) we can subtract the value in each answer to find the points for red and green separately, and see if they add to 15 as stated in the question. (A) is correct: subtracting 5 blue from 12 red leaves 7 red. 5 blue from 13 green leaves 8 green. $7 + 8 = 15$.

7. **E**   Use the graph. Where are the y-coordinates the same? There are two where $y = 2$, three where $y = 1$, and two where $y = 0$. Now check to see if the x-value of one point is 3 times the value of another at the same y-value. The answer is (E). If $c = 9$, we get $f(9) = f(3)$, which is true because both have a y-value of 0.

8. **C**   Small sides are opposite small angles and big sides are opposite big angles. Eliminate (A) and (B) because BC is the hypotenuse: it's across from the biggest angle. Neither b nor c can be equal to or larger than $90°$, eliminate (E). The question states that $AB < AC$, b must be bigger than c, so eliminate (E), in which $b = c$. (C) is correct.

9. **8** The formula for area of a triangle is $\frac{1}{2}bh$. We are given the area (40) and AC is the base, so $b = 10$. Now we can solve for height, since $h = BD$. $40 = \frac{1}{2}(10)h$, so $40 = 5h$ and $h = 8$.

10. **0** Plug $x = 5$ into the function. $2(5) - 10 = 10 - 10 = 0$.

11. **20** Be careful! The question asks only about the number of female students at the two schools, though the data is given for the females at Gateway, and the males at Riverdale. For Gateway we are told that 60% of 300 students are female. We can translate this into math: $\frac{60}{100} \times 300 = 180$ female students. Because we are told that 60% of Riverdale's students are male, we know that 40% of the 400 students are female: $\frac{40}{100} \times 400 = 160$. $180 - 160 = 20$, so there are 20 more female students at Gateway than at Riverdale.

12. **$\frac{4}{3}$ or 1.33**

Remember to distribute the number in front of the parentheses to all parts within the parentheses:

$$2(x + 2) + 4(x - 1) = 8$$
$$2x + 4 + 4x - 4 = 8$$
$$6x = 8$$

so $x = \frac{8}{6}$. If you grid in an equivalent, such as $\frac{4}{3}$ or 1.33, you also get credit for the question.

13.   9   The question asks for x^2, so find x first. In $3^{x+1} = 9^2$, we can turn 9 into a number with a base number of 3 to simplify the comparison: $3^{x+1} = (3^2)^2$, so $3^{x+1} = 3^4$. Because the bases are the same, we know that $x + 1 = 4$, so $x = 3$. We need to find x^2, so the answer is 9.

14. $\dfrac{1}{3}$ or .333

The slope formula is $\dfrac{y_2 - y_1}{x_2 - x_1}$. The points in the graph are at $(-3, 0)$ and $(0, 1)$ so $\dfrac{1-0}{0-(-3)} = \dfrac{1}{3}$. The slope formula can be simplified as $\dfrac{rise}{run}$ so if you see that the line rises 1 unit up while it runs 3 units sideways, you also get $\dfrac{1}{3}$.

15. $\dfrac{1}{2}$ or .5

Simplify the equation by multiplying everything by 2 to get rid of the fractions: $n + \dfrac{n}{2} = \dfrac{n+1}{2}$ becomes $2n + n = n + 1$. Get n by itself: $3n = n + 1$, so $2n = 1$ and $n = \dfrac{1}{2}$.

16.   60   The formula for circumference is $2\pi r$, so a circle with a circumference of 32π has a radius of 16. We know that $AB = 16$, so triangle ABO, made up of two radii and AB is actually equilateral (remember, the figure is not drawn to scale). Since all angles of an equilateral triangle are 60°, and angle BAC is an angle of that triangle, the answer is 60.

17. **30** It is easier to deal with minutes than with fractions of hours. $3\frac{1}{3}$ hours × 60 minutes = 200 minutes. So the trip to the beach + the trip home = 200 minutes. If we make the way home is x, then the way to the beach is $1\frac{1}{2}x$. Solve for x: $1\frac{1}{2}x + x = 200$, so $\frac{5}{2}x = 200$, $5x = 400$, and $x = 80$. So now we know that x (the way home) took 80 minutes and the way to the beach took $1\frac{1}{2}$ times that, or 120 minutes. Now we know that the 60 miles to the beach took 2 hours, for a rate of 30 miles per hour.

18. **90** Notice that the height for both triangles is the same (it would be a line straight down from point X). The base is the only difference between the triangles. The areas of the triangles are proportional to the bases of the triangles. Since UZ is 30 percent of UY, the area of triangle UXZ is 30 percent of triangle UXY. That makes the area of triangle XYZ 70 percent of the area of triangle UXY. The question states that XYZ has an area of 210. Set up a proportion: $\frac{30}{70} = \frac{x}{210}$. Solve for x: $x = 90$.

Section 6

1. **C** The *landlords* were *unable to finance* what they wanted to do, so they do not have enough *resources*. We need a word for the blank that means "not enough." Only (C), *inadequate* has a close meaning.

2. E   Mrs. Smedley's worry is that the daughter is marrying *beneath her*. The blank and *herself* refers to the daughter, so "lower" is a good word for the blank. If you don't know all the words, eliminate answers that have words you know couldn't mean "lower." Only (E) *demean* matches in meaning.

3. A   We know that the words for the blanks must be opposite, because *the director did not* consider the description in the first blank to be correct, and the second blank is the director's (opposite) opinion of her film. The part of the sentence after the colon lets us know the director believes her movie is *fair*: a good word for the second blank, so the first blank must mean "unfair". Only (A) *biased… equitable* matches "unfair"…"fair."

4. D   Finding the correct answer depends on the relationship between the blanks. If the *Japanese artists* were liked *Western contemporary art* they would "copy" its *bold expressiveness*. If they disliked the art, they would "reject" its traits. For the second blank, neither (B) *disclose* or (E) *overrun* makes sense in either case, and (A), (C), and (D) are all somewhat close to "copy" so we need to find a match for the first blank that indicates "liking" the art. (A) and (C) are negative, leaving only (D) as a match for both blanks.

5. A   The nurses were able to *uplift* sad people, so they must have "uplifting" or "upbeat" *personalities*. There is some tough vocab in the answers. (A) *winsome,* which means "charming; winning; engaging" is correct.

6. D   The passage describes the history of the word "boycott." (A) is incorrect, because the passage doesn't state why the word is *popular*. (B) is incorrect, because it tells about the incident that inspired the word, not the history of its *usage*. There is no *unrelated story* (C) here, and no *shift* in the word's meaning is given.

7. **B** Inference questions must be supported by evidence in the passage. Eliminate (A) because Boycott may have done it himself or found someone who wasn't protesting. (B) is true: the townspeople refused Boycott service and so were taking the farmers' side. The *all* in (C) and *never* in (E) is extreme. (D) *physical harm* is not mentioned in the passage.

8. **B** The passage is about how and why "The Little Mermaid" changed over time. No *unscrupulous publishers* are mentioned so eliminate (A). (B) is true: reasons for the changes are given. (C) is extreme and too broad. (D) is mentioned, but it is not the main point. (E) is not supported by the passage.

9. **D** The first mention of *sea foam* in line 4 states what happened at the end of the fairy tale, and the second mention in line 14 describes what happened to Andersen's *original meanings* so there is a comparison being made, using a phrase from one of his stories. (A) *obsession* is too strong. (B) is incorrect, because we are told only of one work, not enough to discover *a prevalent theme* among his stories. There is no evidence for (C), and (E) *prove* is too strong. (D) is correct, a *metaphor* is a figure of speech that compares one thing to another.

10. **B** A *primary purpose* question like this one asks "Why did the author write this passage?" The passage talks about both the British and Zulu sides of the war without taking one side over the other. The second through fourth paragraphs in particular discuss why some British soldiers decided to join the war, and also why the Zulu took part. This is paraphrased nicely in (B). (A) does not mention the Zulu at all. The *myths* in the passage refer to reasons why the British were defeated, not about *relations* so eliminate (C). (D) is incorrect because *loyalty* is not the main focus of the passage and (E) is much broader that what's covered in this short text.

11. **D** Private Moss joined the war *for the Queen's shilling,* or in other words, for the money. Only (D) mentions *money.*

12. **D** The paragraph that contains the quote from the question begins *Neither side had a clue as to why they were involved,* and (D) captures this with *uncertainty about the reasons for their participation.* None of the other answers address the soldiers' cluelessness about *why they were involved.*

13. **B** The fourth paragraph is primarily about the attitudes of the British officers compared to that of the Zulu. The British thought it was a *game* and the Zulu *fought to defend land, homes, and families.* These are opposite, so eliminate (A) because *both* describes similarity. (B) paraphrases "game vs. defense" well. Eliminate (C) because *aristocrats* describes only the officers, not the whole *military force.* (D) and (E) come from other parts of the passage, and the question is only about the fourth paragraph.

14. **B** Lines 38–43 describe how *massacre* and *victory* mean the same thing, but *massacre* is used to avoid saying that the Zulu had won a victory. (B) comes closest: the word *massacre* makes it sound like the Zulu are doing something particularly bad or evil, when the British are doing the exact same thing. (A) goes against the passage: the British are described as *brutal* in the paragraph. (C) is opposite of what is stated in the passage. There is no evidence for (D) or (E).

15. **C** The *myth* was the reasons that were created to explain how the British could be defeated by a supposedly inferior force. This is paraphrased best in (C). (D) may be tempting, but it describes the myth itself, not why it was created.

16. D   Lines 3 and 4 state that *her translations were highly praised throughout her literary career*, making (D) the correct answer. (A) may be tempting, but her poetry had a negative reception, so eliminate (A).

17. E   In line 19, *Panaev* is described as a *utilitarian* critic who felt poetry should be *useful*. Of all the answers, only (E) *offer solutions* could be considered *useful*.

18. B   Only (B) *unwilling to develop* contradicts the passage. Lines 27–29 state that these poets still were part of the romantic tradition, but *their work was nevertheless developing*.

19. D   The third paragraph is about how poets' works were developing, then *A Double Life* is given as an example of a work that encompasses these trends. This is best described in (D). (A) is incorrect: it tell how Pavlova's work was like her contemporaries'. There is no support for (B) or (E), and (C) is opposite of what is stated in the passage.

20. B   The "stories in verse" *helped keep poetry alive* when readers preferred prose. Adding the elements of a story to poetry is best paraphrased in (B) that it drew *from non-poetical works*.

21. C   The passage states that the critics *did not consider* the issue of women's education to be a problem. They are more concerned with *the oppression of Russia's peasant class*. (A) seems close because it mentions *peasants*, but *education* is too specific a focus; the critics are more concerned with *oppression*. (B), (D), and (E) are not mentioned in the passage. Only (C) discusses *class*.

22. A   Go back to the passage and use the context to come up with a word to replace *address*. A good phrase might be "focus on." The only answer that works in the context of the passage is (A) *attend to*.

23. **E** The *main criticism* of *A Double Life* was that is *lacked substance* (lines 43–45) and did not focus on class. The author states that *these critics obviously overlooked the point* of her work and describes that it did indeed evoke *her class*. The phrase "*overlooked* qualities of her writing" can be paraphrased as *inability to recognize* seen in (E). There is no evidence in the passage for the other answers.

24. **A** The critics were concerned that Pavalova's work took focus away from the peasant class. Only (A) and (D) mention anything about the peasant class, but (D) would actually strengthen the criticism, rather than weaken it as the question states. This makes (A) the best answer.

Section 8

1. **C** First eliminate any number that does not fulfill the first part of the statement. All of the numbers are divisible by 4, but (B) and (E) are not divisible by 8, so eliminate them. Now that we have just the numbers that are divisible by 4 and 8, we can disprove the statement by finding one that is not divisible by 12. (A) and (D) are both divisible by 12, but (C) 40 is not. (C) is correct.

2. **B** All radii are equal, so since *BC* has a length of 5 (the distance between *y*-values of 2 and 7) *AB* must also have a length of 5. The distance between the *x*-values of *x* and 1 must be 5, and *x* is a negative number, so $x = -4$, answer (B).

3. **B** The equations in the answers are in the $y = mx + b$ format. From the image, we know that the *y*-intercept (*b*) is negative. Eliminate (A) and (C) because they show a positive *y*-intercept, and eliminate (E) because it shows none. The slope of the line (*m*) is pointing up, and is positive, so eliminate (D) for having a negative slope. (B) is correct.

4. **D**   We need to translate this word problem into math. If dress socks is d and athletic socks are a, we want to find $a + b$. We can show the first statement as $3d + 4a = 27$ and the second as $4d + 3a = 29$. If we stack these equations on top of one another and add them together to get the same number of dress and athletic socks:

$$3d + 4a = 27$$
$$\underline{+\ 4d + 3a = 29}$$
$$7d + 7a = 56$$

Divide all parts of the final equation by 7 to see that $a + b = 8$, answer (D).

5. **D**   We know the variables for x and f are the price and number of brownies per hour, respectively. Because f is the y-value on the coordinate plane, sketch the line they make on the coordinate plane. Selling brownies that cost \$1.50 at a rate of 7 brownies an hour gives a coordinate pair of (1.5, 7), and selling brownies that cost \$2.00 at a rate of 5 brownies an hour gives a coordinate pair of (2, 5). The line that connects these points slants downward, so it has a negative slope. The $f(x)$ in the answers can be replaced by y, and then it's more clear that the answers are the equation of a line, $y = mx + b$. Eliminate (A) and (B) because they show a positive slope. The slope formula can be simplified as $\frac{rise}{run}$, with the difference in y-values as the rise, and the difference in x values as the run. The negative slope means we need the negative difference between 5 and 7 as our rise. The run is positive 0.5: $\frac{-2}{0.5} = -4$. Eliminate (C) and (E). (D) is correct because is has a slope of -4.

6. **E** Come up with some numbers that fulfill the statements in the question, and see which answers you can eliminate. Both a and b must be negative, and a negative times a negative is positive, so that eliminates (A), and (B). If $a = -2$ and $b = -\frac{1}{2}$, then $ab = 1$. That gets rid of (C) and (D) because they don't include 1, only (E) is left, and it is the correct answer.

7. **A** Use your own numbers to replace the variables to make this problem easier to solve. If $p = 4$ and $w = 30$ that means we can purchase 4 items for \$60, and we need to find out how many items we can purchase for \$30. For half the amount of money, we can get half the number of items, so we can get 2 items. Now replace the variables in the answers with $p = 4$ and $w = 30$, and the answer that gives 2 is correct. Only (A) gives 2, while (B) and (D) are too small and (C) and (E) are too large.

8. **B** Get rid of the answers that are not true based on information in the graph. Eliminate (A) because reducing from \$10 to \$5 resulted in the same number of sales. (C) is not true, because there is a difference in sales based on price. (D) states the opposite of what is seen in the graph. (E) can not be confirmed from the chart's information. (B) is true: between \$20 and \$10, the lower the price, the higher the sales. A lower price than \$10 did not change sales. (B) is a good paraphrase of this.

9. **B** Replace the x in the answer choices and eliminate any that give a result of 1—we're looking for what CANNOT be $f(x)$. (A), (C), (D), and (E) all give 1, but (B) gives −1. (B) is correct.

10.   E   Out of the 27 questions Cathy answered, she has missed 9 questions. Since we want to find out the <u>least</u> number of questions on the test, so we won't add any more misses. If $\frac{5}{6}$ of the answers are correct, then $\frac{1}{6}$ were missed. 9 is $\frac{1}{6}$ of what? Translate that question into $9 = \frac{1}{6}x$ and solve for x: $x = 54$, (E).

11.   A   The 10 tiles form a box without overlapping, so there are 2 tiles on each of the 4 sides, and one tile each at top and bottom. Each tile has a perimeter of 24, so the edge of each tile is 6. If the box is 2 tiles tall, that's a height of 12 centimeters. The bottom is one tile, so that's a width and depth of 6 for each dimension. $12 \times 6 \times 6 = 432$, answer (A)

12.   E   The easiest way to solve this is to use each of the answers in place of x and see which makes the equation true. Since we are taking a square root, the easiest answers to check are those that are perfect squares (A) gives $4 = 0$ which is not true. Hold on to (B) since its root is not an integer. (C) gives $8 = 6$ which is not true. (D) gives $10 = 9$ which is not true. (E) gives $12 = 12$ which is correct. (No need to go back to check (B) now.)

13.   B   Come up with some numbers to serve as an example of the situation described to figure this one out. One example of a list in which mean, median and mode are all equal is {2, 4, 4, 6}. If we add a 4 to the list, it changes nothing, thereby eliminating (A). If we add a 0 and an 8 to the list, it also adds nothing, thereby eliminating (C). Adding 2 to each number leaves us with {4, 6, 6, 8}, which has a mean of 6, mode of 6, and median of 6, which lets us get rid of (D). Removing the first and last numbers would leave us with {4, 4}, which is fine; therefore, eliminate (E). Remember, we're looking for the thing that CANNOT

be done to the original list. Adding a number such as 11 does change the mean to a 7, while the mode is still 4, so (B) definitely is the correct answer.

14. E Draw out the possibilities: If points L, M, and N are in a straight line in that order, LN has a length of 13. Statement III is true, so eliminate (A) and (B) because they have no III. If L is between M and N, the whole line has a length of 9, LM takes up 4 of that, leaving LN to be 5 units long. Statement I is true; eliminate (C) because it had no I. Statement 2 is true: If LMN is a triangle, we know that one side is 4 and another is 9. The third-side rule is that the length of the third side of the triangle must be less than the sum of the other two legs (13) but greater than the difference between the legs (5). Since 8 is between 5 and 13, II is true and (E) is correct.

15. D The radius of the circle is also the height of the triangle. A line that is tangent to a circle is perpendicular to the radius of the circle, so drawing the height splits AOB into two 30-60-90 triangles. Angle B must be 30° because AB is a line, so angle B added to the 150° shown must add up to 180°. A 30-60-90 triangle has sides in the ratio of x : $x\sqrt{3}$: $2x$, respectively. Since the height of 6 is opposite the 30° angle, the base of each 30-60-90 triangle is $6\sqrt{3}$. Since we want to find the area of the larger triangle AOB, double the base of the 30-60-90 triangle and use the area formula: $\frac{1}{2}bh = \frac{1}{2}(12\sqrt{3})(6) = 36\sqrt{3}$ and (D) is correct.

16. D Because $y + 1$ is within the absolute value brackets, that means the correct graph will have 2 y-values for every x value, a positive y and a negative y. For example, if $x = 0$, then $|y+1| = 3$. The value within the

brackets could be 3 or −3, which means that the correct graph shows y as 2 and −4 when x is 0. (A), (B), and (D) show only one of these points. Now go back to the equation, but this time make y = 0. The inside of the brackets is positive, as is absolute value, so x can be 2 only when y = 0. Eliminate (E) because it shows (−2, 0) and (−4, 0). (D) is correct.

Section 9

1. **A** *Piercing* and *primordial fears* indicate something unpleasant. Only (A) fits. (C) is positive; (B) and (D) are neutral; (E) is negative but not unpleasant.

2. **C** The phrase *the real name…is Daniel Handler* indicates that the blank must mean "not a real name." Only (C) *a pseudonym* means "fake name."

3. **B** The *Quan Yin symbol* is known for its *purifying qualities*, and it is used *after an argument or disagreement* so the symbol can "remove bad feelings from" *an environment*. We need a word that means something similar to "remove bad feelings from." That's a positive quality, so we can eliminate (A) and (E) for being negative. (B) *harmonize* means "to bring into harmony, accord, or agreement" so it removes *disagreement*.

4. **C** The word *but* indicates that *Heather* and *Ms. Shockey* feel differently about something. The portion of the sentence after the colon indicates that Ms. Shockey *did not find Heather's essay particularly exceptional* so the second blank means "not impressed." Eliminate (A) (neutral) and (B) and (D) (positive). (C) and (E) both have negative words, but only (C) *indifferent* is close in meaning to "not impressed." We need a positive word for the first blank and *confident* fits well. (C) is correct.

5.   E   The *policy changes* resulted in something bad. The word *seemingly* indicates that the first blank means something positive and the bad result of the changes let us know that the second blank is something negative. The first word in (B) and (C) are negative, so eliminate them. The second word in (D) is positive so eliminate it. The words in (A) are neither positive nor negative, while (E) fits the positive negative pattern. (E) is correct.

6.   E   The clue *could not be verified* indicates that the blank should mean "not verified" or "untrue." (E) *specious* is the only choice that means "untrue." (A) *substantiated* and (D) *indubitable* mean the opposite of untrue.

7.   C   The *company* refers to the audience, the people there *to see the new performer*. Only (C) talks about the audience.

8.   B   The passage describes the audience as *stimulated by curiosity* but having no hopes for good entertainment. This is paraphrased in (B) *expected a mediocre performance*. (A) and (C) are the opposite of what's indicated by the passage because they describe the show positively. There is no evidence for (D) or (E).

9.   A   The *novelty and propriety* of Garrick's acting style *threw the critics into some hesitation* because it was different from common acting styles of the day. (A) is a good paraphrase of this. The rest of the answers are not supported by the passage.

10. A   The paragraph that describes *the applause* also mentions *the triumph of the actor,* so it was a good show and the audience liked it. Only (A) describes this situation.

11. C   Go back to the passage and use the context to come up with a word to replace *manly*. The word is defined after the dash: *there was nothing of the trick about it.* So *honest* (C) is a good replacement. Some of the

other words are meanings for "manly" but they do not fit the context of the passage.

12.   **D**   The facial expressions are described as *rigid, cold,* and *colorless* this is closest to (D) *stoic and unfeeling.*

13.   **A**   The passage indicates that *never until his time* did anyone act like Garrick. (A) describes a time before Garrick during which actors acted in the same way, which would weaken the idea that Garrick *introduced* the style. (C) strengthens the argument, while (B), (D), and (E) don't have any bearing on the argument.

14.   **B**   The passage states that Macklin criticized Garrick because he used *action and his gestures* to draw attention to himself. This is paraphrased in (B).

15.   **C**   In the last paragraph of Passage 2, the author agrees with Macklin that Garrick called too much attention to himself, and gives a reason for why Garrick was motivated to do so. Only (C) *justifiable* indicates agreement with Macklin's opinion.

16.   **E**   The passage gives *public applause* as the *palm* Garrick desired. This is closest to *symbol of triumph* (E). (B) and (C) are overly literal meanings of *palm* and do not fit the context.

17.   **B**   The author of Passage 2 criticizes Garrick for hogging the spotlight. If the author saw Garrick perform and he did not try to hog the spotlight, the author would like Garrick better. This is paraphrased in (B).

18.   **A**   The descriptions *familiar* and *natural* are part of larger descriptions that state that this acting style had not been seen before Garrick. Only (A) captures this. The other answers do not mention Garrick's style of acting.

19. **A** The statement referred to in the question is about Garrick being the first person to act in a natural style. The closest match to this is (A), from the portion of Passage 1 that describes how Garrick surprised the critics with this novel acting style.

Section 10

1. **B** The word *Since* at the beginning of the sentence conflicts with the conjunction *as* after the comma. Eliminate (A) and (C). In (E) *be counting* creates an awkward and wordy. (B) is correct; it is shorter and clearer than (D).

2. **C** Keep the sentence short and simple. The underlined part explains why Wallace founded the group. (C) gets that across simply. (A) is wordy and uses an incorrect idiom, (B) lacks a comma before *and*, which makes it sound like the goal was doing the generating, (D) adds the unnecessary *therefore*, and (E) loses the meaning and incorrectly links the phrases.

3. **B** The word *that* is unnecessary and prevents the sentence from being parallel. (B) removes *that* and so is correct. (C) changes the meaning of the sentence. (D) and (E) are not parallel.

4. **A** The sentence is correct as written. The phrase *In 1982* indicates that the verb needs to be in the past tense. Eliminate (B) because it is in the present tense. (C) and (D) are in the past tense, but *was* and *were* indicate that a different band was *the first* in other years, which is not true: the first to do something is always the first. (E) changes the meaning of the sentence.

5. **D** The sentence as written has a misplaced modifier. The subject right after the comma is what is described before the comma, so we need *Ryan* not *Ryan's commute*. Only (D) starts with *Ryan*.

6.   D   The underlined portion of the sentence contains the redundant pronoun *it*. (B) has the same problem. (C) and (E) use a verb form, *roaring* that does not agree with the rest of the sentence. (D) removes the unnecessary *it* and remains in the proper tense.

7.   E   The sentence as written has a misplaced modifier. The subject right after the comma should be someone who can carry something, not the *manager's search*. Only in (E) is a person mentioned: *the equipment manager*. (E) is correct.

8.   C   (A), (D), and (E) all lack the necessary part of the idiomatic phrase "but also." (B) is wordy, redundant, and lacks parallelism. (C) corrects all of these problems.

9.   D   The sentence switches pronouns, using both *your* and *one's*. Eliminate (A); (E) has the same problem. In (B), *their* doesn't agree with *a prospective applicant*. (C) lacks a subject for *proofread*. In (D), *their applications* and *their essays* agree with *prospective students*.

10. E   The noun *variedness* is incorrect: *variety* matches the form of *beauty*, the other quality of *aquatic life*. Only (E) finishes the idiom *such…that* and the verb is in the present tense as it is in the non-underlined portion of the sentence.

11. B   The sentence as written is wordy and redundant. Most of the answer choices share this problem, but (B) is short and simple while giving us all the information we need.

12. D   This is an incomplete sentence: the comma begins a descriptive phrase in (A), (B), and (C), but never finishes the idea that was begun before the comma. (E) uses an inappropriate conjunction *and*. Only (D) is a complete sentence that correctly uses *where* to link the actions described in the second part of the sentence to *certain countries*.

13.   C   This sentence uses the wrong transition *and*. The second part of the sentence describes a situation opposite to that described in the first part, so we need a transition that shows an opposing relationship. This is seen in (B) *but* and (C) *however*. (B) is unnecessarily wordy, so (C) is correct.

14.   A   There are no errors in the sentence as it is written. As you can tell from the way the first word of each answer choice switches between *contributes* to *contribute*, the first issue you need to deal with is subject-verb agreement. The subject of the sentence is *choices*, which is plural. Therefore, we need the plural verb *contribute*. Eliminate (B) and (C). (E) incorrectly uses the pronoun *it*; it is unclear to what it is referring, so eliminate (E). The big difference between (A) and (D) is the verb *do*. (A) uses the singular verb *does*, while (D) uses the plural verb *do*. The subject of this verb is the singular noun *decor*, so (A) is correct.

SAT SCORING WORKSHEET

For directions on how to score your SAT practice test, see pages 5–7.

SAT Writing Section

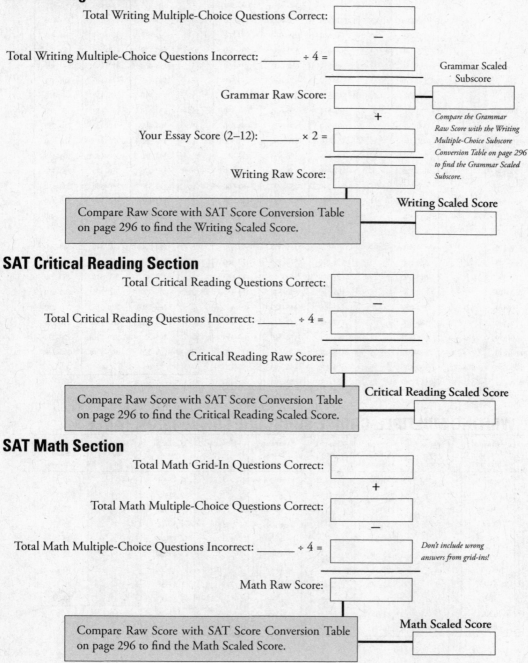

Total Writing Multiple-Choice Questions Correct: [   ]

−

Total Writing Multiple-Choice Questions Incorrect: _____ ÷ 4 = [   ]

Grammar Raw Score: [   ]

Grammar Scaled Subscore [   ]

+

Your Essay Score (2–12): _____ × 2 = [   ]

Compare the Grammar Raw Score with the Writing Multiple-Choice Subscore Conversion Table on page 296 to find the Grammar Scaled Subscore.

Writing Raw Score: [   ]

Compare Raw Score with SAT Score Conversion Table on page 296 to find the Writing Scaled Score.

Writing Scaled Score
[   ]

SAT Critical Reading Section

Total Critical Reading Questions Correct: [   ]

−

Total Critical Reading Questions Incorrect: _____ ÷ 4 = [   ]

Critical Reading Raw Score: [   ]

Compare Raw Score with SAT Score Conversion Table on page 296 to find the Critical Reading Scaled Score.

Critical Reading Scaled Score
[   ]

SAT Math Section

Total Math Grid-In Questions Correct: [   ]

+

Total Math Multiple-Choice Questions Correct: [   ]

−

Total Math Multiple-Choice Questions Incorrect: _____ ÷ 4 = [   ]

Don't include wrong answers from grid-ins!

Math Raw Score: [   ]

Compare Raw Score with SAT Score Conversion Table on page 296 to find the Math Scaled Score.

Math Scaled Score
[   ]

SAT SCORE CONVERSION TABLE

Raw Score	Reading Scaled Score	Math Scaled Score	Writing Scaled Score	Raw Score	Reading Scaled Score	Math Scaled Score	Writing Scaled Score	Raw Score	Reading Scaled Score	Math Scaled Score	Writing Scaled Score
73			800	47	580–620	650–690	540–580	21	410–450	440–480	380–420
72			780–800	46	570–610	640–680	530–570	20	410–450	430–470	370–410
71			770–800	45	570–610	630–670	520–560	19	400–440	420–460	360–400
70			750–790	44	560–600	620–660	520–560	18	390–430	420–460	350–390
69			740–780	43	550–590	610–650	510–550	17	390–430	410–450	350–390
68			730–770	42	550–590	600–640	500–540	16	380–420	400–440	340–380
67	800		720–760	41	540–580	600–640	500–540	15	370–410	390–430	330–370
66	780–800		710–750	40	530–570	590–630	490–530	14	370–410	390–430	320–360
65	770–800		700–740	39	530–570	580–620	480–520	13	360–400	380–420	310–350
64	760–800		690–730	38	520–560	570–610	480–520	12	350–390	370–410	310–350
63	750–790		680–720	37	510–550	560–600	470–510	11	340–380	360–400	300–340
62	730–770		680–720	36	510–550	550–590	460–500	10	330–370	350–390	290–330
61	710–750		670–710	35	500–540	550–590	460–500	9	330–370	340–380	280–320
60	700–740		660–700	34	500–540	540–580	450–490	8	320–360	330–370	270–310
59	690–730		650–690	33	490–530	530–570	440–480	7	310–350	320–360	260–300
58	680–720		640–680	32	480–520	520–560	430–470	6	300–340	310–350	260–300
57	670–710		630–670	31	480–520	510–550	430–470	5	290–330	300–340	260–300
56	660–700		620–660	30	470–510	510–550	420–460	4	280–320	290–330	250–290
55	650–690		610–650	29	460–500	500–540	420–460	3	270–310	270–310	250–290
54	640–680	800	600–640	28	460–500	490–530	410–450	2	250–290	260–300	240–280
53	630–670	760–800	590–630	27	450–490	480–520	400–440	1	240–280	240–280	230–270
52	620–660	740–780	580–620	26	450–490	480–520	400–440	0	220–260	230–270	220–260
51	610–650	710–750	570–610	25	440–480	470–510	390–430	–1	200–220	210–250	200–220
50	600–640	690–730	560–600	24	430–470	460–500	390–430	–2	200–220	200–210	200–220
49	600–640	670–710	560–600	23	430–470	450–490	380–420	–3	200	200	200–220
48	590–630	660–700	550–590	22	420–460	450–490	380–420				

WRITING MULTIPLE-CHOICE SUBSCORE CONVERSION TABLE

Grammar Raw Score	Grammar Scaled Subscore	Grammar Raw Score	Grammar Scaled Subscore	Grammar Raw Score	Grammar Scaled Subscore	Grammar Raw Score	Grammar Scaled Subscore	Grammar Raw Score	Grammar Scaled Subscore
49	78–80	38	60–64	27	49–53	16	40–44	5	30–34
48	77–80	37	59–63	26	48–52	15	39–43	4	28–32
47	74–78	36	58–62	25	48–52	14	38–42	3	27–31
46	72–76	35	57–61	24	47–51	13	38–42	2	25–29
45	70–74	34	56–60	23	46–50	12	37–41	1	24–28
44	68–72	33	55–59	22	45–49	11	36–40	0	22–26
43	66–70	32	54–58	21	44–48	10	35–39	–1	20–22
42	65–69	31	53–57	20	43–47	9	34–38	–2	20–22
41	64–68	30	52–56	19	42–46	8	33–37	–3	20–22
40	62–66	29	51–55	18	42–46	7	32–36		
39	61–65	28	50–54	17	41–45	6	31–35		

NOTES

NOTES

NOTES

NOTES

NOTES

NOTES

NOTES

NOTES

Navigate the admissions process with more guidance from the experts.

Get the scores you need:

1,296 ACT Practice Questions, 3rd Edition
978-0-307-94570-9 • $19.99/$23.99 Can.
eBook: 978-0-307-94592-1

Cracking the ACT, 2013 Edition
978-0-307-94535-8 • $19.99/$23.99 Can.
eBook: 978-0-307-94540-2

Cracking the ACT with DVD, 2013 Edition
978-0-307-94536-5 • $31.99/$37.99 Can.

Cracking the SAT, 2013 Edition
978-0-307-94478-8 • $21.99/$25.99 Can.
eBook: 978-0-307-94479-5

Cracking the SAT with DVD, 2013 Edition
978-0-307-94480-1 • $34.99/$41.99 Can.

English and Reading Workout for the ACT, 2nd Edition
978-0-307-94594-5 • $16.99/$19.99 Can.
eBook: 978-0-307-94596-9

Math and Science Workout for the ACT, 2nd Edition
978-0-307-94595-1 • $16.99/$19.99 Can.
eBook: 978-0-307-94597-6

Essential ACT (Flashcards)
978-0-375-42806-7 • $17.99/$19.99 Can.

Essential SAT Vocabulary (Flashcards)
978-0-375-42964-4 • $16.99/$21.99 Can.

Find and fund the best school for you:

The Best 377 Colleges, 2013 Edition
978-0-307-94487-0 • $23.99/$27.99 Can.
Enhanced eBook: 978-0-307-94601-0
Enhanced eBook (iBooks):
978-0-307-94600-3

College Essays that Made a Difference, 5th Edition
978-0-307-94521-1 • $13.99/$16.99 Can.
eBook: 978-0-307-94522-8

The Complete Book of Colleges, 2013 Edition
978-0-307-94492-4 • $26.99/$32.00 Can.

Paying for College Without Going Broke, 2013 Edition
978-0-307-94532-7 • $20.00/$24.00 Can.
eBook: 978-0-307-94533-4

Boost your scores on the SAT Subject Tests:

Cracking the SAT Biology E/M Subject Test, 2013–2014 Edition
978-0-307-94552-5 • $19.99/$23.99 Can.
eBook: 978-0-307-94572-3

Cracking the SAT Chemistry Subject Test, 2013–2014 Edition
978-0-307-94556-3 • $19.99/$23.99 Can.
eBook: 978-0-307-94576-1

Cracking the SAT French Subject Test, 2013–2014 Edition
978-0-307-94557-0 • $19.99/$23.99 Can.
eBook: 978-0-307-94577-8

Cracking the SAT Literature Subject Test, 2013–2014 Edition
978-0-307-94553-2 • $19.99/$23.99 Can.
eBook: 978-0-307-94573-0

Cracking the SAT Math 1 & 2 Subject Tests, 2013–2014 Edition
978-0-307-94554-9 • $19.99/$23.99 Can.
eBook: 978-0-307-94574-7

Cracking the SAT Physics Subject Test, 2013–2014 Edition
978-0-307-94555-6 • $19.99/$23.99 Can.
eBook: 978-0-307-94575-4

Cracking the SAT Spanish Subject Test, 2013–2014 Edition
978-0-307-94559-4 • $19.99/$23.99 Can.
eBook: 978-0-307-94579-2

Cracking the SAT U.S. & World History Tests, 2013–2014 Edition
978-0-307-94558-7 • $19.99/$23.99 Can.
eBook: 978-0-307-94578-5

NOTES

Ace the APs:

Cracking the AP Biology Exam, 2013 Edition (Revised)
978-0-307-94633-1 • $18.99/$21.99 Can.
eBook: 978-0-307-94580-8

Cracking the AP Calculus AB & BC Exams, 2013 Edition
978-0-307-94486-3 • $19.99/$23.99 Can.
eBook: 978-0-307-94451-1

Cracking the AP Chemistry Exam, 2013 Edition
978-0-307-94488-7 • $18.99/$21.99 Can.
eBook: 978-0-307-94452-8

Cracking the AP Economics Macro & Micro Exams, 2013 Edition
978-0-307-94509-9 • $18.00/$21.00 Can.
eBook: 978-0-307-94581-5

Cracking the AP English Language & Composition Exam, 2013 Edition
978-0-307-94511-2 • $18.00/$21.00 Can.
eBook: 978-0-307-94582-2

Cracking the AP English Literature & Composition Exam, 2013 Edition
978-0-307-94512-9 • $18.00/$21.00 Can.
eBook: 978-0-307-94583-9

Cracking the AP Environmental Science Exam, 2013 Edition
978-0-307-94513-6 • $18.99/$21.99 Can.
eBook: 978-0-307-94584-6

Cracking the AP European History Exam, 2013 Edition
978-0-307-94489-4 • $18.99/$21.99 Can.
eBook: 978-0-307-94453-5

Cracking the AP Human Geography Exam, 2013 Edition
978-0-307-94514-3 • $18.00/$21.00 Can.

Cracking the AP Physics B Exam, 2013 Edition
978-0-307-94515-0 • $18.99/$21.99 Can.
eBook: 978-0-307-94585-3

Cracking the AP Physics C Exam, 2013 Edition
978-0-307-94516-7 • $18.99/$21.99 Can.

Cracking the AP Psychology Exam, 2013 Edition
978-0-307-94517-4 • $18.00/$21.00 Can.
eBook: 978-0-307-94586-0

Cracking the AP Spanish Exam with Audio CD, 2013 Edition
978-0-307-94518-1 • $24.99/$28.99 Can.

Cracking the AP Statistics Exam, 2013 Edition
978-0-307-94519-8 • $19.99/$23.99 Can.

Cracking the AP U.S. Government & Politics Exam, 2013 Edition
978-0-307-94520-4 • $18.99/$21.99 Can.
eBook: 978-0-307-94587-7

Cracking the AP U.S. History Exam, 2013 Edition
978-0-307-94490-7 • $18.99/$21.99 Can.
eBook: 978-0-307-94447-4

Cracking the AP World History Exam, 2013 Edition
978-0-307-94491-7 • $18.99/$21.99 Can.
eBook: 978-0-307-94445-0

Essential AP Biology (Flashcards)
978-0-375-42803-6 • $18.99/$20.99 Can.

Essential AP Psychology (Flashcards)
978-0-375-42801-2 • $18.99/$20.99 Can.

Essential AP U.S. Government & Politics (Flashcards)
978-0-375-42804-3 • $18.99/$20.99 Can.

Essential AP U.S. History (Flashcards)
978-0-375-42800-5 • $18.99/$20.99 Can.

Essential AP World History (Flashcards)
978-0-375-42802-9 • $18.99/$20.99 Can.

Available everywhere books are sold and at PrincetonReviewBooks.com